—— CONSPIRACY NARRATIVES IN ROMAN HISTORY ——

# CONSPIRACY NARRATIVES
# IN ROMAN HISTORY

VICTORIA EMMA PAGÁN

UNIVERSITY OF TEXAS PRESS

*Austin*

Requests for permission to reproduce material from this work should be
sent to Permissions, University of Texas Press, P.O. Box 7819, Austin, TX
78713-7819.

⊗ The paper used in this book meets the minimum requirements of
ANSI/NISO Z39.48-1992 (R1997) (Permanence of Paper).

Library of Congress Cataloging-in-Publication Data
Pagán, Victoria Emma, 1965–
Conspiracy narratives in Roman history / by Victoria Emma Pagán.
p.      cm.
Includes bibliographical references and index.
ISBN: 0292722338
1. Rome—Historiography.    2. Conspiracies—Rome—Historiography.
I. Title.
DG205.P24    2005
937'.0072—dc22        2003027597

*For Andrew Wolpert*
*alpha and omega*

# CONTENTS

ACKNOWLEDGMENTS ix

INTRODUCTION 1

PART ONE
**BETRAYED CONSPIRACIES**
25

1. SALLUST 27
*The Catilinarian Conspiracy*

2. LIVY 50
*The Bacchanalian Affair*

3. TACITUS 68
*The Pisonian Conspiracy*

PART TWO
**SUCCESSFUL CONSPIRACIES**
91

4. JOSEPHUS 93
*The Assassination of Caligula*

5. APPIAN 109
*The Assassination of Julius Caesar*

CONCLUSION 123

ABBREVIATIONS 133

NOTES 135

BIBLIOGRAPHY 163

GENERAL INDEX 177

INDEX LOCORUM 188

# ACKNOWLEDGMENTS

Completion of this project was made possible by generous grants from the Ford Foundation, the Woodrow Wilson National Fellowship Foundation, the University of Wisconsin Institute for Research in the Humanities, and the University of Wisconsin Graduate School. I would like to thank Rhiannon Ash, Susanna Morton Braund, Robert Kaster, Andrew Laird, David Potter, Steven Rutledge, Patrick Sinclair, and my colleagues in Madison, James McKeown, Silvia Montiglio, Carole Newlands, Patricia Rosenmeyer, and Andrew Wolpert for reading drafts and for their candid responses. For invaluable assistance securing several items of bibliography, I am fortunate to be able to thank John Dillon and Mike Clover. For technical assistance, I am grateful to my research assistant Michael Nerdahl and to Megan Bryant of the Sixth Floor Museum at Dealey Plaza. I am most indebted to the University of Texas Press, and to Humanities Editor Jim Burr, in particular, for his vision and energy; to Nancy Moore, my copy editor; and to the anonymous readers for their encouragement and constructive suggestions. Both readers envisioned a different book than what emerged, proof that the study of conspiracy in ancient Rome has just begun.

Finally, I wish to thank the remarkable families of Pagáns and Wolperts who have supported my career patiently, practically, intellectually, and spiritually. The kindness of Lindsey Hebel and Brooke Ocken granted me the peace of mind to write this book.

Please do not assume that the scholars mentioned here agree with my ideas; the faults herein are mine alone. Anything of value, however, ultimately derives from the abiding happiness bestowed on me by a loving husband, a delightful son, a treasured daughter, and a gentle Saint Bernard, those with whom it is a joy untold to conspire daily.

# INTRODUCTION

*What we said during the morning meeting will never be known
completely because the tape of that conversation is the one
with the 18 ½–minute gap.*

— RICHARD M. NIXON[1]

On October 12, 1973, the United States Court of Appeals ordered President
Richard M. Nixon to produce White House tapes and documents that had
been subpoenaed in July. Ten days later, Nixon announced his compliance.
District Court Judge John J. Sirica requested, among others, tapes for June 20,
1972 (three days after the burglary at the Watergate Hotel). But there was a
problem. Rose Mary Woods, Nixon's personal secretary of twenty-three years,
told him that she "might have caused a small gap" in the recording of a conversation that took place on June 20 with H. R. Haldeman, White House
chief of staff and one of Nixon's closest advisors. Her story was unclear, but it
seems that while transcribing, she reached for the telephone to place a call and
inadvertently hit the delete button on the tape recorder. She did not notice
the mistake until she finished her phone call of "about five minutes."

The gap actually ran for eighteen and a half minutes. Haldeman's successor, White House Chief of Staff Alexander Haig, publicly disparaged Miss
Woods: "Typical of a woman," he said, "she did not know the difference between five minutes and one hour of talking."[2] Although the charges of ob-
struction of justice and tampering with evidence were dropped, her reputation was damaged. A panel of scientific experts examined the tape and
concluded that it was unlikely that the erasure was accidental. Did she deliberately erase the tapes? Was she willing to take the blame for someone else's
actions? Or was she forced to take the blame for someone else's actions?

The covert operations of Nixon and his accessories came to be known
as "Watergate" only once the burglars were apprehended. Whatever their
schemes, the actions of the conspirators were brought to a halt, and all their

attention turned to covering up evidence of illegal activity. Hence someone, possibly a woman, felt it necessary to erase part of the tape. The silence of eighteen and a half minutes became the focal point for debate, conjecture, and controversy.

In 1997, historian Stanley Kutler, with the help of Public Citizen, a national nonprofit public interest organization, succeeded in obtaining the release of the remaining Nixon tapes from the National Archives. Kutler edited and telescoped the conversations, eliminating what he believed to be "insignificant, trivial, or repetitious."[3] His selection is most fascinating when it comes to his transcription of the gap. Although the tapes preserve more than an hour of conversation for the morning of June 20, Kutler chooses to transcribe only the silence:

> June 20, 1972: The President and Haldeman, 11:26 a.m.–12:45 p.m., Executive Office Building
>
> This is the highly publicized "18 ½–minute gap." Technical and scientific investigations determined that the tape had been electronically erased by unknown persons some time after Alexander P. Butterfield revealed the existence of the Nixon Administration taping system in 1973. H. R. Haldeman's diary entry for this date talks about lengthy meetings with John Ehrlichman, John Mitchell, and John Dean, which concluded that it was necessary to keep the FBI from going "beyond what's necessary in developing evidence and that we can keep a lid on that." Haldeman said that he and the President talked about "our counterattack" and "PR offensive."[4]

Where we hear the white noise of erasure, we read the words, "This is the highly publicized '18 ½ minute gap.'" Notice too that Kutler's transcription is as cryptic as the silence of the erasure. The phrases that he chooses from Haldeman's diary to supplement the gap only highlight the secrecy. "Keep a lid on that" reaffirms the clandestine operations of the conspirators, while "our counterattack" suggests a counterconspiracy. Although over two hundred hours of taped conversations have been released to the public, eighteen and a half minutes of silence nevertheless conceal important information about one of the most elaborate cover-ups of the American presidency.

On November 22, 1963, in Dallas, Texas, 268 men and women witnessed the assassination of President John F. Kennedy. Twenty-two photographers, both amateur and professional, captured the event in still and moving pictures. Abraham Zapruder, with his primitive home-movie equipment, recorded the most complete film, twenty-two seconds beginning from the moment the motorcade turned from Houston onto Elm Street, until the final, fatal shot killed the president, and the limousine accelerated toward the triple underpass.[5] The Zapruder film has become an icon of the turbulent 60s, a nationally recognized image of the violent murder emblematic of the demise of an entire generation hopeful for the social improvement advocated by Kennedy and known as the "New Frontier." For those too young to recall where they were when Kennedy was shot, the movie provides a common experience and unites the gaze of all generations of citizenry on a single focal point.[6]

In the years following the assassination, the Zapruder film became the cornerstone of both the Warren Commission (the board of inquiry created by President Lyndon Johnson on November 29, 1963, to investigate the assassination and headed by Chief Justice Earl Warren) and its detractors. It was believed to be the most objective piece of evidence, capable of providing answers that plagued investigators. Yet, like the break of eighteen and a half minutes in the Nixon tapes, the Zapruder film too contains a significant gap. At the crucial moment of the assassination, the presidential limousine passed in front of a large street sign (now gone), reading *Stemmons Freeway Keep Right*, which blocked Zapruder's view. President Kennedy, Texas Governor John Connally, and their wives disappeared from sight. Each frame of the film has been scrupulously examined in conjunction with other photographs and eyewitness testimony. At frame 207, the President is seen before the street sign, waving at the crowds. At frame 224 the limousine emerges from behind the street sign, and the president's arms are raised to his neck. He is obviously hit. In the time between frames 207 and 224 (no more than four seconds), in the space behind the Stemmons Freeway sign, an event occurred that will remain unknown. Forensics, ballistics, acoustics, optics: every available scientific method has been applied and reapplied to the evidence. Nevertheless, the street sign in the middle of the screen hides crucial information.

In both examples, the information needed to complete the story and to ensure the continuity of an accurate narrative, one that represents the historical event from beginning to end, cannot be recovered. The erasure of the tape and the disappearance of the limousine behind the sign cause a gap in our knowledge of the sequence of events. In the etymological sense, the evidence, with its root in the Latin verb *videre*, "to see," is *in*visible. At these evidential blind spots, the historian, whose etymology is rooted in the Greek *idein*, "to see," is compelled to conjecture about what really happened. In the absence of fact, the historical accounts of Watergate and the assassination of JFK are left to the Aristotelian devices of probability and necessity.[7] I do not claim that if the eighteen and a half minutes of tape or the four seconds of film were available, then the clouds of conspiracy would dissipate and all chains of causation would be patently clear. But it is around the gaps in the Nixon tapes and the Zapruder film that debates about the details of the conspiracies rage most fiercely. The better a historian is at negotiating these gaps, the more successful he or she is at creating a narrative that is likely to be accepted as the authoritative version, one that leaves little room for the skepticism, opinion, or imagination that can divide and thereby corrode society. A successful conspiracy narrative accounts for all the links in the chain of cause and effect and thereby contains fear and deters citizens from further unrest.

It is no doubt daring—and intentionally startling—to begin a book on conspiracy narratives in Roman history with a discussion of Watergate and the assassination of JFK, but these irresistible modern American events clearly illustrate the problem that compels this study. On the one hand, history is a forum in which to exhibit the deeds of men and women, so that they not fade into oblivion.[8] But because conspiracy is a hidden, secret event, it resists— defies—exposition. In recording any conspiracy, important facts always remain in the shadows; to tell the tale of a conspiracy is to guess at a very great deal. So how does one reveal something that is deliberately kept secret? How does one speak with any authority on matters about which one knows little or nothing for certain? Of course, all historians face uncertainty and ignorance about their subject matter at some point. For all these reasons, I maintain that a conspiracy is an ideal circumstance in which to observe how a historian confronts the limits of knowledge.

Conspiracy plagued Rome from its beginning. According to Livy, the mysterious death of Rome's founder Romulus gave rise to rumors that the senators had plotted against him (1.16.4). The disaffected sons of Rome's fourth king, Ancus Marcius, conspired to assassinate Tarquinius Priscus because he was grooming his adopted son Servius Tullius for the throne. Servius was, they argued, nothing but a foreigner and the son of a slave woman (1.40). Immediately upon the assassination of Tarquinius Priscus, his wife Tanaquil concealed the death until the position of her stepson Servius was secure (1.41). The change from kingdom to republic also occasioned a conspiracy, for members of the family of the expelled Tarquinius Superbus plotted to restore him as king. They sent envoys supposedly to recover Superbus' property, but they in fact enlisted conspirators in secret. A slave, overhearing conversations and intercepting letters meant for Superbus, betrayed the conspirators to the consuls (2.3–5).

At the height of Roman expansion, the senate enacted a *senatus consultum* that called for the dissolution of the large-scale worship of Bacchus. Livy reports that more than seven thousand men and women were participants in the so-called Bacchanalian conspiracy (39.17.6). The restive last days of the republic were fertile ground for malcontents like Catiline who recruited the aid of foreigners. Calpurnia tried in vain to warn Caesar of the Ides of March; his assassination precipitated a course of events culminating in the reign of Augustus, who was himself vulnerable to repeated threats of conspiracy.

Of course, the successive Julio-Claudians fell prey to murderous plots. The suspicious circumstances surrounding the death of Augustus, Livia's concealment of it, and her schemes to secure the position of her son Tiberius echo the death of Tarquinius Priscus and the way Tanaquil jockeyed for her stepson's position.[9] Josephus' lengthy account of the assassination of Caligula attributes the incipient conspiracy in part to the maltreatment of a woman. Agrippina the Younger plotted to kill her husband Claudius; she was, in turn, murdered by her own son Nero. Domitian was assassinated in a plot that involved his wife. According to the late antique collection of biographies known as the *Historia Augusta,* the tyrannical actions of the emperor Commodus drove his sister to conspire to assassinate him; according to Dio, her motives were suspect. The plan backfired, resulting in her exile and execution.

Clearly conspiracies and assassinations in Roman history are not hard to find, and many more examples could be added to this abbreviated catalogue. Roman politics appear to be synonymous with intrigue, and no conspiracy is complete, it seems, without the involvement of a woman, a slave, or a sometimes even a foreigner. Conspiracy is a particularly dangerous crisis of legitimacy, because the conspirators' clandestine actions run counter to the most fundamental principle of *res publica:* that all actions concerning Rome be conducted in public. The secrecy of conspiracy completely undermines the general operation of Roman politics and society. Therefore, conspiracy carries especially heavy emotional and moral burdens. This book seeks to understand how the Roman historians talk about conspiracy; how they articulate, in the open and public forum of history writing, the closed and secret event of conspiracy. As we shall see, conspiracy is betrayed—and thereby revealed to the public—by people trusted with access to the private chambers of the conspirators: bedfellows and slaves.

This principle is demonstrated in three of the most famous conspiracies of ancient Rome: the betrayed Catilinarian, Bacchanalian, and Pisonian conspiracies. Sallust's *Bellum Catilinae,* Livy's Bacchanalian affair (39.8–19), and Tacitus' Pisonian conspiracy (*Annales* 15.48–74) are strikingly similar. In each account, the historian struggles to construct a continuous chain of causality of an event that is shrouded in secrecy and silence. Moreover, women play an important role in each conspiracy narrative. By comparing the depiction of women, their various actions and motives, we can see how conspiracy was a corruption of all that Roman aristocratic life stood for.

But these conspiracies were betrayed. What happens when a conspiracy is successful in achieving its aim? The assassinations of Julius Caesar and the emperor Caligula provide instructive contrasts. While Sallust, Livy, and Tacitus tried to construct a coherent narrative about a secret event, Josephus (*Jewish Antiquities* 19.1–273) was at liberty to describe the assassination of Caligula in its entirety, precisely because the conspiracy was neither detected nor suppressed; its secrets were exposed only once the deed was successfully completed. Our study concludes with an analysis of Appian's narrative of the murder of Julius Caesar (*Civil Wars* 2.111–117), perhaps the most famous event in Roman history, which haunted the Romans and structured their perception of conspiracy, tyranny, and freedom.

In these five conspiracy narratives, a rhetoric of conspiracy contributes to what I call a strategy of containment. Conspiracy is dangerous and threatening, morally, politically, economically, and socially. It arouses fear, both in those in power, who risk being overthrown, and in those who conspire, who risk being discovered and punished. A historical account of a conspiracy controls these fears by solidifying them in written word and disengaging other possible narrative outcomes. Conspiracy narratives operate as palliatives; well-constructed accounts of the worrisome events assure the reader that the conspiracy was a rare exception and will not happen again, if everyone remains vigilant. In this sense, conspiracy narratives both contain fear and deter future attempts at revolution. Other types of events in Roman historiography are celebratory, lauding identity and power. The foundation stories of Aeneas, Romulus, and Lucius Junius Brutus, for example, extol the establishment of Roman rule. Great battles, sacks of cities, kings routed and captured, internal discord between consuls and tribunes, agrarian legislation, the struggle of the orders—these were the topics that made for good old-fashioned history, according to Tacitus (*Ann.* 4.32.1). There is no room for internal threats of conspiracy in this list. Closest to civil war, conspiracy reveals Roman society at its worst and Roman politics at its weakest. But unlike civil war, when difference explodes into fraternal bloodshed like a violent volcanic eruption, conspiracy is more like an earthquake, whose unseen forces suddenly and unexpectedly shift the ground beneath one's feet. Hovering between stability and revolution, conspiracy is most important for understanding how the Romans maintained continuous authority in the face of internal threats of violence and disruption.

## CONSPIRACY IN THE ROMAN LITERARY IMAGINATION

These five conspiracies may at first seem a rather disparate collection, ranging from 186 B.C.E. to 65 C.E., and concerning economic distress, religious worship, party politics, and imperial disaffection; indeed, each conspiracy narrative is its own constellation of substantive and stylistic factors. I have selected these five based on three interconnected criteria: their historical importance, their narrative extent, and the variety of sources that document them. So the texts merit comparison for several significant reasons. First of all, Sallust, Livy, Tacitus, Josephus, and Appian represent the temporal range of Roman historiography from the end of the republic through the age of the Antonines. Considered diachronically, the conspiracy narratives exhibit development and change over time. These five historians also represent a range of socioeconomic backgrounds, from the senatorial to the provincial. In spite of differences in native language and place of origin, these historians nevertheless choose to construct narratives in the face of the limits of knowledge that conspiracy imposes. The narratives themselves manifest similar elements, including a list of conspirators, reasons for discontent, secret meetings and intrigue, revelation of the plot or perpetration of the murder, torture or punishment, and reward of the informants.

Furthermore, these conspiracies are attested in more than one source, allowing us to compare the historians' narratives with other accounts. Sallust's full-length monograph, the *Bellum Catilinae,* is supplemented by Cicero's four speeches *In Catilinam,* the speeches *Pro Murena* and *Pro Sulla,* together with the commentary of Asconius on Cicero's speeches *In Toga Candida, In Pisonem,* and *Pro Cornelio.* In Latin, the summaries of Velleius Paterculus (2.34–35) and Annius Florus (2.12) supplement the biographical material in Suetonius' *Divus Iulius* (14, 17); in Greek, Diodorus Siculus (40.5), Appian (*Civil Wars* 2.1), Dio (37.29–42), and Plutarch's *Life of Cicero* (14–22) also recount the events. Yet, while the Catilinarian conspiracy may be one of the most fully documented events in republican history, the sources remain irreconcilable on several counts. This is precisely because the secretive nature of the event precludes full disclosure.

The famed Bacchanalian affair of 186 B.C.E. is presented by Livy as a conspiracy to upset the stability of Rome by means of frenzied Bacchic worship introduced by foreigners from the East. The senatorial decree banning the cult survives in an inscription (*CIL* I² 581 = *ILS* 18) and provides a primary source against which to measure Livy's lurid account. Tacitus' account of the aborted attempt on Nero's life is supplemented by the brief mentions in Suetonius'

*Nero,* the epitome of Dio (62.24–28), and Plutarch's *De Garrulitate* (*Moralia* 505c–d).

A generation before Tacitus, Josephus wrote his account of the death of Caligula, an event that surely occupied Tacitus in the lost portion of the *Annales.* Our understanding of the assassination of Caligula is aided by Suetonius' *Caligula* and Dio (59.29). The assassination of Julius Caesar is documented in the works of three historians: Velleius Paterculus (2.56.3–59.1), Appian (*Civil Wars* 2.111–117), and Dio (44.12–22). These are supplemented by Plutarch's and Suetonius' biographies of Julius Caesar. In addition, Nicolaus of Damascus' biography of Augustus (the oldest surviving source) was written during the 20s B.C.E. and presumably reflects the version of the assassination given by Augustus in his *Memoirs.*[10] The interconnections of the ancient sources demonstrate the historical and literary importance of these five conspiracies. Throughout the book, I draw on these other sources to clarify what is distinctive about the narratives of Sallust, Livy, Tacitus, Josephus, and Appian.

Most importantly, however, these conspiracies fascinated the Romans themselves. Catiline became emblematic of evil.[11] Vergil commemorates him on the shield of Aeneas as one of Rome's most famous criminals.[12] Civil war, like conspiracy, pits fellow citizens against one another; Horace, Lucan, and Martial compare the destruction of civil war with the wrath of Catiline.[13] In his account of the conspiracy of patrician women who concocted poison in secret, Livy names Sergia and Cornelia. The allusion to the evil conspirators Lucius Sergius Catilina and the members of the house of the Cornelii— Publius Cornelius Cethegus, Publius Cornelius Lentulus Sura, Publius and Servius Cornelius Sulla—would not have been lost on Livy's audience.[14] The moralizing satirist Juvenal includes the conspirators in an abbreviated, but pointed, catalogue of infamous historical figures.[15] Avidius Cassius, who conspired against Marcus Aurelius, is called a "second Catiline," while Clodius Albinus, who plotted against Septimius Severus, is called the Catiline of his times.[16]

The achievements of Cicero, and especially his suppression of the conspiracy, were eulogized in an epic poem by Cornelius Severus,[17] and Lucan invokes the eloquence of Cicero, "beneath whose authority fierce Catiline trembled" (2.541). Seneca, Tacitus, and Martial attest the canonical status of Cicero's speeches *In Catilinam.*[18] Along with the speeches, Sallust's monograph was also widely read in antiquity.[19] Valerius Maximus twice draws upon Sallust's account for anecdotes. His example of A. Fulvius as a severe parent who visits harsh punishment upon his son derives no doubt from Sallust, as does his example of Catiline as a man of luxury and lust.[20] Quintilian notes that Lentulus was the third Cornelius to rule Rome, a detail found in both the *Bellum Catilinae* and Cicero's third Catilinarian; in Ampelius, the conspirators are proverbial.[21] Orosius, contemporary of Augustine of Hippo, declares in his history that the Catilinarian conspiracy was well known to all because of Sallust's monograph.[22] Eventually the year 63 B.C.E. became synonymous with the conspiracy.[23] Suetonius erroneously reckons that Augustus was born "on the day the conspiracy of Catiline was before the senate."[24] The error belies the degree to which the Catilinarian conspiracy dominated the year 63 and cast a shadow across the imagination of Roman writers for centuries.

The worship of Bacchus also holds a prominent place in Latin literature, where it is depicted as unbecoming of a proper Roman. The frenzied Bacchanalia, characterized by madness, intoxication, and extreme physicality, appears often in the slapstick comedies of Plautus.[25] Vergil twice compares the love struck Dido to a Bacchant, a convention taken up by later epic poets.[26] The unbridled lasciviousness of the Bacchic revelers enrages the satirist Juvenal, who contrasts proper moral behavior with the wanton revelry of the Bacchanalia.[27] Tacitus describes the Dionysiac garden party at which Messalina, wife of Claudius, behaved like a maenad (*Ann.* 11.31). Pliny's letter to Trajan on the Christians recasts the republican problems of religious worship under the empire; his description of worship recalls the dangers of such secretive societies.[28] On the other hand, later Christians also co-opted the Bacchanalian affair for their own moralizing discourse.[29] Clearly, the severity of the senate's response to Bacchic worship had lasting repercussions on the Roman mindset.

In the aftermath of the Pisonian conspiracy, Nero's brutal retaliation against some of Rome's most talented writers of the day came to symbolize the harsh circumstances of life under tyranny. Three of the greatest names of Neronian literature, Seneca, Lucan, and Petronius, were forced to commit suicide. Their works are a testimony to their literary genius and their precarious position in the Neronian circle.[30] The late antique biography of Clodius Albinus reproduces a letter of the emperor Septimius Severus to the senate in which he chastises them: "You have not returned to me the gratitude which your forefathers showed in the face of the Pisonian conspiracy against Nero, which they likewise showed Trajan, and which they showed lately in opposing Avidius Cassius."[31] The letter is no doubt the product of the biographer's imagination. Nevertheless, the statement is good evidence that the aborted Pisonian conspiracy had become legendary enough to be an effective point of comparison.

Like the foundation myths and legends that occupied Vergil in the *Aeneid* and Livy in Book I, the prominence of the Catilinarian, Bacchanalian, and

Pisonian conspiracies in Roman literature is testimony to their significance in the Roman literary imagination. As the ancient myths of Aeneas and Romulus allowed Romans to celebrate their origins, so the stories of the conspiracies allowed Romans to commemorate their preservation from the most pernicious danger of all: one's own fellow citizens.

It is by the hands of those closest to him that Caligula fell. Yet his assassination is not commemorated in the literature to the same extent that the Catilinarian, Bacchanalian, and Pisonian conspiracies were, no doubt because immediately upon his death, the senate desired to disgrace Caligula and refuse him honors. Although Claudius formally rejected a motion declaring Caligula a *hostis* (a public enemy), nevertheless he caused statues of the former emperor to be removed. Ample evidence of the defacement of Caligula in statues, inscriptions, and coins suggests a popular renunciation of him.[32] As a Julio-Claudian, Caligula was assured his place in history, but he never seems to have been a favorite of the poets.

The assassination of Julius Caesar, on the other hand, fascinated the ages and provided ample material for literary productions.[33] In the *Georgics*, Vergil gives one of the most extensive lists of portents in ancient literature, the omens attending the assassination of Caesar. Indeed, the foreboding indications of his death captivated the ancients.[34] They also seem to have had a morbid fascination with the actual number of wounds. Appian, Suetonius, Livy, Florus, Zonaras, Eutropius, Valerius Maximus, and Plutarch all record that Caesar was stabbed twenty-three times.[35] Twice Ovid speaks of the conspirators; in the *Metamorphoses*, Venus spies the incipient conspiracy (*Met.* 15.763), while in the description of the temple of Mars Ultor in the *Fasti*, Augustus vows to avenge Caesar's death at the hands of the conspirators (5.518). In the aftermath, Brutus and Cassius were canonized as the Liberators, as evidenced in the Tacitean speech of the Tiberian historian Cremutius Cordus: "There will be plenty of people who will remember not only Cassius and Brutus but even me, should destruction fall upon me."[36] We shall see that the Flavian historian Josephus alludes to the murder of Caesar in his account of the assassination of Caligula. Indeed, the memory of the Ides of March runs deep in the Roman collective memory.

## THE VOCABULARY OF CONSPIRACY

Conspiracy is a paradoxical phenomenon, for it can be identified and named as such only once it has been brought to light. Disclosing a secret plot and calling it a "conspiracy" gives substance to the covert event, enabling it to be narrated. In this sense, conspiracy resides in the space between concealment and revelation, between silence and speech. This interstitial nature is manifested fundamentally in the vocabulary of conspiracy.

The Latin conspiracy narratives featured in this study denote the event with the noun *coniuratio*.[37] Etymologically and in its earliest attested meaning, the verb *coniurare* refers to the act of taking an oath or joining in league with others for a common purpose. Poets use the term to designate the oath sworn by the Greeks against the Trojans at Aulis at the outset of the Trojan war. *Coniurare* is also the verb used by Statius for the oath that the women of Lemnos swore against their husbands. In a speech in favor of the Oppian law, Livy's Cato alludes to the Lemnian conspiracy.[38]

In military contexts, *coniuratio* denotes the oath that soldiers took before a campaign. In the republic, there were two distinct military oaths. The consul administered to all soldiers upon enlisting the compulsory *sacramentum*, which had religious implications; violation incurred the wrath of the gods. This primary oath bound the soldier to the republic, his commander, and his comrades. A soldier took a second oath before a tribune when he actually joined his unit; in the *ius iurandum* the soldier swore to uphold discipline and to obey his immediate commanders.[39] According to Livy, before the battle of Cannae in 216 B.C.E., the two oaths were combined for the first time and administered by the tribune.[40] In his commentary on the *Aeneid*, Servius preserves a vivid description of pageantry of this bygone ceremony:

> Surely if there is some uprising, namely, the Italian or Gallic war, causing great fear because of the proximity of danger, since there is no time to ask each [soldier] individually, the one who would have led the army used to proceed to the Capitol, holding up two standards; one red, calling forth the infantry, the other blue, summoning the cavalry (for blue is the color of the sea, from whose god it is commonly held the horse originates). Then he used to say, "Who so wishes the republic to be safe, let him follow me." And those who were present used to swear allegiance all together [at the same time]. So this type of campaign is called a *coniuratio*.[41]

*Coniuratio* was thus initially a legitimate measure taken by law-abiding citizens dedicated to defending the republic. It was a course of action followed in extreme circumstances, when sudden danger made it impossible to enlist men individually. It was a public act by which members of the community affirmed their commitment to the preservation of the Roman state and to each other. The soldiers who assembled under a *coniuratio* were legitimized to fight the war at hand and would automatically disband at its conclusion.[42]

In contrast to the military *coniuratio,* Caesar uses the term in the *Bellum Gallicum* to designate the treacherous uprisings of Gauls against him. The Remi (the only Belgian tribe to submit to Caesar at once and remain loyal to the end) deny participating in a conspiracy against Caesar (2.1.1, 3.3). As Caesar prepares to cross the channel to Britain, the coastal tribe of the Veneti swears an oath to take no separate action but to endure whatever happens among themselves (3.8.3). In response, Caesar takes harsh measures, justifying his action by equating the *coniuratio* with *iniuriae, rebellio,* and *defectio* (3.10.2). The Britains (4.30.3), the Gauls (5.27.4), and the Senones and Carnutes (6.44.1) are all said to have conspired against Caesar. Even the continuator of the *Bellum Gallicum,* Aulus Hirtius, emphasizes the ever-present threat of foreign conspiracy in the first sentence of Book 8: "Several tribes at that time were reported to have renewed their war councils and to have joined in conspiracies" (cf. 8.2.2, 23.3).

When Caesar established the colony of Urso in the months just before his assassination, a provision was made that "no colonist of the colonia Genetiva, established by the order of G. Caesar the dictator, shall get together any assemblage or meeting or conspiracy. . . ." Caesar had good reason to guard against conspiracy from this particular quarter; the people of Urso had been sympathetic to the Pompeian cause.[43] Although the word *coniuratio* never appears in the *Bellum Civile,* the inscription of the charter of Urso testifies to the growing possibility of citizens engaging in conspiracy. Thus, in the course of Caesar's career, the use of *coniuratio* shifts from foreign to domestic contexts.

The same pattern of usage, from foreign to domestic, is evident in the speeches of Cicero. In only two of his pre-Catilinarian speeches does Cicero use the word *coniuratio.* The voluminous speeches against Verres, governor of Sicily tried for *res repetundae* (extortion) in 70 B.C.E., were not delivered in their entirety before a jury, but their subsequent publication provided a powerful venue for Cicero to voice his views on the corruption within both the provincial and judicial system, while at the same time promoting his own self-image among the Roman élite.[44]

In the fifth book of the second speech, he refutes the argument that Verres ought to be acquitted because he was a good general, on the grounds that he had in fact suborned slave conspiracies while in Sicily. Verres had learned of a slave revolt in Triocala; the participants were convicted and condemned to death by crucifixion. They were bound to the stake, when Verres ordered their release and return to their master—for a handsome price, Cicero alleges.[45]

Just one year later, Cicero defended a former provincial governor from the charge of extortion. In the speech delivered on behalf of Fonteius, former governor of Transalpine Gaul, Cicero demonstrates his rhetorical agility. He argues that Fonteius is not guilty of *res repetundae* because he did not extort money from other Romans living in the province but only from Gauls. Furthermore, in a xenophobic tirade that forms the basis for his entire defense, Cicero discredits the witnesses, on the grounds that Gauls are, in general, untrustworthy. He insinuates that they are greedy, irrational, sacrilegious, and capable of plotting conspiracies.[46]

In both of these speeches, Cicero depends on the prevailing negative attitudes towards slaves and foreigners.[47] By casting opprobrium on the band of *fugitivi* (slaves who have revolted) and by casting the suspicion of conspiracy on foreigners, he reinforces the stereotype that was eventually to form the foundation of his attack against Catiline. Cicero vilified his fellow citizen by comparing him to a foreign enemy. Of course, Catiline was a greater danger precisely because he dwelled among the Romans.[48] Thus, in the course of Cicero's speeches, the direction of the meaning of conspiracy changed, from an external attack by foreigners to an internal attack by citizens.

Habinek argues that in the speeches against Catiline, Cicero mobilizes the polyvalence of the word *coniuratio* and its ability to call to mind both the positive, salutary acts of law-abiding citizens and the negative, destructive acts of bandits and criminals. Relying on the remark of Servius that "*coniuratio* can be used of good things, for the word has a middling sense,"[49] Habinek maintains that the word is "ethically neutral," referring to runaway slaves and bandits as readily as to legitimate Roman citizens.[50] The dual nature of *coniuratio* is captured on republican coinage dating to the first year of the Hannibalic war (218/217 B.C.E.), depicting a ceremonial oath-taking on one side and the head of Janus on the other.[51] Inherent in the portraits of Janus on the coins are his associations with roads and journeys, with beginnings in general, and most significantly for understanding the iconography of these coins, with "the sacrifice preliminary to any important ceremony."[52] Thus, his presence on the coins officiates the military *coniuratio*, bestowing his benediction on the oath-taking. The *tumultus* that necessitates the *coniuratio* puts the community in a state of uncertainty; the sudden onset of danger meets its swift oppression, in a moment that looks both forward and back. The duality of the portrait of Janus also suggests the possibility of a counterconspiracy; for every obverse there is a reverse, for every oath sworn to protect the state there is the possibility of an oath sworn to destroy it.

The summer of 32 B.C.E. saw a radical redefinition of communal oaths:

The whole of Italy voluntarily took an oath of allegiance to me and demanded me as its leader in the war which I afterwards won at Actium. The same oath was taken by the provinces of Gaul, Spain, Africa, Sicily, and Sardinia.[53]

The speaker is, of course, Caesar Augustus, retrospectively recording his career in the monumental inscription known as the *Res Gestae*. In a characteristic ploy, Augustus used an already existing military practice, the act of swearing an oath of allegiance, in a novel way. Not only soldiers but citizens as well felt compelled to pledge their faith to Augustus. But this was not the *coniuratio* of Hannibalic times, taken by soldiers in the face of sudden tumult. Sworn by citizens, this oath was extra-constitutional and did not have the force of law. Surely the notion of *tota Italia* was suspect; according to Suetonius, Augustus excused the people of Bononia from swearing the oath because they had for so long been dependents of Antony (*Aug.* 17.2). The exemption of some suggests the compulsion of others. The phrase *tota Italia* does indicate the globalization of an otherwise localized event. A conspiracy is to be feared when a few swear oaths in secret or when a few swear allegiance to a particular leader, thereby undermining the constitution.[54] The oath to Augustus, on the other hand, assuaged fear because everyone (*tota Italia*) swore the oath openly, indeed, voluntarily (*sua sponte*). Augustus manipulated the concept of "swearing together" so completely and effectively that thereafter a similar kind of oath was taken on the accession of new emperors.[55] But in the turbulent years before Actium, at the moment of his break with Antony in that summer of 32, Augustus claimed that stability was achieved by the very act — an oath of allegiance — that had, within his own lifetime, produced instability and had in fact been deployed simultaneously by his enemy: "Such was the zeal on both sides alike that they made alliances with each leader by oaths of allegiance" (Dio 50.6.6). The oath recorded in the *Res Gestae* (together with its legacy) demonstrates quite forcefully the binary capacity of *coniuratio*, a state of affairs between danger and safety, between conflict and resolution, between old ways and new, between ancestral custom (*mos maiorum*) and revolution (*res novae*).

## APPROACHING CONSPIRACY

A historical study of conspiracy would consider, among other aspects, the causes of the conspiracies, the social implications of rewards and punishments, and the political and economic trends surrounding the phenomenon of conspiracy. While this book makes efforts toward understanding these broader historical issues and may inspire such further work, it is not, in its conception, a historical contribution. Rather, as a literary study, this book is concerned with the way conspiracies are portrayed. Therefore, I approach each conspiracy individually for several reasons. Since we shall be dealing with five different events ranging from 186 B.C.E. to 65 C.E. and involving a wide cast of characters in very different situations, it will simply be easier to engage in the specifics of one conspiracy at a time. Furthermore, each author should be taken on his own terms; the circumstances of production for each were unique, and should remain so.[56]

Individual chapters on Josephus and Appian underscore their importance in the development of Roman historiography; they are treated as essential, not tangential, contributors to the fabric of Roman imperial literature. Josephus and Appian remind us that the Rome of the emperors was a polyglot society that had successfully incorporated the diverse peoples of the Mediterranean basin within its political as well as cultural realm. Josephus and Appian compose their histories in the Greek language but clearly follow lost Latin sources. Thus, they offer a unique opportunity to observe the way Latin literature influences the composition of Greek works.[57] Finally, it is important to take each conspiracy as a whole, for only then can we observe how narrative continuity is achieved by each author.

Since women participate in each conspiracy, it is necessary to identify some basic assumptions that underlie and shape our understanding of their role in the narratives. First, the representations of women are not expected to be wholly accurate portrayals of lived experience but rather fictional constructions designed along certain organizing principles. Women are assigned actions in the sources to serve the interests and the rhetorical strategies of male authors.[58] For instance, in most texts, "woman" is a definitional tool that operates as the opposite of "man." Woman's actions and behavior are always contrasted to man's and are usually found wanting. When women usurp power beyond their means, they constitute a threat that must be controlled.[59]

At the same time, it is important to remember that the ancient sources are notoriously unreliable about women's sexual misconduct. Political invective regularly deploys adultery as a weapon against women; the tropes of satire depend on the stereotypical sexual deviance of women.[60] Before this premise was exposed, the study of ancient literary sources merely reproduced the male-authored point of view. But recognition of this premise allows us to observe the political, sexual, and moral ways in which women serve male discourse. For example, it is not coincidental that the women of the Julio-Claudian dynasty are consistently painted unfavorably by authors who tend to criticize the regime. Thus, attention to women in conspiracy narratives tells us more about male discourse on conspiracies. Any assertion otherwise would simply reinscribe male perceptions rather than expose them.

Second, there exists a persistent tension between the general representation of women and the details of their daily existence.[61] Any reading of women in Roman conspiracies must acknowledge where the text follows certain generic rules for representing women and where the text deviates from the rules to represent a specific woman. These deviations are also constructed along certain organizing principles, for instance, the need to accommodate different social strata, political structures, temporal and spatial settings, and perhaps most obviously, differences in immediate circumstances. In each conspiracy narrative, the participation of specific women is a historical fact; yet the portrayal of these specific women is, to a certain degree, commensurate with the portrayal of women in general.

In this sense, the content of the five conspiracy narratives is not arbitrary or trivial; the presence of women in these conspiracies is not an accident or a rhetorical flourish but an essential fact of the event. Thus, while male authors control the way women are portrayed, the actual presence of women in the conspiracies appears to flex the rules of generally accepted gendered discourse. No doubt women have prominent roles in the outcome of Roman conspiracies. They are portrayed as having made a difference because they actually did influence the course of events.

To this extent, women in Roman conspiracy narratives demonstrate the tendency of Roman discourse on sex to be engrossed with departures from the established norms.[62] Conspiratorial women are anomalies both sexually and morally, and these irregularities serve as symbolic frameworks for identifying and denigrating the fundamental nature of conspiracy. The singularity of women in conspiracy narratives serves to underscore the singularity of the phenomenon of conspiracy. By focusing on the exceptionality of conspiracy, an author can mitigate its effects, tame, and contain it.[63]

Limitations are obvious: I say little of other women in Sallust, Livy, Tacitus, Josephus, and Appian. I do not assume that the other unstudied women are variations of the conspiratorial woman, nor do I want to make conspiratorial women emblematic of women in Roman historiography. My point is to suggest that the strategy of containment evident in Roman conspiracy narratives is strengthened by the portrayal of conspiratorial women.

In an article on Sallust's famous portrait of Sempronia, G. M. Paul remarks in passing that it is customary to include women, especially those of the lower class, on the list of degenerates ready to foment violence against the state.

He goes on to claim that "the ancient reader . . . was fully susceptible to the idea of finding a woman, especially one with sexual charms, at the center of a conspiracy."[64] Rather than take for granted the participation of women in conspiracies, I ask why they were drawn into conspiracies, what purpose their presence served, how they contributed to the overall continuity of the narrative, and most significantly, how they concealed or revealed secrets. While certain common features are readily perceived, individual characteristics emerge. I explore the dialectic between the general notion of a "whore with a heart of gold"[65] and the particular woman's situation in each conspiracy. Some of the women taken up in this study are certainly not whores; others have hearts of lesser metal. It behooves us to pay attention to these differences, for the commonplace is not devoid of meaning.[66] Although such critical practice can be condemned as merely making mountains out of molehills, nevertheless our understanding of Roman women stands to gain from attention to the smallest scraps preserved in an already fragmentary record.

As an intermediate state of affairs, conspiracy confounded categories not only of gender but also of status. As women were privy to the secrets of conspirators by virtue of their intimate contact, so too slaves had access to the secrets of conspiracy. Slave labor provided the basis for the ancient economy; yet slaves' "separate subjectivity," to use McCarthy's terminology, was the very thing that made them both valuable and dangerous.[67] Although slaves could be subdued by the promise of manumission, the threat of slave resistance, both active and passive, was never far from the surface of society. For instance, certain intimate tasks afforded slaves dangerous avenues of contact with the lives of their masters. The barber or doctor had access to the body (indeed, the throat) of the master. A messenger could distort or destroy the entrusted communication. A slave's purposeful idleness or laziness, although difficult to pinpoint, detracted from his value to the master.[68]

Although the threat of punishment deterred such behavior, nevertheless the possibility of revolt remained, giving rise to a persistent undertone of fear and mistrust between slave and master, as a letter of Pliny the Younger attests: "You see with how many dangers, insults, and ridicules we are surrounded; no one can be safe if he is lax and lenient."[69] The constant presence of slaves in the daily lives of their masters gave slaves access to knowledge and so to power that threatened the equilibrium of the slave-master relationship.

Slaves were privy to everything the master said and did. Only their silence ensured the master's privacy, but this silence depended upon either the slave's loyalty or the master's threat of punishment. Between the extremes of loyalty and punishment, the ancient system of slavery interposed judicial torture, the legal, physical destruction of the slave's silence at the expense of his ever-present body.[70] As noncitizen chattel, slaves were subject to corporal punishment and were permitted to give testimony only under judicial torture. In general, slaves could not be compelled to testify against their owners. Slave owners in ancient Rome, however, had the right to call for the torture of their slaves, both male and female, for evidence on criminal matters; Bradley demonstrates the continuity of the practice from early republic to late empire.[71] Although the slave owner risked damaging his own property, presumably the ends justified the loss.[72]

A slave's access to spaces both public and private corresponds to the conception of his body as composed of a deceptive exterior and a truth-bearing interior.[73] So judicial torture was necessary to excavate the truth hidden within the interior of the slave body. Such state-sanctioned, institutionalized violence against slaves afforded the Romans one more way to gloss the unease with the power inherent in the dual nature of the slave's subjectivity and to deny the power caused by this duality.[74]

Torture did not necessarily succeed in elucidating the truth; indeed, some slaves would say anything, even if it were not true, to stop the torture.[75] Others would maintain obdurate silence in the face of cruelty, even to the point of death. According to Tacitus, the slaves of Octavia (wife of Nero) demonstrated the range of responses: examined under torture, some were forced by the intensity of the agony to admit falsehoods, but most persisted to uphold their mistress. When one of the faithful did speak, she chastised her tormentor with an insult, ironically all the more true precisely because delivered under torture: "Octavia's genitals are more pure than your mouth."[76] Thus, evidentiary torture, a formal legal mechanism intended to safeguard the rights and property of the ruling élite, elicits not a dependable outcome of truth but a range of responses that bespeak the duality inherent in the institution of slavery itself.

While the line of demarcation between the slave, subject to evidentiary torture, and the citizen, immune from torture, was clearly discernible in the Republic, the torture of free witnesses is attested under Tiberius, Caligula, Claudius, and Nero. Indeed, the victims, both men and women, were nearly always incriminated in acts of treason, and conspiracy in particular. Garnsey summarizes:

> When treason was the charge, no man was safe from torture, whether as a punishment or as a means of securing the names of possible confederates. The theory was that whoever threatened the life of the Emperor had forfeited his rights and privileges: he could be treated as a slave.[77]

The torture of free persons by emperors was clearly an abuse of power for which they were not held accountable. Thus, the tyrannical response to the suspicion of conspiracy blurred the distinction between free and slave. As conspirators sought to change the political order, so the emperors effaced the social order.

No doubt, élite male conspirators had unlimited access to operate in all spheres of Roman society. But to preserve the integrity of the conspiracy, and indeed to preserve the appearance of their own moral integrity, they could not conduct the plot in open, public spaces. Upstanding Roman citizens led their lives in full view of the public eye. But conspirators had to keep out of sight. Hidden away in private quarters, the conspirators operated in the places women and slaves tended to occupy. Thus, women and slaves were privy to information otherwise inaccessible to the public. As a result, they were both valuable and dangerous to conspirators, for they could either keep or betray secrets. This Januslike quality made women and slaves the ideal participants in the duplicitous act of conspiracy.

The final part of this introduction sets forth my approach to conspiracy in the Roman historians. Although some scholars have paid attention to the rhetorical aspects of the narratives,[78] there has been no unified exploration of the typology of conspiracy narrative. At work in these texts (as I hope to show) is more than literary allusion; resonances among the texts demonstrate more than erudite engagement, competitive emulation, or even self-deprecating admission of secondariness to one's predecessors. Rather, the conspiracy narratives reveal several different tactics for conquering fear and distrust and several different rhetorical strategies for depicting the struggle. I compare and contrast these five conspiracies to understand how the Roman historians talked about the perilous phenomenon of conspiracy and how they managed to construct coherent, continuous narratives of secret events so as to contain fear and deter future revolution. To do this, I employ a narratological method that seeks to discover, describe, and explain the mechanics of conspiracy narratives, the elements responsible for their form and functioning. Narratology takes into consideration three components of the reading experience: author, text, and reader. Attention to all three components yields a composite understanding of the narrative.[79]

By author, I mean the five Roman historians (Sallust, Livy, Tacitus, Josephus, and Appian) who produced historical texts that contain descriptions of conspiracies. In each conspiracy narrative, the presence of the historian is evident in the text. For example, the use of the first-person pronoun, deictic markers of space or time (e.g., "in my day") and even directional signals (e.g., "as I stated above") signal the act of writing and remind the reader of the status of the narrative as written document. The intrusiveness of a given historian helps gage his degree of self-consciousness and his reliability, and this profoundly affects interpretation and the reader's perception of the historian. Does he appear to be objective or subjective? Is he to be regarded with suspicion or is he generally trustworthy?

A definition of text is somewhat more complicated. For my purposes, it refers to the written word that the author produced. The text is further subcategorized. "Story" refers to the events that are to be depicted, while "plot" refers to the chain of causation that dictates how the events are to be linked. But beyond the story and the plot, "narrative" is the revelation of events *in a particular mode* for the purpose of storing knowledge used to create and maintain a collective identity.[80] In classical Greek and Latin texts, the revelation of events occurs either by showing or by telling. This is best exemplified by the presentation of the *Iliad:* the epic advances either by description or by speech. Furthermore, the epic is a storehouse of information that informs a particular cultural identity. Likewise, the historians constructed their storehouses of cultural-historical information on this twofold principle of revelation, namely, speech often in the form of dramatic mimesis, and description in the form of the author's own voice. This duality could also be thought of in terms of scene and summary: scenes in which characters speak for themselves, and summary in which the author speaks.

Despite this simplicity, such representation admits of complex literary productions because of the mode of representation, for it is in the choice of a particular mode that the author exercises his control over the text. There are several ways the author can manipulate the presentation of a narrative.

First, the author can present material either explicitly or implicitly. Either information is imparted in such a way as to be verifiable, or information is communicated by suggestion, innuendo, insinuation, or implication. In conspiracy narratives, implicit information is often more abundant than explicit information.

Second, the author makes presuppositions about what his audience knows. Presuppositions allow the author to shape the reader's world. The author emphasizes certain characters and incidents and not others. Some information is thereby considered shared, common, and therefore not new or revelatory, while other information is perceived as new and even startling.

Third, the author chooses his mode of discourse.[81] In direct discourse, the author indicates that a character speaks. In Latin and Greek, postpositive verbs of speaking serve to mark *oratio recta* (direct discourse), given in an independent clause. In indirect discourse, the character does not speak. Instead, the author reports what the character said. In English, quotation marks are suppressed, and the conjunction *that* is inserted before the reported speech. Personal and possessive pronouns are shifted from the first or second to the third person. The tenses of verbs shift back, converting present tense to past. In Latin and Greek, the introductory verb is followed by a dependent clause; this is traditionally referred to as *oratio obliqua* (indirect discourse). A third category, free indirect discourse, suppresses or delays the reporting verb of saying or thinking. McHale provides a clear example in English: "Oh, no, she was fine, she was just going to stay in bed all day, Mary answered in a dead voice."[82]

Different modes of discourse allow for information to be processed in different ways. Speech that is highlighted by direct discourse or decentralized in free indirect discourse can emphasize certain themes or characterizations, lend a degree of suspense, contribute to the overall sense of aesthetic pleasure, and appeal to the reader's emotions more or less directly. Sometimes the mode of discourse complicates the reader's ability to discern easily who exactly is speaking and whose ideas are being represented. The degree of directness and indirectness of discourse provides a vantage point from which to observe the degree of the author's involvement in the statements being made.

Closely related to the mode of discourse is what has been traditionally referred to as point of view and more recently as focalization.[83] There are two types that the author can adopt in his presentation. From the unrestricted point of view, the author-narrator tells more than any and all the characters could know or tell at the time of the situation described. Such a stance is characteristic of the so-called omniscient narrator. From the internal point of view, however, information is presented strictly in terms of the knowledge perception of one or several characters. The author tells the story through the eyes of one or more characters who know and can reveal only so much at any given time. Our Roman historians present much of the conspiracy narratives from the unrestricted point of view; however, they do shift to the internal point of view. Such shifts to internal focalization alert the reader to the limits of knowledge. Who speaks and who perceives the information that is presented shape the reader's understanding of the progress of the narrative.

Finally, the author chooses his mode of description. For instance, description can take the form of *ekphrasis* or allusion. The author perspicuously chooses the sequence, the temporal ordering, in which he presents events. Indeed, historians are by no means bound to strict chronological order; elsewhere I have demonstrated the effect, for example, of Tacitus' temporal ordering of events in the first book of the *Annales*.[84] *Ekphrasis*, allusion, indeed all the tropes of description contribute to the overall aesthetic pleasure of the reading experience. No doubt pleasure is a fundamental aspect of literature.

Yet the amusement of the reader is seldom innocuous; Horace links delight to admonition.[85] Thus, in a conspiracy narrative, a pleasurable mode of presentation is an effective way to discourage thoughts of further uprising. By anesthetizing the reader to the realities of the violence of conspiracy, the aesthetics of a conspiracy narrative can also defuse the fear that a conspiracy engenders. Once reading a conspiracy narrative becomes fun, the conspiracy is no longer dangerous, fearful, or insidious.

Above all, the author chooses the degree to which the progress of the events is impeded. Delay, detour, digression, diversion — these techniques add an element of pleasure by entertaining the reader, and an element of suspense, or even frustration, by withholding information from the reader. For Barthes, the suspension of information is one of the key features of the hermeneutic principle,[86] and it is largely on this principle that my investigation of conspiracies rests. A hermeneutic reading of a text interrogates the suggestions or assertions that there is a mystery to be solved. To what extent does the author formulate that mystery? Does the author propose a possible solution? To what extent does information presented contribute or hinder the solution of the mystery? As we examine the modes in which the Roman historians choose to reveal or suspend information, we will be forced to consider a more pressing question: What happens when the events themselves are withheld from the author who is trying to create a narrative?

At last we come to the third and final component of the act of reading, the reader. All the techniques of representation at the disposal of the author have profound effects on the reader's interpretation. Interpretation depends to a large extent on the mode of representation; at a fundamental level, the reader's understanding is constrained not only by his or her ability to decode the text but also by the content of the text. A text that presents information implicitly is more opaque than a text that presents information explicitly. Presuppositions, indirect discourse, internal focalization, temporal displacement, and extensive use of delay complicate the task of interpretation by making it difficult for the reader to answer certain questions and so to gain knowledge from the narrative.

Most readers assume that the author strives to be understood, that he chooses modes of presentation that limit interpretive possibilities. Indeed, I argue that Sallust, Livy, Tacitus, Josephus, and Appian all strive to limit interpretive possibilities and thereby contain the phenomenon of conspiracy within a strict code, so as to deter readers from entertaining the notion of conspiring against Rome. Yet the historian's ability to construct such an airtight narrative depends on his own knowledge of events and his ability to present the events — secret, hidden events at that — in a fully plausible way.

In other words, the strategy of containment rests upon the historian's ability to construct a continuous narrative.

Studies of beginnings and endings in literature seem to take for granted the basic question of how an author gets from the opening to the last words.[87] The inaugural moment of a text breaks a silence; closure is a retreat back into silence. Generic considerations often determine the ways an author treats these moments. An epic poet traditionally declares his subject up front; some-times lyric poets employ the priamel (or preamble, a series of statements that gradually ascend to the goal of the poem) as an introductory tool. Histori-ans often begin by justifying their endeavor in superlatives — "the greatest war ever waged" — and by stating claims of impartiality — "with neither animus nor eagerness."[88] Often endings are signaled with such closural language as references to night, mourning, or death. But once the author has solved his problem of how to begin and end his text, the more abiding problem of how to maintain narrative continuity presses at every turn.

Continuity is the quality of a text that creates the sense of advancement from beginning, to middle, to end, following a chain of causality that gives the impression that the story "hangs together."[89] Continuity is achieved in sev-eral ways. Repetition of information keeps the subject in the forefront of the reader's mind and assures the reader that the subject of the narrative is united. Yet variations in the repetitions advance the narrative; the same material is re-presented but with new qualifications that add to the reader's knowledge. Anaphora is a particularly useful rhetorical device for achieving continuity; the repetition of a word or phrase at the beginning of successive paragraphs helps keep the reader's place in the narrative sequence. Transitional words and phrases help ease the reader from one subject to the next. Structural and logi-cal phrase and clause markers lend cohesiveness to a text by accounting for the succession of propositions that lead to a conclusion. The historian deter-mines the connections between discrete events that bind them together in a continuous narrative; in short, he asserts causality.[90]

In sum, three principles govern my approach to conspiracy narratives in Roman historiography. First, the author controls the mode of representation of the narrative. The author chooses to give information explicitly or im-plicitly. He chooses his presuppositions. He decides whether information is transmitted by description or by dialogue, and if by dialogue, whether it is reported in direct or indirect discourse. He selects the point of view and can shift it within the course of the narrative. He decides the order for presenting information. Second, the hermeneutic principle accounts for the constraints placed on the reader's knowledge; it also explains the creation of suspense in the narrative. The author suppresses or delays information so as to guide the reader toward a particular conclusion. Until that conclusion is reached, the reader remains in a state of uncertainty. Finally, according to the principle of continuity, the narrative unfolds from beginning to end, logically. Making sense of conspiracies in narrative is a key step in the process of averting fear and keeping conspiracies from surfacing in real life.

After comparing how Sallust, Livy, and Tacitus construct their accounts of the betrayed Catilinarian, Bacchanalian, and Pisonian conspiracies, the three chapters of Part I culminate in a typology of conspiracy narrative. The continuous narrative of a secret event depends upon the transmittal of information from a private setting to the public sphere, and women are the ideal conduits for the transfer of sensitive information. Because the conspiracies to assassinate Caligula and Julius Caesar were not betrayed, the focus of Part II shifts to elucidate the hermeneutics of assassination, that is, the ways Josephus and Appian maintain suspense throughout their accounts, in spite of the reader's prior knowledge of the outcome of the events. Taken together, the narratives of the Catilinarian, Bacchanalian, Pisonian conspiracies and the assassinations of Caligula and Julius Caesar demonstrate that the capacity to expose, and so to narrate a secret conspiracy depends on either the betrayal that halts it or the success that brings it to fruition.

# PART ONE

# BETRAYED CONSPIRACIES

# ONE

# SALLUST

## *The Catilinarian Conspiracy*

Cicero's invitation to Lucceius to write an individual monograph about his consular year and its most famous event, the Catilinarian conspiracy, indicates that such a narrow topic was considered a suitable subject for a shorter historical monograph:

> So you may also likewise isolate the domestic conspiracy from the external foreign wars. Indeed I see it matters little to my reputation, but it does matter to my impatience, that you not wait until you come to that place but immediately seize that event in its entirety. And likewise, if all your attention is turned toward one plot and one character, I already detect how much the more everything will be luxuriant and highly wrought.[1]

Of course, Cicero himself was willing to meet the need for a history glorifying his consulship. Based on his four speeches *In Catilinam,* it is not difficult to imagine the connections Cicero would have drawn between causes and effects, and the way he would have achieved narrative continuity. Lucceius did not answer the call to write about the year 63 B.C.E.;[2] but two decades later, the Catilinarian conspiracy proved irresistible to Sallust.

The first part of this chapter traces the political background and sketches the story of the Catilinarian conspiracy. The second part dissects some of the rhetorical devices Sallust uses in the *Bellum Catilinae* to achieve narrative continuity. Some of these devices stand outside the narrative; others are embedded within. The third part of the chapter surveys the way Sallust creates suspense in the monograph. Digressions and character sketches, for example, impede the progress of the narrative. But the results of two episodes in particular impel the narrative forward: the affair of Fulvia and Curius and the skirmish at the Mulvian Bridge.

## POLITICAL BACKGROUND

Our picture of the years 66–62 B.C.E. relies especially on two sources, Sallust's *Bellum Catilinae* and Cicero's no-doubt revised speeches *In Catilinam*.[3] Thus, from a historiographical standpoint, the Catilinarian conspiracy is unique; the rest of our conspiracy narratives are written by later historians, removed from the events by as much as two hundred years.

Social, economic, and political factors each contributed to the climate of unrest in the 60s. In Cicero's time, according to Plutarch, the situation in Rome was such that "matters needed only a slight impulse to disturb them, and it was in the power of any bold man to overthrow the commonwealth, itself in a diseased condition" (*Cic.* 10.5). The incipient cause of this corruption is traditionally traced to the destruction of Carthage and the subsequent conquests of the East that expanded the geopolitical scope of the empire and overburdened a system of government designed for a localized city-state. The vast amount of wealth that poured into Rome was concentrated in the hands of only a few who used it to their political and social advantage, bestowing rather than electing magistracies and military commands. With the rise of latifundia (extensive estates resulting from an aggregation of properties too large to manage according to traditional slave-staffed methods), the number of small farmers decreased, while the urban population steadily increased. Too much wealth in the hands of too few aristocrats contributed to an eventual polarization within the aristocracy. Some strove to consolidate power in the hands of an élite oligarchy, while others attempted to establish personal supremacy.[4]

In addition to these general conditions of fierce aristocratic competition and extreme financial distress, Yavetz points to two immediate political factors that contributed to Catiline's insurrection. In 70, during the consulship of Pompey and Crassus, the senate list was revised. For the first time since 86, censors were appointed. Gellius Publicola and Lentulus Clodianus carried out their task with unmitigated severity, expelling no fewer than sixty-four members. Although Sulla had packed the senate with unworthy nominees, it is assumed that the censors made their selection under the guidance of the consuls Pompey and Crassus. Then in 65, the *lex Papia* legislated the expulsion from Rome of all aliens who were not permanently domiciled in Italy.[5] Economically, the wars against Mithridates, first conducted by Sulla, Murena, Lucullus, and finally ended by Pompey, had profoundly lowered credit facilities, while increased activities of pirates in the Mediterranean raised the cost of shipping and therefore the cost of grain.[6]

Within this climate of political rivalry and economic disaster, Pompey and Crassus emerged as bitter rivals, each with a strength, each with enough sense to use the other to his advantage. As early as 72, the wealth of Crassus was overshadowed by the military might of Pompey; although Crassus effectively crushed the slave revolt of Spartacus, the credit for subduing the rebellion redounded to Pompey, who merely intercepted enough of the fugitives to claim victory for himself. Clever enough to know his limitations, Crassus joined with Pompey, and in 70 the two obtained the consulship. Appian vividly describes the détente: "Crassus yielded first. He came down from his chair, advanced to Pompey, and offered him his hand in the way of reconciliation. Pompey rose and hastened to meet him. They shook hands" (*B.C.* 1.121). This was the year that an aspiring lawyer from Arpinum successfully prosecuted a former governor of Sicily named Verres—so Marcus Tullius Cicero earned the reputation as the foremost orator in Rome. The following year he was elected aedile.

In 69, Lucullus invaded Armenia and captured the city of Tigranocerta, but his attempt to gain territory even further north and east ultimately failed at Artaxata because of hesitation, mismanagement, and even insubordination.[7] The hope of conquering Armenia and increasing its status from a client-kingdom to a province prompted the assembly to pass the *lex Manilia* in 66, commissioning Pompey against all Roman enemies in Asia.[8] Cicero, as praetor, supported the bill and delivered his speech *De Lege Manilia*. With this mandate, Pompey campaigned in the East until 62 and therefore was not in Rome during the Catilinarian conspiracy. Crassus tried to use Pompey's absence to his advantage.

Attempting to counter Pompey's ascendancy, Crassus sought to gain influence abroad. As censor in 65, he proposed to grant full citizenship to the Transpadanes, and he tried to pass a bill through the tribal assembly making Egypt a province under the command of Caesar. Crassus' colleague Lutatius Catulus objected so strongly that the two censors laid down their office (Suet. *Jul.* 11; Plu. *Crass.* 13). Thwarted, Crassus sought the aid of the desperately poor but solidly aristocratic Lucius Sergius Catilina. Thus, the rivalry of the powerful Pompey and Crassus was deflected onto Cicero and Catiline, the former a man of lesser rank, the latter of lesser means. Marcus Tullius Cicero was a *novus homo*, the first in his family to achieve the office of consul. Lucius Sergius Catilina, on the other hand, was from an old, yet deeply impoverished, patrician family.[9]

Few things can bring the lived experience of the Catilinarian conspiracy closer to the modern person than standing in the Mamertine Prison, relishing the cool underground refuge from the baking heat of the Roman forum, while contemplating the place where five Roman citizens were strangled to death for conspiring against Rome. What led to the execution of Lentulus, Cethegus, Statilius, Gabinius, and Caeparius? The struggle that ended on the battlefield near Pistoria actually began in the heart of Rome, on the political battleground of the consular elections.

In the year 66, the consuls-elect, Publius Cornelius Sulla and Publius Autronius, were charged with electoral bribery and disqualified from office (Sal. *Cat.* 18.2). A second election was held, for which Catiline offered himself as candidate. His application was rejected on the grounds that he had not yet been tried for extortion committed during his governorship of Africa the year before (Sal. *Cat.* 18.3). Aurelius Cotta and Manlius Torquatus were returned as consuls. In retaliation, a plot was supposedly formed to assassinate them on 1 January 65 and declare Catiline and Autronius the new consuls. One of the conspirators, Cn. Calpurnius Piso, a supporter of Crassus (*adnitente Crasso,* Sal. *Cat.* 19.1), was sent to secure Spain in Pompey's absence. But Piso was murdered shortly after his arrival (Sal. *Cat.* 19.1; Asc. *Tog.* 93.10). This coup (the so-called first Catilinarian conspiracy) was discovered; according to Asconius (92), Catiline, in his impatience, signaled the conspirators prematurely. Catiline was acquitted of the charges against him and was eligible to stand for office the next year (in 64), along with Cicero.

The first Catilinarian conspiracy raises unanswerable questions. It is clear that Piso was one of the conspirators; yet he was sent to Spain by order of the senate (*Sal.* Cat. 19.1; Asc. *Tog.* 92). Did the senate send him to his death in Spain to rid the state of a dangerous upstart? Although the plot was discovered, no official inquiry was made and no one was punished. Some have doubted whether there was even a first conspiracy at all.[10] Secrecy and silence so tightly envelop the events as to obscure them permanently; such is the essence of conspiracy. At the very least, the events of late 66–early 65 ushered in a sense of apprehension and suspicion that was to pervade the rest of the decade.

At the uneventful elections held in 65, L. Julius Caesar and G. Marcius Figulus were returned as consuls. In 64, Cicero was elected consul for the year 63 with Antonius, beating Catiline by only a narrow margin. Apparently the stalwart oligarchy preferred to admit a newcomer to office than to abide the debt-ridden Catiline. Crassus thereupon discarded the defeated Catiline, who nonetheless persisted in his bid for the consulship. In the late summer of 63, when elections for the following year were held, Catiline stood again for the consulship, on a platform of debt cancellation—a promise one hardly imagines Crassus sanctioning. He was again defeated by D. Junius Silanus and L. Licinius Murena, and he finally turned to force to achieve his ends.

With a band of dissatisfied men, he formed a conspiracy. On October 18, Crassus received an anonymous letter threatening bloodshed and advising him to escape Rome. Crassus immediately brought it to Cicero (Plu. *Cic.* 15), and by October 21, the senate proclaimed a state of emergency and passed a *senatus consultum*. Yet, they did not apprehend Catiline, who was planning a series of insurrections throughout Italy to coincide with organized arson in Rome. Catiline intended to march on the city on the appointed day (October 27) with an army from Etruria led by Gaius Manlius. Cicero mobilized troops but lacked sufficient evidence to bring Catiline to justice.

On November 6, the conspirators met at the house of Marcus Porcius Laeca on the Street of the Scythemakers to delegate tasks and finalize their plans. Catiline instructed two of the conspirators to call on Cicero the next morning on the pretense of paying their respects, and there they should murder him unsuspecting. This is the information, according to Plutarch, that a woman named Fulvia passed along to Cicero.

Armed with this knowledge, Cicero delivered his first oration against Catiline to the senate on November 7. The next day, Catiline left Rome to muster his forces in Etruria, and Cicero addressed the people in a second oration. In Catiline's absence, the zealous conspirators enlisted the aid of a Gallic tribe, but these Allobroges denounced the conspiracy to Cicero. Cicero seized the ringleaders at the Mulvian Bridge on December 2 and disclosed the entire affair, complete with witnesses and documentation, to the senate on December 3.

That afternoon Cicero addressed the people again to proclaim the revelation of the conspiracy and the salvation of the state. Two days later the senate debated the punishment of the conspirators, and Cicero delivered his fourth speech against Catiline. Caesar argued forcefully that the five prisoners not be executed, but convinced by Cato, the senate consented to their immediate execution. Cicero himself escorted Lentulus from the aedile's house on the Palatine hill, along the Via Sacra, across the forum, to the prison where the other four had been brought. The *vindices rerum capitalium* (executioners), dispatched the five in the Tullianum, the dungeon under the prison. With his army, Catiline was defeated by the legate Marcus Petreius in January near Pistoria. In the end, it is a marvel that a man who accomplished so very little continues to baffle us as much as he fascinated the historian who first attempted to understand him, Sallust.

## CONTINUITY "AND OTHER THINGS OF THIS SORT"

A historiographical narrative of a conspiracy eventually must come to terms with the secrecy that pervades the events. Sallust, however, cannot simply interrupt his narrative with a self-imposed lacuna when silence overshadows the progression of causes and effects. He can admit uncertainty and even defeat, but he still draws connections where there are gaps in the sequence of cause and effect. The better he is at negotiating these limitations, the more successful he is in creating a continuous narrative of the conspiracy that is convincing.

Therefore, our first concern is to observe how Sallust maintains narrative continuity from the opening words of the monograph, the magisterial *omnis homines* of the great moralizing preface (*Cat.* 1.1), to the bitter end, the *luctus atque gaudia agitabantur* (61.9) that closes the final scene of Catiline's last stand. To a large degree, rhetorical devices form the connective tissues and fibers that bind the story together, allowing the author to advance the narrative and compelling the reader to continue. Some of these rhetorical figures stand outside the action of the plot and call attention to the status of the text as a written document.

The most familiar rhetorical flag is the assertion of authority in the first person. Sallust uses the first person thirty-one times in the course of fifty pages of Latin.[11] By comparing the frequency of the first person in the *Bellum Catilinae* to the later *Bellum Iugurthinum*, Skard attributes this overwhelming presence of the author in the earlier work to his development from ethical subjectivity to historical objectivity in the later monograph.[12] But objectivity is not the goal of the ancient historian. Instead, the highly self-conscious first person so prevalent in the *Bellum Catilinae* is a symptom of the difficult subject matter at hand. For example, seven of the first person uses generally direct the reader to other parts of the text with a simple aside, "as I said above" (*supra memoravi*, 5.7, 57.1; *supra diximus*, 16.1, 57.2; *ante memoravi*, 20.1, 26.4; *ut dixi*, 55.1), and one use simply brings the digression on the so-called first Catilinarian conspiracy to a close (*in medio reliquemus*, 19.5 ["we shall leave off in the middle"]).

One may object that these ordinary uses of the first person are negligible. But they give a preponderance of direction in a monograph devoted as it is to a single subject. The troublesome years from 66 to 62 appear to demand a good deal of direction from Sallust. Furthermore, with such directional signals, the author can help the reader, reminding him of previously supplied information. Statements like, "as I mentioned above," explain how newly provided data, seemingly conflicting, is actually consistent with the overall course of events. In a sense, such statements partially do the reader's work for him, by drawing connections between prior and present information. Therefore, such seemingly unimportant first-person directional statements confirm the reader's confidence in the author as one who is helpful and willing to impart information.

The first person also validates Sallust's research efforts. He has heard (*ipsum Crassum ego . . . audivi*, 48.9), read, and actively sought out the facts (*sed mihi multa legenti, multa audienti . . . ac mihi multa agitanti*, 53.2–4). He has pieces of evidence at his disposal (*quarum rerum ego maxuma documenta haec habeo*, 9.4), and he can rely on his own memory (*memorare possum*, 7.7; cf. 13.1). Three times he professes to relate events to the best of his ability. At the beginning of the monograph, he levels the customary claim to impartiality with the phrase "as truthfully as I can" (*quam verissume potero;* 4.3), and his account of the so-called first Catilinarian conspiracy echoes the claim: *de qua quam verissume potero* (18.2). Likewise, in the comparison of the characters of Cato and Caesar towards the end of the monograph (the *synkrisis,* 54), he promises to relate the nature and habits of each *quantum ingenio possum* (53.6). By the end of the work, however, we come to realize with Sallust that this degree of veracity is only as high as the historian's ability (*ingenium*) permits.

Rhetorical devices that stand outside the narrative range from these closely engaged first-person statements, spoken by the author himself, to statements framed in the third person, without any named subject. Information is imparted without the interference of the author's own voice. This technique lends a degree of sophisticated realism to the narrative; the events narrated are revealed to the reader without the intrusion of authorial opinion. Yet, by attributing causes or effects to nameless spokesmen, Sallust not only maintains narrative continuity, he also shapes the ideological message of his text. Sallust uses the grammatical construction of a third-person verb with an unnamed subject followed by indirect discourse ten times in the *Bellum Catilinae;*[13] four of these uses record contemporary views.[14] For example, with the formula, "There were those at that time who said," Sallust records the rumor that the conspirators sealed the oath by drinking human blood (*fuere ea tempestate qui dicerent*, 22.1). This incredible act of barbarism is mitigated in the text by the third-person, impersonal introduction. Sallust appends his own opinion to the conclusion of the paragraph: "As far as I am concerned, not enough has been discovered about the matter, given the seriousness of the allegation" (*nobis ea res pro magnitudine parum conperta est*, 22.3). Similarly, the digression on the so-called first Catilinarian conspiracy begins with an impersonal expression and ends with a first-person resignation (*relinquemus*, 19.5).

In reporting the rumor that Catiline seduced young boys, however, the two techniques are combined. Sallust embeds the impersonal relative clause of characteristic within a first-person statement: "I know there were some who so believed" (*scio fuisse nonnullos qui ita existumarent*, 14.7).[15] Sallust puts the incredible information contained in the relative clause, namely, that Catiline debauched young boys, at a remove. But he owns up to reporting the rumor by framing the entire sentence in the first person. The reader is assured that Sallust is wise enough to recognize a rumor and honest enough to admit when he is repeating one. In this way, the scandal does not go unreported. The reader is given yet another glimpse of the wicked character of Catiline and another opportunity to exercise his righteous indignation at the debased morals of the times.

Likewise, the formula that frames the rumor of human sacrifice, *fuere ea tempestate qui* ("there were those at the time who"), distances Sallust from the ghastly detail. It also implies that no right-thinking person would even contemplate such an action. The formula recurs in the conclusion of the lengthy catalogue of conspirators:

> At that time, members of the senatorial order Publius Lentulus Sura, Publius Autronius, Lucius Cassius Longinus, Gaius Cethegus, Publius and Servilius Sulla the sons of Servius, Lucius Vargunteius, Quintus Annius, Marcus Porcius Laeca, Lucius Bestia, and Quintus Curius came together; moreover, from among the equestrian order Marcus Fulvius Nobilior, Lucius Statilius, Publius Gabinius Capito, and Gaius Cornelius joined. To this were added many from the colonies and municipalities, men from noble stock. Furthermore, there were several nobles, whose participation in the plot was a little less obvious, who were encouraged more by the hope of greater power than by poverty or another pressing need. But several youths, especially young men of the noble class, were in favor of Catiline's plan: they had in their means the ability to live in leisure, either in a grand fashion or at least comfortably. They preferred instability to certainty, war to peace. Likewise there were those at the time who believed that Marcus Licinius Crassus was not ignorant of this plot. . . .[16]

Unsurprisingly, the list of participants is arranged in predictable order of descending social status. It begins with the actual names of senators and equestrians. Then the specificity of the catalogue quickly begins to dissolve, for the provincial nobility is mentioned but not enumerated by name (*ad hoc multi ex coloniis et municipiis, domi nobiles*, 17.4), and several conspirators were simply "a little less obvious" (*paulo occultius*, 17.5). Their names are kept from the record for any number of reasons: the list is too long and therefore too tedious to reproduce;[17] the list is too short and therefore not as alarming; their names were never formally recorded; they were not members of families with the kind of "name recognition" to merit attention. Sallust continues to list the youth (*iuventus*, 17.6), and especially those of noble birth. Of all the participants in the conspiracy, however, the most elusive is Crassus. Evidence of his participation is admittedly flimsy and rests on the belief of unnamed contemporaries. So this catalogue of conspirators begins with assured specifics and ends in hesitation and doubt.

It would be naïve to think that Sallust always invoked unnamed spokesmen because he was unable to give more reliable testimony. Rather, in a manner common in ancient historiography, the technique allowed the historian to criticize his sources without naming them. Moreover, by supplying information implicitly, Sallust guides the reader toward a particular interpretation. The use of unnamed spokesmen contributes to a generally sinister impression of a character, most notably Catiline.[18] Sallust also resorts to impersonal expressions when discussing Crassus' implication in the plot (17.7, 48.3, 48.7). While not definitively proving that Crassus participated in the Catilinarian conspiracy, the insinuation conveys an unfavorable impression of him.

In addition to the more obvious framing devices outlined above, moments embedded within the narrative also betray the rhetorical maneuvers Sallust employs to achieve narrative continuity. It is also no surprise that this continuity is freighted with ideological significance. Sallust embellishes the narrative for purposes of continuity in two distinct ways. First, he often caps a list of people or actions with a form of the indefinite pronoun *alius*. Sometimes the indefinite neuter plural pronoun is simply a shorthand, neatly rounding off a tricolon. In one instance, Catiline ordered the conspirators to prepare for the slaughter, arson, and other crimes of war (*aliaque belli facinora*, 32.2). Caesar bemoaned the state of the republic in which factions grow strong, lawyers victimize innocent men, and other things of this sort (*alia huiusce modi*, 51.40). Thus, Sallust inflates the sinister nature of these events.

Like the impersonal expressions, this tactic also contributes to the negative impression of a character. Sallust tells of the many unspeakable acts Catiline committed with a noble woman, with a Vestal Virgin, "and other things of this sort" (*alia huiusce modi*, 15.1). Decorum perhaps prohibits any further explanation; the indefinite pronoun crowns the ascending tricolon. Likewise, Sempronia's talents are enumerated. She could read Greek and Latin, play the lyre, sing, and many other things designed for a life of luxury (*multa alia quae instrumenta luxuriae sunt*, 25.2).

The disposition of Catiline's troops is similarly exaggerated using the distributive pronoun. He sent Manlius to Faesulae, Septimius to the region of Picenum, Julius to Apulia, and others to various districts deemed useful (*alium alio*, 27.1). How many or where does not matter; rather, the number and location, kept indefinite, arouse fear the more. As a result, rumor took hold of the city, and some (*alii*) reported omens while others (*alii*) declared that military operations were afoot (30.2). The indefinite subjects increase the sinister nature of these rumors.[19] Thus Sallust uses the indefinite pronoun to give a negative impression. But it also pads the story with information that does not necessarily advance an empirical understanding of the course of the conspiracy, although it adds quite successfully to the growing suspense.

Second, throughout the monograph, Sallust shifts the point of view of the narrative, from his own authorial standpoint to the limited point of view of a particular character. The author, who knows, if not everything, at least more than the characters know at a given time, shifts to reveal only what a given character feels or knows.[20] According to Bal, such a transition signals a shift in the "narrative's center of interest," from plot to character, and in the shift, "knowledge diminishes." As the narrator hands over the point of view to a character, he sees and knows only as much as that character, and not more.[21] Thus, Sallust impels the narrative forward by attributing a cause or an effect to the inner thoughts of a character, again most notably Catiline.

Yet it is unlikely that Sallust had direct recourse to the thoughts of one who died twenty years before he took up the task of writing the monograph. Instead, he can posit the intentions of a character based on the rules of probability, but he does so without calling attention to his role in the formulation of the statement or its status as less than factual. Nominative singular participles ("believing," "reckoning," "judging," "understanding," etc.) are particularly effective: *Catilina . . . credens* (20.1), *ipse [Catilina] secum volvens . . . credens* (32.1), *Catilina . . . ratus* (57.5), *[Lentulus] . . . existumans* (40.1), *[Cicero] intellegens . . . dubitans* (46.2), *consul . . . ratus* (55.1), *Celer . . . existumans* (57.2). As these participles shift the narrative point of view from Sallust to Catiline, Lentulus, Cicero, and Celer, so they shift the source of information from the omniscient narrator to the character with limited knowledge.

The characterization of Catiline throughout the monograph is based on such psychological inferences; Sallust reports his desires (5.5), fears (15.4, 31.4), and beliefs (24.4). The historian did not have recourse to the thoughts of the conspirator, but he could rely on the probability of unspoken intentions as likely motivations for action. Once Catiline's profligacy is suggested, a reasonable conjecture about his lusts easily follows. Yet we do well to remember that Sallust padded the crimes of Catiline with the indefinite *alia*. Whatever follows from that list is speculative. Rather than indict Sallust with the charge of historical inaccuracy, however, it is better to understand these techniques as contributing to a different goal: verisimilitude. By reporting the inner thoughts of a character, Sallust reaches this goal with arresting skill. By reporting the inner thoughts of a character, the author can synthesize his discourse with that of his characters. Thus, the technique allows Sallust an opportunity to infuse the narrative with an ideology that pits good against evil. Point of view is a property of all narrative, to be sure, but the patterns of shifting points of view in conspiracy narratives allow us to distill the effectiveness of the technique in a situation that is deliberately secretive.

First-person and third-person impersonal statements frame the narrative and stand outside the action and the plot. The statements provide no information about the course of the conspiracy per se but only information about the methods used to narrate it. By these methods, the historian calls attention to the act of writing history and his active role in the process. Sometimes Sallust employs this traditional rhetoric of authority as *apologia* for moments of greater improbability, for instance, the rumor of human sacrifice. The two types of internal markers, indefinite pronouns and psychological inferences (internal focalization), denote a shift from factual to nonfactual information. *Inventio* (contrivance) is at work, attributing causes and effects that although they cannot be verified, are nonetheless believable.[22]

### THE ROAD TO PISTORIA

The reader who picks up the *Bellum Catilinae* is never in doubt as to the outcome of the conflict. Sallust wrote the monograph twenty years after the fact. It was not a blow-by-blow journalistic report from the field but a retrospective rendering of the conspiracy whose final event, the death of Catiline on the battlefield near Pistoria, was already well known to all, before Sallust even took up the task of writing. Why, then, should a reader bother with the *Bellum Catilinae?* How does Sallust maintain suspense throughout the course of the narrative?

Digression, character sketches, and speeches repeatedly delay the progress of the narrative. The first and most obvious diversionary tactic, however, comes at the very beginning of the work, for the preface alone throws one of the biggest obstacles in the way of narrative progress. A *praefatio* is deceptive, for etymologically it purports to "say beforehand," yet it is commonly assumed that an author composes a preface only after completing the work. For the author, then, a preface is an after-word that becomes a foreword only in the hands of the reader. This tension in the direction of progress, forward for the reader but backward for the author, gives a preface its tantalizing force. It is a sneak preview that only hints at the causes behind the events to be narrated. A preface recapitulates the content of the work without disclosing anything about causes and effects. It is inherently repetitious and at the same time uninformative; therefore, it operates as a very efficient kind of delay. It simultaneously entices and frustrates the reader.

The preface to the *Bellum Catilinae* is proportionately the longest extant Latin prose preface; longer historical works begin with much less fanfare. For instance, Tacitus begins his monumental *Annales* with an echo of *Bellum Catilinae* 6.1, effectively dispensing with the first five chapters of the monograph. Indeed, Sallust does not announce the topic of his monograph until 4.3: *igitur de Catilinae coniuratione* ("therefore, about the Catilinarian conspiracy"). Sallust's preface makes it clear to the reader that the outcome of the war with Catiline will not be as important as the moral issues that the conspiracy raises. The lengthy introduction justifies a work devoted to a subject that does not necessarily display all members of the Roman citizen body in the best possible light. Although in the end justice and good prevail, nevertheless the conspiracy demonstrated the grim potential for Roman society and morality to fall prey to violence and lawlessness.

The first sentences engage the distinction between slavery and freedom that pervades the rest of the monograph.[23] The social condition of slavery is transferred metaphorically to the current political crisis. Obedience to the belly characterizes animals, while men are characterized by the slavery of the body to the command of the mind.[24] Here Sallust modifies the usual diction of *servitium* versus *libertas,* contrasting *servitium* instead with the political concept of *imperium.* He maps the social division between slave and free onto the human body and thereby slips into a metaphor of the body politic. Thus, the analogy "mind is to body as master is to slave" corresponds to a social hierarchy. Yet the analogy also expresses a political relationship whose interpretation Sallust leaves open. The power of mind over body could symbolize the command of the senate over the people, the consul over the senate, or even more specifically, the command of the *optimates* (nobles) over the *populares* (so-called demagogues).

The distinction between slavery and freedom is carried throughout the monograph. Both sides claim a loss of freedom, and therefore fear slavery, should they fail.[25] Catiline warns his men of the unspeakable conditions they will live in if they do not assert their claims to liberty; they live under a repressive oligarchy.[26] On the other hand, in his speech to the senate, Cato says that the conspiracy threatens the senators' *libertas*.[27] Cicero's discovery of the conspiracy, moreover, caused the *plebs* to rejoice as if they had been saved from slavery.[28] Such statements do not contribute to the plot of the narrative and the disclosure of the conspiracy. Yet, they are very effective at lending a moral tone to the monograph. The Catilinarian conspiracy turned both moral probity and social order on its head.

The decline of morality prompts Sallust to "go back further (*supra repetere*) and briefly describe the principles by which our ancestors guided their conduct" (5.9). Of course, all historians backtrack; Barthes calls this "zigzag history," history catching up with itself.[29] Too much happens before that the historian must go back and explain. In this case, Sallust barely manages to introduce Catiline and already feels the need to give further background information. The digression may more suitably be called a *retro*gression, for Sallust goes all the way back to the foundation of Rome by Aeneas and his Trojan followers (6.1). Although cursory, the retrogression puts the ultimate goal of the narrative, the defeat of Catiline, even further from the reader's immediate reach. Then, within this retrogression, Sallust artfully inserts yet another digression, comparing the achievements of Athens and Rome (8).[30]

All the material contained in the retrogression/digression is of course integral to Sallust's conception of the *Bellum Catilinae*. It conveys information implicitly rather than explicitly and presupposes that the reader needs the information conveyed. In this sense, it is not extraneous nor does it detract from the coherence of the text. Rather, it contributes a palpable tension to the narrative. A digression is formally set apart from the rest of the narrative with stock recognizable phrases. It intrudes upon the sequence of events and halts progress. It is a removable part. At the same time, the content of a digression is closely linked to, and is reflected in, the rest of the narrative; logical connections often signal a digression (e.g., *igitur*, 9.1). As a preface embodies the tension of forward and backward reading, so a digression materializes the tension between part and whole.

The most memorable digression in the monograph is the account of the so-called first Catilinarian conspiracy, which opens with a disclaimer: "But a few had conspired against the republic before, among whom was Catiline; about this I shall speak as truthfully as I am able" (*de qua quam verissume potero dicam*, 18.2) and concludes with a resignation: "About the earlier conspiracy enough has been said" (*de superiore coniuratione satis dictum*, 19.6). This *satis dictum* has to be one of the greatest disappointments in all Latin literature. He most certainly has not said enough. As a result, the details of the so-called first Catilinarian conspiracy cannot be obtained. Who devised the conspiracy, who participated in it, and why, are questions that produce many different answers. Because the conspiracy never transpired, speculations abound. Nothing explicit can be said; whatever information can be gleaned from the digression is given implicitly.

This is perhaps the most dramatic example of Sallust's negotiation of an epistemological gap. By attempting to narrate the unnarratable, the so-called first Catilinarian conspiracy, Sallust demonstrates to potential conspirators that even their unrealized plans can be detected, if not fully comprehended. There is a tone of finality and closure in the phrase *satis dictum,* as if to say more would challenge, and not advance, knowledge and any authority that knowledge can impart.[31] To this extent, his narrative of the so-called first Catilinarian conspiracy, no matter how imperfect, stops further inquiry and so serves as a deterrent.

Neatly balanced character sketches and speeches constitute another kind of delay in the progress of the action of the narrative. The paragraphs describing Catiline (5) and Sempronia (25) complement one another. The lengthy list of Catiline's followers (36.4–39.5) responds to Cicero's characterization of the disaffected (Cic. *Cat.* 2.8–10). The *synkresis* comparing Caesar and Cato (53–54) is a fitting conclusion to their debate on the punishment of the conspirators, a debate that lends a good deal of suspense to the narrative. After Caesar's speech, the decision still hangs in the balance (52.1). It is not until the end of Cato's speech that we learn the verdict: the senate votes in favor of capital punishment. The two longest speeches in the monograph keep the reader in suspense. Yet the result boils down to just one sentence: "The senate decreed as he recommended" (*senati decretum fit sicuti ille censuerat,* 53.1).

When the reader finally reaches the end of the conspiracy, Catiline's last stand is composed of traditional expressions and motifs.[32] Without further delay, the reader's expectations of the typical battle scene are fulfilled. Sallust describes the terrain and the disposition of the troops on both sides before narrating the attack, but he avoids the tedium of yet another pair of balanced speeches by casting Catiline's battle exhortation in *oratio recta* (58) and Petreius' in *oratio obliqua* (59.5). He ends with a view of the aftermath of the battle and a meditation on the dual nature of this internecine conflict. The civil strife is ended, but the community is only beginning to realize the high price it paid. As the survivors collect their dead, in an intermediate step between war and peace, so they are poised between conflict and resolution. Looking back, they see the danger Catiline posed to the state; looking forward, they see the safety to which they are only just now delivered. In this intermediate state, Sallust's monograph ends with the chiastic flourish of emotions wavering between joy and grief: *laetitia maeror luctus atque gau-*

*dia agitabantur* (61.9). Although narrative resolution is achieved, emotional stability remains in the balance. Sallust's Januslike narrative masterfully maintains suspense to the last word.

### FULVIA ON THE BRINK

In spite of the delays posed by the preface, digressions, character sketches, and speeches, the action of the narrative advances; knowledge about the events is imparted, and the reader gains an understanding of the conspiracy. Two episodes in particular contribute to this advancement. Because of the betrayal by Fulvia and by the Allobroges, Cicero was able to bring down the conspirators.

Women are prominently mentioned in the sources as participating in the Catilinarian conspiracy.[33] In the second Catilinarian, Cicero asked, "In all Italy, what poisoner, what gladiator, what bandit, what assassin, what parricide, what forger of wills, what cheater, what glutton, what spendthrift, what adulterer, what notorious woman (*mulier infamis*), what corruptor of the youth, what corrupt man, what ruined man can be found who does not admit to having lived on the most intimate terms with Catiline?"[34] In this list of those who have no place in respectable public life,[35] Cicero relied upon emotional appeals to his audience, arousing outrage at the illegality of the conspiracy. Cicero equates the women who consort with Catiline in general terms with the worst type of people. Sallust, on the other hand, details the misconduct of the women who participated:

> At that time it is said that he claimed for himself several men of every sort, and even some women who at first supported their enormous expenditures by the prostitution of their bodies; later, when old age restricted their occupation but not their luxury, they ran up a huge debt. With their help Catiline believed that he could stir up the urban slaves, burn the city, and either add their husbands (*viros*) to his cause or kill them.[36]

Sallust implies that the women whom Catiline enlisted were prostitutes, but it is not until the end of the sentence that we learn that these women in fact had husbands (*viros*). Appian's interpretation of the passage ignores the act of prostitution: "He procured much money from many women who hoped that they would get their husbands killed in the rising."[37] But according to Sallust, these married women engaged in illicit, extramarital sex (*stupro corporis*) to maintain a degenerate lifestyle, and when no longer capable of trading sex for goods, they incurred enormous debt. The behavior of these women illustrates the thematic distinction Sallust makes in his lengthy preface between mind and body. Thus, Sallust renders their promiscuity all the more despicable.

From the general, Sallust moves to the specific. Crowning this band of unnamed, adulterous women is the most corrupt of all, Sempronia (*sed in iis erat Sempronia*, 25.1). The celebrated portrait of Catiline's degenerate consort, cast in elegiac terms, depicts a woman who, although descended from the illustrious house of the Sempronii, is nonetheless thoroughly steeped in the very luxuries Sallust deprecated in the beginning of the work (11.6–13). Sallust singles her out as the epitome of the crumbling morals of the republic; she personified the growing distance between a noble birth and an ignoble life. Williams aligns her with other distinguished women of the republic who entertained colorful lifestyles: Fausta, daughter of Sulla, wife of C. Memmius and famed for her lovers; Servilia, half-sister of Cato, mother of Brutus, and mistress of Julius Caesar.[38] But Sallust's Sempronia outstrips them. As the female counterpart to Catiline, she was a classic example of the good woman gone bad.[39] This portrayal of Sempronia is stereotypical and renders her a one-dimensional figure in the text. She induced Decimus Brutus to join the conspiracy, but beyond this gratuitous mention (40.5), she plays no significant role in the course of events.

Fulvia, on the other hand, is crucial to the development of Sallust's story, for the revelation of the conspiracy depended upon her. She provided the link between the conspirators and the consul:

> He [Curius] shared with Fulvia, a woman of social rank (*mulier nobilis*), a longstanding familiarity of illicit sex (*stuprum*). When she was less impressed because he was able to bestow less due to a lack of funds, suddenly bragging, he began to promise the sea and the mountains, and in some instances to threaten her with a sword, if she was not obedient; in short, he behaved more violently than usual. Once the reason for Curius' arrogance was recognized, Fulvia did not keep secret such danger to the republic; withholding the name of her source, she told several people what she had gathered and by what means[40] about the conspiracy of Catiline. This matter particularly enflamed the zeal of men to entrust the consulship to M. Tullius Cicero.[41]

The tryst occurred in the summer of 64, when Cicero would have been campaigning for office. Fulvia's revelations are said to have advanced Cicero's candidacy. But if Cicero knew about the brewing conspiracy from his election into office, why did he wait until November of the following year, seventeen months later, to act on this information?[42] As elsewhere, Sallust uses this story to give a sinister impression, that Catiline had been meditating conspiracy for quite some time. He embellishes the early stages of the conspiracy to heighten suspense and to magnify the impending danger. Thus, he rearranges chronology for emotional effect. Previous explanations of the chronological displacement in the monograph have been content to stop here.[43]

I maintain that this episode is central to the continuity of the narrative of the conspiracy. The account of the affair between Fulvia and Curius provides a venue for the transfer of critical information about the Catilinarian conspiracy. If Cicero had not been informed, then the conspiracy would not have come to light. The failure of the plot depended on channeling the conspirators' secrets to the proper authorities. Fulvia was the first link in the chain between the conspirators and the consul. In his speeches, Cicero went to great lengths to emphasize his thorough investigation and single-handed discovery of the conspiracy.[44] According to Sallust, however, Cicero's omniscience in the first place depended on a woman.

The longstanding affair of the lovers was uneventful, until one night, Curius' treatment of Fulvia was more violent than usual (*ferocius agitare quam solitus*).[45] Curius went so far as to threaten her with a sword. The increased physical abuse she suffered at his hands was enough to convince her that the republic was in danger. According to Sallust, Curius never told Fulvia anything explicitly. Instead, Curius' behavior, more rough than usual, appears to be sufficient cause to deduce the incipient conspiracy. Her suspicion is conveyed by an unnamed source, *sublato auctore* ("with the source removed"). Sallust gives no indication of who Fulvia's other sources may have been.

A comparison of Sallust's austere encounter between Fulvia and Curius with the more colorful version of the Augustan historian Diodorus Siculus is illuminating:

There was one who was in love with a certain girl and who, on being slighted by her, remarked more than once that within a few days her very life would be in his power. The remark puzzled her, and she could not guess what grounds he had for his threat, but still the young man remained insistent. When they were together, therefore, and drinking, she feigned extreme delight at his company and asked him to tell her what in the world his remark meant, and he, wishing in his infatuation to please her, disclosed the whole truth. She pretended to have taken what was said sympathetically and joyfully, and held her peace, but on the morrow went to the wife of Cicero the consul, and speaking privately with her about the matter reported what the young man had said. Thus the conspiracy was brought to light, and the consul, by using now threats and terror, now kindly exhortations, learned from them full details of the plot.[46]

Several differences emerge. First, Diodorus does not mention either man or woman by name. Second, the scene is tempered with wine; the threats of violence are less immediate. Instead of a sword, the young man frightens her with words. Third, the man (Curius) discloses the entire conspiracy to the woman (Fulvia). Moreover, Diodorus specifies the next step in the chain of causation; the information is channeled through respectable means. It is more fitting that Cicero should converse with his wife Terentia than with a courtesan.[47]

In the public sphere, at least, there were proper channels through which women were supposed to register their voices. A woman who eschewed proper channels earned a negative reputation. Valerius Maximus lists women who pleaded before magistrates on behalf of themselves or others. Maesia was nicknamed "Androgyne" because of her boldness. Carfania became such a notorious example of female litigiousness that shamelessly outspoken women were dubbed "Carfania." According to Livy (34.1.7), women desperate for the repeal of the *lex Oppia* dared to approach the consuls, praetors, and other officials. The most well-known woman forced to sidestep proper channels of communication was Hortensia (V. Max. 8.3). The women who protested the triumvir's taxes first attempted to complain to the sister of Octavian and the mother of Antony. But when Antony's wife finally drove them off, their spokeswoman Hortensia had no choice but to address an assembly in the forum (App. *B.C.* 4.32–34). The reign of Tiberius provides yet another example. To secure her acquittal for the murder of Germanicus, Plancina (wife of Cn. Calpurnius Piso) approached Livia, mother of the *princeps,* who interceded with Tiberius successfully on her behalf.[48] Hortensia and her colleagues tried to observe formalities; Plancina's very life depended on adherence to such protocol.

Diodorus portrays the courtesan as following the proper gendered rules of discourse by approaching the wife of Cicero. But Sallust is unclear about exactly whom Fulvia told, specifying only *compluribus* ("several"). Yet for both historians the kernel of the story is the same: the transfer of the crucial information took place in a private, amorous setting. Both historians credit a woman with the origin of the disclosure of the conspiracy to Cicero.

Because of her amorous affair with Curius, Fulvia was privy to the secrets of the conspiracy otherwise inaccessible. Sallust uses this opportunity to introduce the character of Cicero in the *Bellum Catilinae,* leading to speculation about the politics surrounding the rise of a *novus homo.* By betraying secrets to Cicero, Fulvia brought private information into the public sphere. The likelihood that a private conversation took place between two lovers allows Sallust to posit her conjecture for Curius' arrogance (*insolentiae Curi causa cognita*). Thus, the probability of such pillow talk between Fulvia and Curius provides the convincing link in the chain of causality between the conspirators and Cicero. No mention of the first person, no unnamed third-person sources, no evidentiary qualifiers frame the vignette. Curius' promises and threats in the bedroom were no more available to the historian than Fulvia's inner thoughts that led her to deduce the conspiracy. Perhaps Sallust was following a particular source (compare the account of Diodorus), but he does so without the traditional external rhetorical fanfare of the first-person or third-person impersonal subjects. Instead, Sallust uses an indefinite adverbial phrase (*quoque modo*) and a psychological inference (*cognita*). The episode does not compromise the historian's authority or the integrity of the narrative because its sheer verisimilitude is proof enough.

Joshel argues that the founding of the Roman state depended upon the violated chastity of a noble matron, most notably Lucretia: "Livy's narrative of Rome's political transformation revolves around chaste, innocent women raped and killed for the sake of preserving the virtue of the body female and the body politic."[49]

Sex and violence define Lucretia's fate and result in the establishment of the republic. But the suppression of the Catilinarian conspiracy that threatens political stability depends not on rape but on consensual sex. A woman of questionable morality revealed the secrets of the Catilinarian conspiracy and gave information to the consul. How she gained that information was not a matter of public record. Instead, the historian depended on the probability of pillow talk. The *a priori* sexual availability of Fulvia was so probable as to need no rhetorical framework. To this extent, Fulvia serves the purposes of Sallust and Diodorus (i.e., of male authors); her sexual deviance further denigrates the act of conspiracy.

There is no question that Fulvia existed and that she transmitted the secrets of the conspiracy to Cicero. But the way Sallust portrays her in his narrative achieves a particular effect. The timing of Fulvia's disclosure to Cicero differs in Sallust and our later Greek sources Plutarch and Appian. According to Plutarch, she came forward to Cicero after Catiline departed to the camp of Manlius (*Cic.* 16.2). According to Appian, she betrayed the conspiracy to the consul when Catiline was gathering force from among senators, equestrians, plebeians, foreign residents, and slaves (*B.C.* 2.1.3). Sallust alone says that she betrayed the conspirators before Cicero was even elected consul. Because the affair occurs in the year 64 (and not 63), the effect is to exaggerate the origins of the conspiracy and create a picture of a republic plagued by an insidious disease for more than a year. The chronology also allows Sallust to posit a reason for Cicero's success at the polls. Displacement is of course the ancient historian's prerogative.[50] It is nevertheless interesting to note that the differences in these accounts arise when it comes to the involvement of a woman. Fulvia appears at the brink of the epistemological gap in Sallust's narrative of the conspiracy, at the moment when the initial revelation leading to the eventual demise of the conspiracy takes place. To the extent that Sallust strives for a continuous narrative, so Fulvia provides a plausible catalyst for the demise of the conspiracy.

More importantly, the way Sallust narrates the affair allows the conspiracy to move from private, secret chambers to the public, open forum. We have seen that a certain indirectness characterizes Sallust's portrayal of the affair with Curius. The exchange between the two lovers is reported entirely by indirect means and by focalization: because Curius boasts (note the telltale use of the nominative participle, *glorians*), Fulvia ascertains the reasons for his behavior (*causa cognita*). Specific names and intentions are not mentioned at this point. When at last she informs on the conspiracy, Sallust reports only that she told several people (*compluribus*), and even so, she withheld the name of her source (*sublato auctore*). A very different strategy is at work when it comes to Sallust's account of the participation of the Allobroges in the downfall of the Catilinarian conspiracy.

### ALLOBROGES AT THE BRIDGE

According to Sallust, upon the departure of Catiline, Lentulus was left in charge of the conspiracy at Rome. Lentulus enlisted the aid of Publius Umbrenus to solicit the participation of the Allobroges in the conspiracy. The Allobroges were easily persuaded to revolt because of maltreatment by the Roman magistrates and because they were naturally inclined to war. As a businessman, Umbrenus was known to these people, and so he approached the ambassadors who had come to Rome. At first he simply offered them a means of relieving their oppression: "I will show you, if only you wish to be brave, a way by which you may escape these great ills" (40.3). He led them to the house of Decimus Brutus where he and Gabinius divulged the conspiracy and, unlike Fulvia, named its participants (*coniurationem aperit, nominat socios*, 40.6). The Allobroges were uncertain whether to join the conspiracy. Then, says Sallust, the fortune of the republic (*fortuna rei publicae*, 41.3) finally prevailed over them as they contemplated their choices. They decided to report the conspiracy to their patron, Quintus Fabius Sanga, who in turn informed Cicero. Cicero then advised the ambassadors to feign interest in the conspiracy and to lend their aid so that he might apprehend the conspirators. The ambassadors of the Allobroges met with the conspirators and demanded a written oath (*postulant ius iurandum quod signatum ad civis perferant*, 44.1), and suspecting nothing, they gave it (*ceteri nihil suspicantes dant*, 44.2). As the Allobroges then set out for home, Lentulus sent Volturcius with them, to accompany them to Catiline and to witness their allegiance to him. Volturcius also carried a letter to Catiline, which Sallust reproduces: "Who I am you will learn from the one I sent to you. Be mindful of the danger you are in, and remember to be a man. Think what your plans demand, seek help from all, even the most humble" (44.5). Thus, both Volturcius and the Allobroges had in their possession written evidence of the conspiracy.

In the meantime, Cicero enlisted the aid of the praetors to guard the Mulvian Bridge and to apprehend the party as it made its way to the camp of Catiline in Etruria. A brief skirmish ensued; the praetors prevailed. Arrested and brought before the senate, Volturcius had no choice but to reveal the conspiracy. After the testimony of the Allobroges, Cicero produced the written evidence and obtained the confession of Volturcius. Rewards were decreed to the Allobroges and to Volturcius for their aid in bringing down the conspiracy (50.1). In the debate on the punishment of the conspirators, Cato's formal proposal attributes the revelation of the conspiracy to Volturcius and the legates of the Allobroges alone (*indicio T. Volturci et legatorum Allobrogum convicti*, 52.36).

A comparison of the affair of Fulvia and Curius with the involvement of the foreign ambassadors is enlightening. In the first place, we are struck by the directness of Sallust's narrative; information is conveyed explicitly. Umbrenus' initial approach to the Allobroges, although not necessarily indicating a conspiracy, is given in *oratio recta* (*inquit*, 40.3). Moreover, the letter that Volturcius carried to Catiline is said to be reproduced directly (*exemplum infra scriptum est*, 44.4). Thus the narrative at this point depends more heavily on scene than on summary. Second, in telling the Allobroges about the conspiracy, Umbrenus and Gabinius are quite direct: they reveal the conspiracy and even name participants. Curius makes no such clear statements to Fulvia; she infers a conspiracy and withholds names. Third, both Fulvia and the Allobroges transmit information to Cicero indirectly. But the links between Fulvia and the consul are not specified (*compluribus narravit*, 23.4), whereas the connection between the Allobroges and Cicero is detailed.[51] While Volturcius is mentioned in the Greek narratives of Appian and Plutarch and in the third Catilinarian oration of Cicero, only Sallust specifies the activities of this conspirator. Others mention only that he carried letters to Catiline. Sallust alone tells us of Volturcius' special task, to forge an alliance between Catiline and the Allobroges (44.3).[52] Like Sanga, Volturcius is yet another explicit link in the chain of causality.

Furthermore, Cicero's instructions to the Allobroges constitute a counter-conspiracy. Plutarch reports that Cicero, in addition to the secret cooperation of the Allobroges, had employed many men who spied upon the conspirators and helped him learn their activities. Cicero met secretly and confidentially with many who were supposed to belong to the conspiracy[53] to plot the overthrow of Catiline and the suppression of his followers. According to Sallust, the Allobroges were critical to the success of Cicero's counterconspiracy. By demanding an oath (*ius iurandum,* 44.1) from the Catilinarian conspirators, the Allobroges turned the conspirators' own act of swearing allegiance against themselves. Indeed, when Cicero led the Allobroges into the senate as witnesses, they stated that an oath had been sworn.[54]

With the cooperation of the Allobroges, Cicero could arrange to seize evidence and arrest Volturcius at the Mulvian Bridge. Cicero related the encounter in grand detail in his speech before the people. His swift, staccato sentences convey the immediacy of the action: "I summoned the praetors; I exposed the matter; I showed what needed to be done. Meanwhile, the third watch was scarcely over when the Allobroges with a grand retinue began to approach the bridge together with Volturcius; an attack was sprung upon them; swords were drawn on both sides. The matter was known only to the praetors; everyone else was unaware. Then, by the intervention of the praetors, the skirmish that had begun was over" (*Catil.* 4.5). Sallust too devoted a full paragraph to the skirmish at the bridge: Cicero entrusted the praetors with the ambush of the Allobroges, and Volturcius attempted to defend himself but was deserted and so surrendered (45). Finally, the biggest difference between Fulvia and the Allobroges comes down to reward. The Allobroges and Volturcius were granted rewards for their part in bringing down the conspiracy (50); Fulvia was granted no such distinction, in any of the sources.

Two factors account for the differences in Sallust's treatments of Fulvia and the Allobroges as informants: the real and the rhetorical. Sallust provides more information about the involvement of the Allobroges because, as ambassadors, their very presence in Rome was a matter of public record. Unlike the private affair between Fulvia and Curius, the ambassadors' business before the senate placed them in the public arena. In his third Catilinarian oration, Cicero makes their participation in the conspiracy known to all. While their meetings with Umbrenus, Gabinius, Volturcius, and the other conspirators may have taken place behind closed doors, their testimony before the senate revealed all these plans in a public setting.

Rhetorically, the representation of Fulvia (and Sempronia, for that matter) conforms to the expectations of Roman historical writing, established in part by Cato the Censor,[55] who appears to have consistently doubted the moral capabilities of women. He equates adulterous women with poisoners (fr. 240 Malcovati); he disparages women's ability to keep secrets (Plu. *Cat. Mai.* 9.6); he delivers a tirade against women in his speech in favor of the *lex Oppia* (Livy 34.2–4). Given Sallust's tendency to emulate, imitate, and sometimes even challenge the thought of Cato in general, as amply attested by Levene,[56] it is not difficult to imagine that he also imports, whether consciously or unconsciously, the rhetoric of Catonian prejudices against women into his own writing. Fulvia's actions are extraordinary. As a woman capable of saving the republic, she is a departure from Catonian notions of women. Her exceptional behavior serves to underscore the exceptional nature of the conspiracy.


In conclusion, Sallust's chosen mode of presentation (his use of the first and third person, focalization, and indefinite pronouns) shapes the reader's impressions of his own reliability as well as the characters' motives. Sallust maintains a high degree of suspense throughout the narrative by delaying information. The preface, digressions, character sketches, and speeches impede the progress of the action. Fulvia and the Allobroges provide the important avenues through which crucial information about the conspiracy is transferred eventually to the consul. Both exchange information with the conspirators behind closed doors, in secret meetings. Such secrecy threatens the Roman state; therefore, the downfall of the Catilinarian conspiracy and the preservation of the *res publica* depend on the betrayal by Fulvia and the Allobroges. Whereas Fulvia provides information about the Catilinarian conspiracy at the brink of the gap between the conspirators and the consul, the Allobroges bridge the gap, allowing for the revelation of the conspiracy in the public record.[57] In the next chapter we shall see how Livy employs each of these features, namely, continuity, suspense, and betrayal by a woman, in his narrative of the Bacchanalian conspiracy.

# LIVY

## *The Bacchanalian Affair*

The Catilinarian conspirators needed to hide their activities so that their plans could come as a complete surprise to a public caught unaware. Meeting in secret, they depended upon one another's silence to ensure that the conspiracy went undetected. But first, the involvement of a woman brought the matter to the attention of the consul, and then foreign intervention provided the necessary evidence that enabled Cicero to rescue the state from the incipient peril. Unlike Sallust and Cicero, who lived through the Catilinarian conspiracy, Livy is separated from much of his subject matter by hundreds of years. The rest of the authors treated in this book all stand at a remove, distanced from the events they describe by as much as a hundred years or more. Furthermore, Sallust's was the only monograph devoted to a single subject. The rest of our conspiracy narratives are part of larger historical projects; however, they all share in the rhetoric of conspiracy, and in all, women play crucial roles. In Livy's account of the Bacchanalian conspiracy, once again a woman provided the necessary information to the consul, who took excessive precautionary measures on behalf of the state.

After discussing the climate of xenophobia in the post-Hannibalic era, I turn in this chapter to slaves. The participation of slaves in the Bacchanalian affair is not well documented, but Livy's narrative reveals senatorial attitudes and prejudices. In the final section of the chapter, I discuss the key witness for the prosecution: a woman. Just as Sallust depended on the probability of Fulvia's affair with Curius, so Livy depended on the probability of such an amorous exchange to disclose the conspiracy to the consul. Suspense is generated by a woman caught between the silence of conspiracy and the speech of counterconspiracy. Before turning to the specific roles of foreigners, slaves, and a woman in the Bacchanalian conspiracy, however, we must first take into account the particular problems presented by the sources.

## THE SOURCES

Only a fragment remains of Cato the Censor's *De Coniuratione*, a speech that probably concerned the Bacchanalian conspiracy.[1] Unlike the Catilinarian conspiracy, with its plentitude of sources spanning several hundred years in both Greek and Latin, the Bacchanalian conspiracy is attested in only two texts: the historical account of Livy in Book 39 and the inscription of the *senatus consultum de Bacchanalibus* of 186 B.C.E. (*CIL* I² 581 = *ILS* 18), a bronze tablet from the Ager Teuranus from Bruttium in southern Italy. Since we will make recourse to the inscription of the *senatus consultum de Bacchanalibus* in the discussion that follows, it is worth reproducing it here:

The consuls Quintus Marcius, son of Lucius, and Spurius Postumius, son of Lucius, consulted the Senate on October 7 in the Temple of Bellona. The recording officers were Marcus Claudius, son of Marcus, Lucius Valerius, son of Publius, and Quintus Minucius, son of Gaius.

Concerning the Bacchanalia, they decreed that this edict be issued to confederate members:

"None of them is to consent to conduct a Bacchic rite. If there are some who say it is necessary for them to hold such a rite, they must come (5) to Rome to the praetor urbanus, and when their statement has been heard, our Senate is to decide such matters, provided that no fewer than a hundred senators are present when the matter is discussed. No person, whether Roman citizen, or one of Latin status, or one of the allies, must consent to attend Bacchic rites without approaching the praetor urbanus, and without his instruction in compliance with the decision of the Senate; no fewer than a hundred senators are to be present when the matter is discussed. This is their decree.

(10) No man shall be a priest; no man or woman shall be master of ceremonies; none among them shall consent to administer a common chest. *[money]* Nor shall they seek to appoint any man or woman as magistrate or promagistrate; nor henceforward seek to conspire, make vows, or make promises or guarantees in unison; nor seek to plight their faith with one another. (15) No one must seek to celebrate rituals in secret; nor strive to celebrate them publicly, privately, or outside the city, without approaching the praetor urbanus, and without his instruction given in accord with the decision of the Senate, provided that no fewer than a hundred senators are present when this matter is discussed. This is their decree.

No one shall consent to celebrate rites in numbers greater than five (20) in all, men and women; more than two men and more than three women must not attend there, save with the consent of the praetor urbanus and the Senate, as has been written above."

You must proclaim these measures in your assembly at least by the third market day, and so that you may be aware of the decision of the Senate, it was as follows: "If there are any who in this matter act otherwise than has been written above, the senators have agreed that a capital charge (25) be laid against them." The Senate decreed it right that you engrave this instruction on a bronze tablet, and bid it be nailed up where it can most easily be read; and you are to ensure that any Bacchic objects other than what is sacred there should be dismantled, as has been written above, within ten days of your receipt of the tablets. In agro Teurano.[2]

According to Livy, the consuls were assigned to investigate secret conspiracies. It was alleged that a certain Greek introduced questionable religious practices into Etruria; at first only a few were initiated, but the numbers of participants increased. In addition to acts of immorality, members committed perjury, forgery, poisoning, and murder. The cult spread to Rome where it was initially hidden, but a young man named Aebutius eventually disclosed it to the consul Postumius (Liv. 39.8–9.1).

Livy then tells an intricate tale of love and betrayal to explain how the consul learned about the conspiracy. This young Aebutius, raised by his mother and domineering stepfather, had been deprived of his inheritance. Before he could charge his spendthrift guardians for squandering his money, they conspired to initiate him in the Bacchanalia and so prevent him from prosecution. His mother made up a story, that she vowed when he was ill to initiate him into the Bacchic rites as soon as he recovered. Preying upon his sense of piety, she instructed him to abstain from sexual intercourse for ten days, after which he would accompany her to the shrine. Aebutius told his girlfriend Hispala not to be surprised if he did not visit her for several nights in preparation for his initiation. Hispala strenuously objected; she explained that when she was a slave (an *ancilla*), she had accompanied her mistress into the shrine but that she had never returned once manumitted (39.10.5). She described the Bacchic rites to him in detail. Aebutius returned home, refusing to be initiated into such a cult. Driven from the house by his angered parents, he went to the home of his aunt Aebutia, who encouraged him to report the entire matter to the consul Postumius (39.11).

Postumius then contrived a meeting between his mother-in-law and Aebutia. Appearing to drop in by chance, the consul asked about the young man, and the aunt related his sad lot. The consul then summoned and interviewed Hispala, who explained the origin of the cult and its secret rites (39.13). Once both Aebutius and Hispala had informed on the conspiracy, Postumius took the matter before a meeting of the senate, which decreed that the consuls make a special inquiry into the Bacchanalia and the ceremonies and that rewards be granted to anyone disclosing information. A proclamation was made at Rome and throughout Italy (39.14, the substance of the inscription). After the senate meeting, Postumius delivered a speech to the people (39.15–16). Conspirators were captured and condemned to capital punishment (39.18), and a final senatorial decree rewarded the informants handsomely, especially Aebutius and Hispala (39.19).

Livy's account differs from the inscription on a critical point. According to the inscription, the senate met once to discuss the matter. Livy, however, reports two senatorial meetings. According to Gelzer, Livy exaggerated and embellished this meeting by reporting it at two different points in the story.[3] This, together with the novelistic quality of Livy's narrative, has led some to doubt Livy's reliability. According to Méautis, the cumulative details of Livy's imaginative account serve two important purposes. By constructing the fanciful story, Livy can display the prudence and circumspection of the consul, while he simultaneously renders the informants so much the more sympathetic.[4] On the other hand, McDonald supports Livy, stating that his style need not deter our trust in his report; indeed, the historian's account accords with the inscription. Instead of relying on philological or stylistic considerations, McDonald interrogates the two documents to determine just how the senate was able to get local authorities to carry out its repressive measures.[5]

Some suggest that the differences between the inscription and Livy's account can be attributed to the fortunes of textual transmission, which surely depleted the resources to which Livy had access. Tarditi argues that Livy was limited by his sources, as well as by the moralizing tone of his history. Having suggested a consular ancestor of Postumius as a possible source,[6] Tarditi also identifies sections of the episode that derive from the lost works of Valerius Antias, Claudius Quadrigarius, and Cato.[7] But rather than ask how Livy is wrong when he differs from the inscription, we ought to consider instead why he has chosen to portray the events as he does. I argue that Livy embellishes the words and actions of a woman, in order to explain how a private matter came into the public arena and thereby to achieve narrative continuity. The continuous narrative of the Bacchanalian affair strives to make sense of this singular crisis and to assure the reader of its singularity. This unique event will not be repeated, provided everyone remains vigilant.

## THE ENEMY WITHIN

Because of the close-knit relationship between the state and religion in republican Rome, it is difficult to sort out the religious and the political aspects of this conspiracy.[8] Toynbee turns to historical circumstances for understanding this intricate relationship. He ascribes the rise in mystery religions in peninsular Italy during the second century B.C.E. to the social, political, and economic climate of the post-Hannibalic era. Entire populations were displaced by the turmoil of the Second Punic War. Mass movements of slaves and prisoners of war dramatically changed the complexion of the Italian countryside and the city of Rome.

According to Toynbee, these disaffected people sought comfort and support not in the state regulated religions of Rome but in the personal worship of mystery cults. Imperial expansion necessitated government regulation on all fronts, and the "collision between the Roman Government and the private worshippers of Dionysus in the Roman Commonwealth was thus perhaps almost inevitable."[9] The year 186 B.C.E. was a watershed moment. Gruen discounts the hypothesis of Toynbee and attributes this turning point to a shift in foreign policy coincident with an assertion of collective authority by the senate.[10] Even if Toynbee's direct connection between the influx of foreign persons and the Bacchanalian affair of 186 is tenuous, nevertheless it accounts for a pervasive atmosphere of xenophobia.

Conspiracy was not recognized as a criminal offence until the decade following the wake of Sulla, and specific accusations under the *lex Plautia de vi* accumulate in the years 63–51.[11] Catiline's supporters were tried under this law.[12] Before this time, *coniuratio* was not a crime per se, although it could lead to the accomplishment of any number of punishable criminal acts.[13] By swearing an oath together, in secret, the Bacchantes by definition forged a conspiracy, which left them open to accusations of public enmity.[14] Although women and slaves aided the causes, the Catilinarian and Pisonian conspiracies were named after the élite citizen leaders whose bid for power was exclusively Roman and male.[15] The Bacchanalian conspiracy, on the other hand, was a religious association of men and women, patricians and plebeians, Romans and non-Romans. The senatorial decree preserved in the inscription prohibits the Bacchantes from conspiring, making vows, promises, or guarantees in unison (*coniourase neve comvovise neve conspondise neve conpromesise*, lines 13–14). The meaning of *coniurare* is amplified by verbs with the same prefix, and it stresses the communal aspect of the cult. This secret coexistence of men and women of all sorts posed the greatest threat in the eyes of the senate.[16]

When the consuls were charged with investigating the practices of the cult, Livy reports that they discovered "the indiscriminate debauchery of youths and women was not the only kind of crime, but perjury of witnesses, forgery of documents and wills emanated from that training school, likewise such poisonings and murder within households that often not even the bodies survived for burial" (39.8.7–8). Bauman believes that in this passage Livy describes the financial operation of the conspiracy. The Dionysiac orgies led to murder, whereupon wills were forged or falsified to redirect inheritances into the coffers of the cult. It is no coincidence, according to Bauman, that a will needed five witnesses, and the decree limited the number of participants to five.[17] This theory still does not explain why the senate found the Bacchantes such a threat. For perjury, forgery, and murder there was legal recourse; but for *coniuratio* there was only prejudice and fear.

The *senatus consultum* (itself a vague institution, according to Lintott[18]) provides some insight into the charges against the conspirators. First of all, the inscription lists several prohibitions and threatens with capital punishment those who disobey (lines 24–25). One could circumvent the edict by direct appeal to a quorum of the Roman senate (lines 4–6). This shows, according to North, that the senate did not intend to obliterate the cult and that it did not object to individual participation.[19] Rather, the senators objected to organization on such a large scale. Rome was a state where only citizen men were elected or appointed to the public offices of priesthoods; the indiscriminate mix of men and women as priests in this mystery cult ran counter to Roman religious sensibility.[20] Thus the *senatus consultum* forbids that any man be a *sacerdos* and any man or woman be a *magister* (line 10). While the responsibilities of the *sacerdos* versus the *magister* elude us, the precise terminology is testimony to a well-articulated organizational structure. The senate reacts not to the threat of a religious cult but to the threat of an organized counter-state. Indeed, the senate takes special care not to offend the god by forbidding worship altogether; ample provision is made in the *senatus consultum* for worship to continue on a small scale (lines 19–20). In addition, although worship of Bacchus appears to have diminished in the years immediately after 186, worship continued in Italy on a small scale and was even revived under Caesar.[21] The *senatus consultum* dismantled merely the apparatus of the cult.

In the end, senatorial prejudice appears to be the most pressing cause for the strong reaction against the cult. Such prejudice finds expression in the prefaces of Livy and the *Bellum Catilinae*. Livy promises to trace the moral decline of Rome from its beginning, to its rapidly increasing disintegration, finally to its collapse (pr. 9). For many generations, Rome was free from foreign *avaritia luxuriaque* (greed and indulgence).[22] It is not until Book 39 that Livy fixes the turning point for the degeneration of morals, in the year 187 B.C.E. (39.6.7). Sallust attributed the moral crisis at Rome to the destruction of Carthage in 146 B.C.E. (*Cat.* 7-10) and to the domination of Sulla (*Cat.* 11.4). Both authors agree that the causes were sustained contact with the material prosperity emanating from the East, the elimination of an external threat, and the opportunity for increased individual wealth.[23] Both Livy and Sallust imply that contact with foreigners hastened conditions that left Rome ripe for conspiracy.

Exceptional measures are justified, when one considers that a band of foreigners, women, and young men were conspiring against the state.[24] "It is evident," writes Nilsson, "that the Senate considered the Bacchic associations a genuine threat to public security."[25] Whatever the Bacchanalians were doing, by calling it a *coniuratio,* the consul and the senate instantly defamed the cult and its participants.[26] The senate reacted to the cult the way it did because of prevailing fear of those who participated. A strategy of containment is at work in Livy's narrative that assures the reader of the senate's all-pervasive power to halt conspiracy in its tracks.

## DON'T ASK, DON'T TELL

Given the evidence, it is surprising how many scholars have asserted the participation of slaves in the Bacchanalian affair. Frank proposed that the cult was brought to Rome by the hordes of prisoners taken captive and enslaved after the sack of Tarentum in 208 B.C.E.: "The devotees were now to a great extent in miserable slavery in a foreign country."[27] He was followed by McDonald, who conjectured that "a considerable number of Greeks from the South, including many slaves from Tarentum, must have moved up into Central Italy, bringing their cults with them."[28] When Tarditi said that "citizens and foreigners, patricians and plebeians, freedmen and slaves were found together in the cult,"[29] he was following the words of Bruhl: "The Dionysiac groups were revolutionary, because they united different types of conditions, citizen and foreign, patrician and plebeian, freed men and slaves."[30] In a careful reconsideration, Gruen dismantled the arguments for slave participation. The inscription of the *senatus consultum* makes no explicit reference to slaves, and Livy's only reference to a slave is the heroine Hispala. Yet she was manumitted, and she could be an exception.[31] The evidence does not show whether slaves were involved in the Bacchic cult, but it does reveal the suspicion of slave participation. Thus the cult produced a deep-seated status anxiety. Bacchic worship and the physical act of its initiation rituals in particular blurred the distinction between free citizen and slave. The *senatus consultum* responded to this category crisis with singular resolve.

Literary evidence points to a well-established cult of Bacchus between the end of the Second Punic War and its suppression in 186.[32] Six plays of Plautus specifically mention either *bacchantes* (the worshipers) or *bacchanalia* (the shrines):[33] the *Menaechmi, Miles Gloriosus, Aulularia, Amphitryo, Casina,* and *Bacchides.* Two examples are particularly illuminating. In the *Amphitryo,* the slave Sosia says:

> What do you want? Don't you know? If you wish to oppose a raging Bacchant, you make her the more insane, and she will bang you more often![34]

Sosia appears to have first-hand experience of Bacchanalian behavior; the abuse is physical. In the *Aulularia,* the slave cook Congrio rushes on stage, exclaiming about his rough treatment among Bacchantes:

> This is the first time I ever came to cook for Bacchantes at a Bacchanal. O dear, what an awful clubbing I and my disciples did get! I'm one big ache! I'm utterly ruined! The way that old fart took me for a gymnasium![35]

Both Sosia and Congrio imply that they have suffered physical abuse among the Bacchantes. Strikes and blows are often metaphors for sexual acts, and the vocabulary here ( *feriet,* "bang"; *contuderunt,* "make sore"), together with the mention of a gymnasium, a place associated with the Greek pursuit of young men, evokes sexual imagery.[36]

Pailler points out that it is difficult to depend on Plautus for precise evidence about the senatorial suppression of the cult for three reasons. First, the chronology of the plays is uncertain, especially in relation to 186; Plautus may have died before the *senatus consultum* was issued. Second, all the references are extremely brief, only one or two lines. Third, the cultural overlap between Greek and Roman comedy makes it impossible to discern any explicit references to a distinctly Roman cult. The context may be more Greek than Roman.[37] At the very least, the plays of Plautus reveal that it would not have been surprising to a Roman audience to hear a slave refer to frenzied Bacchic worship of the type mentioned in Livy's account[38] and that this Bacchic worship involved physical, even possibly sexual, abuse.

Livy details the ritual and adumbrates an anxiety about the participation of free persons in such physical abuse. After introducing the consular year in the traditional way, Livy describes the activities of the cult:

This indiscriminate debauchery of freeborn boys and of women was not the only kind of vice. . . . Many outrageous acts were performed by guile, and not a few by violence; but the violence lay hidden, for no cry of those protesting (*vox quiritantium*) could be heard amidst the debauchery (*stuprum*) and slaughter because of the howling and the din of drums and cymbals.[39]

Hispala repeats these details of the initiation:

When someone is initiated, he is handed over to priests just like a sacrificial victim; they lead him to a place that resounds with shrieks and the music of instruments and the blasts of cymbals and drums, to drown out the shout of him crying out (*vox quiritantis*) as he is raped (*stuprum*) violently.[40]

Her eyewitness account of the initiation echoes Livy's introductory remarks about the nocturnal activities. Both passages highlight the physical abuse and in particular the *stuprum* to which the initiates are subject.

Several studies have sought to arrive at a definition of the capacious term *stuprum,* each approaching the term from a different angle. Adams' lexical study finds that *stuprum* originally meant disgrace in general but later came to specify sexual disgrace, whether adulterous or forcible.[41] Gardner's legal study traces *stuprum* as a category of prosecution; in general, *stuprum* denoted any sexual immorality, including adultery.[42] In her social history of Roman marriage, Treggiari says that *stuprum* was used for any irregular or promiscuous act, especially rape or homosexuality.[43] Fantham's study of attitudes toward sexual offenses in Republican Rome traces the use of the word *stuprum* to designate the notion of penetration as an assault on the person who is penetrated. The opposite of such *stuprum* is *pudicitia,* the confinement of one's sexual activity to appropriate, conventionally sanctioned partners.[44] Most recently, Williams' cultural study of Roman homosexuality challenges a definition that distinguishes between homosexual and heterosexual acts. Rather, *stuprum* is the violation of the sexual integrity of freeborn Romans of either sex. Without specific reference to either homosexual or heterosexual activity, *stuprum* is bound to Roman notions of the inviolability of the citizen male and the impenetrability of his body.[45]

The initiation as described in Livy appears to involve sexual penetration of a male (*introductus* is distinctly masculine gender). Furthermore, in his speech before the people, the consul Postumius says, "If you knew at what tender ages the males are initiated, you would feel not merely pity but also shame for them." The Latin is clear: *si quibus aetatibus initientur mares sciatis* (39.15.13). The consul is most disturbed by the men who participate in the rituals (39.15.14): "Will these men, caked with the defilement of themselves and of others, fight with the steel to defend the chastity of your wives and children?" Clearly the act of *stuprum,* the main component of the ritual initiation, renders men incapable of performing their civic duties and serving the state.[46] This produces an anxiety in the consul.[47]

Initiation at its core consists of three phases: separation, liminality, and reaggregation. Separated from the rest of society, the initiate is deprived of his old status and awarded a new status after the ritual.[48] Individual initiates are brought back together into a new community; the newly reaggregated society is permanently metamorphosed.[49] Ritual initiation can be compared to conspiracy in many ways. As initiation is an interm diate step between secular and sacred, so conspiracy is a liminal state between danger and safety. As initiation permanently changes individuals, conspiracy threatens permanent change. As initiation rituals, often involving transvestism, mystify gender and status, so conspiracy confounds gender and status. As initiation rites are closely guarded secrets, so conspiracy is a clandestine, secret act; it is as difficult to speak of mystery cults as it is to speak of conspiracy. And so for both phenomena, the most interesting part of the process is the middle: the unseen actions and untold words that effect this profound and permanent change.

Suppression of the Bacchanalia depended upon revealing and publicizing the secret rituals; such is the purpose of Postumius' speech. Furthermore, insofar as initiation marks an irreversible passage from one social status to another, it marks a boundary. In this case, I suggest it is the passage from a freeborn to a servile status, a passage from a position of greater to a position of lesser power, that evokes senatorial anxiety. Normally the body of the Roman male is protected from physical abuse by virtue of his status as a freeborn citizen. Slaves, on the other hand, were not protected from violation and were in fact perceived as available for sexual abuse at any time by a master.[50] The *stuprum* of the Bacchic cult initiation violated the body of the citizen male and confused his status with that of a slave.

Citizens were protected from physical abuse by the *lex Porcia de provocatione.*[51] Caesar invoked this law in his speech against capital punishment of the Catilinarian conspirators.[52] Thus, both conspiracies register a concern with the inviolability of the citizen body. Furthermore, to describe the cries of the initiates, Livy twice uses the rare verb *quirito* (39.8.8, 10.7), apparently derived from *Quirites,* the name given to the citizens of Rome collectively. Varro (*L.* 6.68) defines *quirito* as *dicitur is qui Quiritum fidem clamans inplorat* ("[*Quiritio*] is used of one who, crying out, begs for help from fellow citizens"). In a letter to Cicero, Asinius Pollio describes the arrogant Balbus' outrageous punishment of a Pompeian veteran, forced to be a gladiator, who exercised his right of *provocatio* (appeal) and called to the people of Gades for release:

> Then he [Balbus] half buried him [the veteran] at a show . . . and surrounded him with fire . . . and to that miserable one crying out (*quiritanti*), "I was born a Roman citizen," he replied, "Go then and beseech the protection of the people."[53]

The language of a passage from Cicero's second oration against Verres reminds us of Livy's description of the drowned out cries of the victims of the Bacchic initiation:

> No other cry of the miserable one was heard among his grief and the sound of the whips but "I am a Roman citizen."[54]

The letter of Asinius Pollio and the speech of Cicero preserve the formulaic expression of the *provocatio: civis Romanus sum.* In a society without the formal mechanisms of a police force, citizens relied on the self-help of an ancient formula for personal protection. The *quiritatio,* the formal beseeching one's fellow citizens, played an important role in the early Republic in the struggle of the orders.[55] In these passages of Livy's Bacchanalian affair, the victims cried out to their fellow citizens, and the use of the verb *quirito* points to the boundary between citizen and slave, even as that boundary was being violated.

Gruen argues that the senate's extraordinary measures as enumerated in the inscription prove slaves did not participate. Legal proceedings complete with indictments, hearings, trials, judicial pronouncement, and sanctioned punishment would have been unnecessary if slaves had composed virtually all of the victims.[56] The argument, however, is *ex silentio.* Their absence from the inscription does not prove their absence from the cult; it proves only that the senate did not need to justify the capital punishment of slaves who might have participated. The evidence still does not support a conclusive answer. Instead, it is useful to consider what the suppression of the Bacchanalian affair tells us about Roman attitudes. Flower argues that the *senatus consultum* is an attempt to "put men and women in their proper places." Her gendered reading rises to the evidentiary challenges of the inscription.[57] No doubt the cult produced gender anxiety.[58] But I argue that status anxiety also lurked behind the suppression of the cult. As the *senatus consultum* explicitly reinforced the distinction between men and women, so it also implicitly reinforced the distinction between citizen and slave. Citizens must not subject themselves to *stuprum*, and if they do, their capital punishment must be highly regulated.

In sum: mention of Bacchic worship in the plays of Plautus highlights the physical abuse of the cult. The consul's speech as reported by Livy testifies to a preoccupation with the inviolability and especially the sexual integrity of citizen males. *Stuprum* is objectionable because it is servile; just as the organization of the cult elided the difference between male and female, so the initiation ritual threatened the distinction between free and slave. Thus, while it is impossible to verify the participation of slaves, we can assert that servile behavior took place, to which the senate objected with the utmost vehemence. In the end, the sources reveal less about the actual participation of slaves in the Bacchanalian affair and more about prevailing senatorial attitudes toward them. In an account that devotes a great deal of space to the consul's denunciation and the senate's suppression of the cult, we see the strategy of containment at work again.

## WITNESS PROTECTION

While Livy spends little effort substantiating his own research efforts or his reliability for the account of the Bacchanalian affair, he goes to great lengths to validate his eyewitness, Hispala Faecenia. Originally a Spanish slave from Hispalis (now Seville), she took the name of her patron upon manumission.[59] Livy introduces her as "a noble prostitute, a freedwoman named Hispala Faecenia." Although she continued to live as a prostitute even after her manumission, her character was better than her occupation.[60] Scafuro explains the catachresis *scortum nobile* ("noble prostitute") from the perspective of the stereotypical characterizations of New Comedy: "Because we must assume, on the basis of Livy's account, that Aebutius has no funds of his own, we must conclude that Hispala supports her lover from her earnings as a prostitute." And because she was *nobilis*, well known in the Aventine neighborhood (39.12.1), she earned a handsome living.[61]

Still, the connotations of ethnicity and status in the phrase *scortum nobile Faecenia Hispala* cannot be overlooked. Her name betrays a familiarity with foreign ways. In the atmosphere of xenophobia surrounding the conspiracy, the name Hispala confirms that such a woman would have had access to the foreign rites that were polluting the city. Scafuro also argues that status is a key factor in explaining the mechanics of Livy's account of the Bacchanalian affair. By manumission, Hispala gains a fluid status; neither completely free nor still a slave, she is "a perfect witness for the state," capable of garnering the sympathy of both slaves and free.[62] In the phrase *scortum nobile,* Livy valorizes Hispala as a source of information and softens the effect of her presence in the narrative.[63] Despite the questionable social status of her occupation, with the adjective *nobilis* Livy renders her a suitable witness and prefigures her as an acceptable savior for the Roman state.

Furthermore, when Aebutius tells Hispala that he will not visit her for ten days, he explains his mother's intention to initiate him into the cult because, as Livy says, there are no secrets between them: *nec quicquam secretum alter ab altero haberent* (39.10.1). With this subtle clause, the historian confirms that the lovers keep an open channel of communication. Livy further authenticates the reliability of their intimate conversation when Hispala, having objected quite strongly to Aebutius' initiation, begs forgiveness if compelled by affection for him she disclosed things better kept silent (*si coacta caritate eius silenda enuntiasset,* 39.10.5). We are assured that all secrets are fully disclosed in the privacy of the lovers' chamber.

In the previous chapter, I suggested that while the foundation of the republic depended on the actions of high-born, noble women of distinguished social rank and means, the women who preserve the republic from the internal threats of conspiracy belong to a different category. Hispala's actions stand in stark contrast to the deeds of two principal women of the foundation narrative of Livy's Book 1: Tullia, exemplum of evil, and Lucretia, paragon of probity.

The sons of Lucius Tarquinius Priscus, Lucius Tarquinius and Arruns, were married to the daughters of Servius, the elder and the younger Tullia. Tarquinius was fiercer and more ambitious than his brother; the younger Tullia fiercer and more ambitious than her sister. But Tarquinius married the elder, while the mild Arruns was likewise mismatched with the younger. Tarquinius and the younger Tullia were each dissatisfied with their weak and feeble partners, and so Tullia took action. The trouble began, says Livy, with the woman: *sed initium turbandi omnia a femina ortum est* (1.46.7). Tullia frequently met Tarquinius in secret, demonstrating the subversive power of a woman's speech in a private setting, for she aggressively goaded Tarquinius, and not without results. Swiftly her boldness inspired him; with funerals in rapid succession, both were suddenly widowed and subsequently married each other. Inflamed by her ambition, Tarquinius solicited support; at last, surrounded by armed men, he burst into the forum and commanded the senate to convene. In the midst of his harangue, the aged Servius reproached him. Tarquinius threw the king from the steps of the senate house and dispatched a band of thugs to murder him. Tullia arrived at the Curia and was the first to hail her husband as king, but Tarquinius dismissed her. As she was making her way home, her driver spotted the murdered corpse of her father, over which she drove her carriage herself, foul and frenzied. The place bears eternal testimony to the outrage, for the Romans called it the Street of Crime. Tullia incited a violent change in rule. Through her agency, Tarquinius Superbus became king. Because of Lucretia, he was to be the last king.

The story of Lucretia begins with the siege of Ardea, a break in fighting that afforded the officers more leisure than usual. One night, Sextus Tarquinius, son of the king, and Tarquinius Collatinus, his cousin, were drinking, when the topic of conversation turned to wives. Each boasted his own, but Collatinus proposed that the men see for themselves whose wife was best. The men first rode to Rome to find the royal wives enjoying themselves in great luxury. They proceeded to Collatia and espied Lucretia, in contrast to the other women, virtuously spinning wool. Collatinus feasted his companions in celebration of her victory as the best of wives.

Her beauty and her chastity (*castitas*, 1.57.10) inflamed the passion of Sextus Tarquinius, who returned after a few days to rape her in her chamber. She sent word to her husband and father, and when they came she told them what had happened and then committed suicide before their eyes. Lucius Junius Brutus then swore to avenge her death, and all were driven to overthrow the king: "By this woman's blood, by the gods, I swear that with sword and fire, and whatever else can lend strength to my arm, I will pursue Lucius Tarquinius the Proud, his wicked wife, and all his children, and never again will I let them or any other man be king in Rome" (1.59.1). Lucretia's body was carried from the house to the public square; crowds gathered. Anger at the criminal brutality of the king's son stirred the populace. When Brutus called for a coalition against the tyrants, every man answered. Brutus in command marched on Rome. When news of the rebellion reached Tarquinius Superbus, still camped at Ardea, he too set out for Rome, arriving at the same time as Brutus and his force. Tarquinius was repelled and exiled, and Brutus was proclaimed Liberator. The monarchy was over, the republic begun.

The bold Tullia incites rebellion, suborns murder, and defiles the dead. She manipulates her husband, a very effective way for those without franchise to assert a high degree of influence in the public sphere. The timid Hispala, on the other hand, uses pillow talk, not for destructive purposes but to save the republic from the threat of the Bacchantes. Hispala is likewise the polar opposite of the noble Lucretia. As the founding of the Roman republic rests ultimately on the violated chastity of Lucretia, raped and defiled but true to her husband and her father, so the salvation of the republic rests on the low-born, promiscuous Hispala, a woman with no husband and no father. Whatever noble actions she performs are extorted from her by threat of torture or by promise of reward. The high-born Tullia and Lucretia, formally excluded from political power, nevertheless effect radical changes; the lowly Hispala, on the other hand, is deployed for the salvation of the state.

Given the degree of detail that Hispala recounts about the initiation rites, it is interesting to note the utter lack of detail in Aebutius' report to the consul: "He then reported the matter to the consul Postumius on the following day with no witnesses present."[64] Perhaps Livy compressed Aebutius' information into this indirect statement to avoid redundancy; however, Livy does not shrink from repeating the grisly details of the initiation. The rites are first described in the opening paragraph of the account (39.8.8). Only two paragraphs later, Hispala closely echoes the same details (39.10.7). "Repetition only diminishes credibility," according to Gruen.[65] Perhaps, but repetition helps create narrative continuity by keeping *stuprum* at the forefront of the reader's attention. The repetition also shapes the reader's interpretation. The exceptional behavior is attested by an exceptional character. Hispala gives a lurid description, but Aebutius simply delates the affair to the consul, *rem detulit*. No witnesses are present before whom he must humiliate himself. Livy does not require him to utter the word *stuprum*. A gentlemen's code of silence prevails; Aebutius' integrity remains intact.[66]

Because of her first-hand knowledge of the initiation rites, Hispala is in a position to save the Roman state from the so-called conspiracy of the Bacchantes. But a counterconspiracy is underway. By informing Aebutius, she thwarts his parents' conspiracy to deprive him of his patrimony once and for all. Furthermore, Scafuro argues that Livy presents Postumius as the leader of a counterconspiracy. As the Bacchantes plot, supposedly, to upset the stability of Rome, so the consul carries out an elaborately constructed plan to destroy the Bacchantes.[67] Naturally his counterplot also hinges on Hispala.

Hispala is the key witness for the prosecution; she is also a hostile witness. Postumius summons her to an audience, and in the presence of his mother-in-law Sulpicia (in contrast to the private interview with Aebutius), a scene unfolds in which Postumius and Hispala each reluctantly reveal by degrees what they know of the conspiracy. He demands her information. When she demurs, he offers some assurance for her safety. She then admits to having been initiated but claims ignorance since her manumission,[68] whereupon he admits that he already knows of her participation in the lurid initiation. Again she hesitates and begs that the casual banter between lovers (*cum amatore sermonem*, 39.13.2) not be admissible evidence in a capital case.[69] She flatly denies that she has knowledge; this sends Postumius into a fit of rage. Sulpicia finally resolves the conflict. As a result, Hispala agrees to testify once offered protection.

To suppress the conspiracy, Postumius must extract its secrets hidden within Hispala. She is clearly unwilling to testify. Not only does she protest verbally, but physically she also resists speaking. In a scene not unlike that in *Aeneid* 6, in which Vergil's Cumaean Sibyl is possessed by the god,[70] Hispala falters before the entrance and nearly faints:

> When she saw the lictors, the crowd of consular men, and the consul himself in the entrance, she nearly fainted.[71]

> When she was told that she had been summoned to tell all she knew about the Bacchic initiations, such fear and trembling of all her limbs seized the woman that she was for some time unable to open her mouth.[72]

Hispala's fear and hesitation constitute a delay in the progress of the narrative. The lictors and the crowd of consular men serve as obstacles, both to the entrance and to her disclosure. Unable to open her mouth, Hispala avoids having to speak and thereby halts the action altogether, until she gains her composure. The very next word, *tandem,* signals that "at last" the narrative is about to advance. The adverb marks a stark contrast between Hispala's silence and her speech. Like the Sibyl, Hispala was forced by a higher power to reveal what she had seen. Once emptied of her knowledge, she collapsed, exhausted and no longer of any use.[73] Her body performed its duty for the Roman state, and she fades from the story. Armed with her testimony, Postumius has no more use for her. In the end, she is permanently metamorphosed into a suitable savior for the republic by a generous monetary reward, the right to dispose of her own resources, and the right to marry outside her *gens.*[74]

So although Livy does not substantiate his own credibility for the tale he tells, he takes great care to validate Hispala's testimony. The story depended on one eyewitness whose reliability had to be established. Her knowledge of the violation of male citizen bodies put her own body in physical danger. If she informed, she ran the risk of being torn to bits by the Bacchantes (39.13.5). If she kept silent, however, she ran the risk of the consul's wrath (39.13.3). Her authority as a witness rested on her capacity to speak "solely in the name of an incapacity to speak."[75] She was the more reliable precisely because her capacity as a witness put her in double jeopardy. She was threatened from both sides, by both conspirators and counterconspirators.

Her double jeopardy finds a modern counterpart in the case of Jean Hill, witness to the assassination of President Kennedy. This ordinary woman, a divorced elementary school teacher, was the closest civilian to the presidential limousine. She stood across the street from the School Book Depository, opposite the grassy knoll and the stockade fence, with an unrestricted view. The general public had been kept on the other side of Elm Street, but she was granted permission to cross because of her personal relationship with a member of the Dallas police force, whose friend allowed her this privileged vantage point. Her eyewitness testimony contradicted the findings of the Warren Commission, that one man (Lee Harvey Oswald) shot the president from the sixth floor of the book depository. She asserted that several shots were fired, and one from behind the stockade fence. She gave this testimony to both the media and the Secret Service on the day JFK was shot. Her information and her insistent testimony put her in grave danger from both sides. Both the assassins and the authorities, intent on constructing a foolproof version of the murder, had good cause to silence her. She was summoned before the Warren Commission to testify, and she recalls that her interview with Arlen Specter (at the time, assistant counsel to the commission) was both intimidating and humiliating:

> She clearly recalls Specter telling her, frostily, however, that he knew "all about" her. She says he accused her of engaging in a "shabby extramarital affair" [with the Dallas police officer], thirsting for publicity and notoriety, refusing to cooperate with the federal authorities, and proving herself "totally unreliable" as a witness. Unless the commission received her full cooperation from now on . . . she would be "very, very sorry."[76]

Hispala and Jean Hill had the same problem. Both women were unwittingly drawn into vast conspiracies during eras of volatile foreign policy; the influx of Greek culture threatened Roman stability, while Communism, and especially Cuba, frightened the United States. Both women possessed knowledge that the authorities needed—but did not necessarily want—to hear. Both women were physically threatened if they did not support the official versions. In both cases, the consul and the attorney had already decided what the testimony was to be and merely needed the woman to corroborate the story. Both unmarried women, by virtue of their low social status and illicit affairs, were deemed unreliable sources.

The differences are of course significant. To ensure her survival, Hispala had no choice but to tell the consul what she saw; silence was not an option. On the other hand, silence ensured the survival of Jean Hill's dissenting voice. For more than fifteen years she refused to talk to anyone about the assassination, thereby denying her extraordinary role in the investigation. Thanks to her silence, she survived the "accidents" that befell other witnesses to the events in Dealey Plaza on November 23, 1963, so that her dissenting voice would eventually be heard.[77] Moreover, Hispala's story has a happy ending. The consul's counterconspiracy succeeded, and for her part Hispala was rewarded. On the contrary, for the strong patriotic convictions that bound Jean Hill to defy the official report of the Warren Commission, she received no compensation and a lifetime of woe instead. As we shall see in the next chapter, the intricacies of an exceptional woman's speech and silence in the face of conspiracy were not lost on that most ironic of historians, Tacitus.

# THREE

# TACITUS

## *The Pisonian Conspiracy*

Perhaps no other extant Roman historian is as obsessed with conspiracy as Tacitus. From the outset, the *Annales* would have us believe that Tiberius owed his rise to power to secret machinations. In the first ten chapters alone, Tacitus casts suspicion on the rise of Augustus and the deaths of Lucius, Gaius, Hirtius, and Pansa—all before Tiberius even becomes emperor, thanks to his scheming mother Livia. The first act of Tiberius' principate was the murder of Agrippa Postumus. Much of Books 2 and 3 is dominated by the mysterious death of Germanicus. With Sejanus around, no one was safe; Tacitus scornfully tells of senators hidden in the rafters above the ceiling in order to spy on an enemy. Tiberius was smothered; Claudius was poisoned. Treachery, prevarication, dissimulation—such is the subject matter of the *Annales*. With so many secretive events, several episodes demand skepticism, and Tacitus must confront the limits of knowledge. Nowhere is continuity more difficult to achieve, and nowhere does Tacitus employ the rhetoric of conspiracy more fully, than in his narrative of the aborted plot to assassinate Nero.

Yet to what extent are the difficulties manifested in the Pisonian conspiracy a function of the nature of history writing in general? It will be useful to start with an analysis of another moment of narrative diffidence in the *Annales:* the trial and death of Gnaeus Calpurnius Piso in the aftermath of the death of Germanicus in Book 3. With this in mind, in the second part of the chapter we examine Tacitus' admissions of ignorance or uncertainty about the facts of the Pisonian conspiracy, which suggests it is particularly difficult to narrate. The narrative of the Pisonian conspiracy is distinguished from other moments of dubiety in the *Annales* and is allied with other conspiracy narratives because of the transfer of information via women. The third and fourth sections of this chapter take in turn Epicharis, who protected the conspirators with her silence, and the wife of the freedman Milichus, who betrayed the conspirators with her speech. The one ensured the conspiracy would continue;

the other ensured it would be narrated. The chapter closes with a typology of conspiracy narrative based on our readings of Sallust, Livy, and Tacitus.

## THE TRIAL OF PISO

Just as the account of the Pisonian conspiracy is the longest episode, so the trial of Gnaeus Calpurnius Piso (3.10–19) is the longest and most detailed narrative of a legal proceeding in the extant *Annales*.[1] In the year 20 C.E., Calpurnius Piso faced a threefold indictment. Fulcinius Trio prosecuted him for provincial mismanagement. Then Servaeus, Veranius, and Vitellius charged him with treasonable tampering with the army in Syria and with the murder by poison of Germanicus (3.13.1–2). The first charge was negligible, but the other two were brought forth with *multa eloquentia* (3.13.2); these were the charges for which the Roman people eagerly awaited Piso's conviction. In the course of the trial, the defense was able to refute only one charge, that of poisoning (3.14.2). When the people were informed of this, they threatened to riot, and Piso had to be escorted home under guard from the senate house to ensure his safety (3.14.3–4).

Piso's wife Plancina was apparently a co-defendant on the charge of murder; she secured for herself the protection of Livia and separated her defense case from his (3.15.1). Although disheartened by his wife's desertion, Piso endured another day of the trial; when it became obvious that he was in great peril, he retired to his home and ended his life. Tacitus then records the contents of his suicide note (3.16), in which Piso begs pardon for his children, omitting any mention of his wife. Tiberius acquitted the boys and deferred to Livia in the case of Plancina (3.17). Even after Piso's death, the trial continued. He was convicted, and Tiberius mitigated the punishments proposed by the consul Cotta. The senate then voted offerings of thanks because the death of Germanicus had been avenged.

The inscription of the *senatus consultum de Cn. Pisone Patre (SCPP)* records the findings of the senate's fourfold investigation of (1) the death of Calpurnius Piso and whether he committed suicide, (2) the case of his son, (3) the case of his wife Plancina, and (4) members of his staff.[2] Then, recognition goes to Tiberius for his determination in finding the truth. The inscription describes Calpurnius Piso's rivalry with Germanicus, his insubordination, and his punishments.

One detail of the *senatus consultum* regarding thanksgivings after the trial elicits a curious comment from Tacitus. Messalinus proposed that official thanks be given to Tiberius, Livia, Antonia, Agrippina, and Drusus for avenging the death of Germanicus (3.18.3). Asprenas corrected the omission of Claudius, whose name is in fact recorded in the inscription.[3] This prompts Tacitus to share a personal reflection on the matter:

> For me (*mihi*), the more I go back (*revolvo*) over several events of the present or the past, the more the mockeries of mortal affairs in all matters are evident. For in rumor, hope, and homage, all intended for *imperium* another rather than him whom fortune was keeping hidden for the future principate.[4]

We can only imagine how Tacitus would have narrated the ascension of Claudius, cloaked behind a curtain and plucked from obscurity by a soldier. The allusion to the emperor Claudius allows Tacitus to transgress the temporal limit of the consular year 20 C.E. and include within its narrative material belonging properly to the year 41. But in anticipation of the event, Tacitus alludes to the future emperor without mentioning his name. The irony, that the one who would one day command the Roman world was overlooked, is recapitulated in Tacitus' own omission of the name Claudius in the sentence beginning with *mihi*. But the irony does not undercut the historicity of the passage; even the external reference provided by the inscription confirms Asprenas' addition of Claudius to the imperial roster. The information in 3.18.3–4 is on firm historical ground. The intrusion and prominence of the first person (*mihi, revolvo*) remind the reader that even when the facts are sound, the historian still controls how they are narrated.[5]

Tacitus records the stories surrounding the mysterious death of Piso, which he heard from men of his day:

> I recall that I heard from my elders that a folder was often seen in Piso's possession . . . and that he did not die of his own will but an executioner was sent. Neither of which I would assert (*adseveraverim*), nevertheless I ought not hide what was told by those who survived until my youth.[6]

The syntax and diction of the disclaimer are noteworthy. The verb *adseveraverim* is a potential subjunctive expressing cautious assertion. Tacitus takes the time to say that he must not hide (*occulere*) the information he heard, regardless of its validity. He reports what he has heard from unnamed, first-hand sources of the previous generation (*ex senioribus . . . qui duraverunt*, 3.16.1). The evidence of a *percussor* (executioner) is not proven to Tacitus' satisfaction.

In fact, Piso's death preempts the verdict of the trial:

Although he thought about continuing the defense for another day, he wrote a few things down, sealed the note, and gave it to his freedman; then he attended the care for his person in the customary way. Finally, deep in the night, after his wife left the bedroom, he ordered the doors to be shut, and at daybreak he was found with his throat cut and a sword lying on the ground.[7]

The death of Piso presents a difficulty for the historian. Since the act was hidden within a private chamber, no one saw exactly what happened. Even his wife, the most probable witness, and the one who could most likely reveal the actual manner of his death, was not present.[8] Tacitus sidesteps this difficulty by adding details that do not necessarily help uncover the mystery. On the one hand, Piso wrote what could be considered a suicide note;[9] on the other hand, the deed was carried out behind closed doors. The *sword* may have belonged to the executioner as easily as to Piso, and it is impossible to determine who wielded the weapon. Thus, the inconclusive description of the circumstances surrounding Piso's death affirm Tacitus' statement that he cannot say whether reports of suicide were true. He is at a loss as to how exactly Piso died, but he is still able to narrate the event, in all its uncertainties.[10]

Indeterminacy in the text, like the ambiguity of the death of Piso, is an inescapable component of any narrative.[11] Because a text cannot capture every single aspect of the event it attempts to record, some elements must remain undefined. But to maintain the momentum of the story, to avoid silence, the author must create continuity where there is none, and the reader must infer continuity where the author is unable to sustain it explicitly. Paradoxically, such moments of indeterminacy can also be thought of as the most stable moments in the text. Both author and reader must confront the limits of knowledge.

The only thing that is certain is that we do not know exactly what happened. In the description of Piso's mysterious death (3.15), Tacitus stitches together the various pieces of information available to him, and the reader is left to choose for himself how Piso died. In the very next paragraph (3.16), Tacitus exonerates himself, as he will do in the case of the Pisonian conspiracy, and in doing so he draws attention to the representational quality of the narrative. He asserts his control over this representation by inserting himself into the text in the form of the first person. Claims to historical veracity about the death of Piso are dropped in favor of verisimilitude. The facts lay elsewhere than in the representation, but the failure of historical discourse does not keep the historian from relating the event. Tacitus achieves narrative continuity by depending on the reader's ability to leap across the furrows of indeterminacy.[12]

Some moments of indeterminacy are more extreme in the *Annales* than others. In the coda to the episode of the trial of Piso, Tacitus notes that the integrity of his sources for the event may be suspect:

> This was the end of the avenging of the death of Germanicus not only among men who lived then but even according to the various rumors bantered about in later times. To such an extent (*adeo*) are great things uncertain, because some regard what they have heard from whatever source as verified, while others turn the truth into its opposite, and both gain credence over time.[13]

Nearly one hundred years separate Tacitus from the event. The reality of the trial of Piso is far removed from its representation, and this distance produces an anxiety in the historian.[14] The anxiety of representation generates statements such as these, in which attention is drawn to the representational features of the text. Martin and Woodman note that the sentence beginning with *adeo* is "variously paradoxical," particularly in its claim that great things are ambiguous.[15] If this was indeed the end of the avenging of Germanicus, then why did rumors continue to circulate later? Although Tacitus attempted to provide a satisfactory account of the trial and death of Piso, he knows he has failed to answer for every link in the chain of causality.[16] In addition, Tacitus seems to discredit those who rely on what they have heard, and yet he reports hearsay above, *audire* (3.16.1). It is also strange that "some turn truth into its opposite." Tacitus credits the manipulation of the truth to unnamed sources. If this episode is any indication of the historian's ability to overcome the difficulty imposed by secret events, then the betrayed Pisonian conspiracy meets and exceeds this example.

## OUTRIGHT ADMISSIONS

Nero's reign began in 54 C.E. with a murder, and the Tacitean portrait of the emperor's abominations is relentless. Junius Silanus and Claudius' freedman Narcissus were the victims of Nero's mother Agrippina; the former was poisoned, the latter forced to commit suicide. Nero repeatedly humiliated Britannicus before finally poisoning him. The freedman Atimetus paid with his life for his part in a complicated plot between political rivals Agrippina and Domitia. Julius Montanus, mugged by Nero, committed suicide. Octavia, too frail to bleed to death, was suffocated in the bath and subsequently be-headed. Acerronia was an innocent victim in the attempt on Agrippina's life; Agrippina was, of course, murdered. The praetorian praefect Burrus died under suspicious circumstances. Seneca, Lucan, and Petronius were just a few of the victims in the aftermath of the Pisonian conspiracy. Poppaea died from a violent outburst of Nero's rage. This is an abbreviated list of the more memorable victims, a deranged take on the epic *aristeia*.[17] Tacitus' rhetoric gives the impression of an endless, steady stream of blood. This establishes but one of the many motives for conspiring to kill the emperor.

Book 14 closes with the murder of two of Nero's most powerful freedmen, Doryphorus and Pallas, and the notice of an unsuccessful prosecution. Romanus accused Seneca of an affiliation with Piso,[18] but Seneca won his case by imputing the charges to Romanus. Thus already in 62, Piso was a political lightning rod, dangerously attracting opposing forces. As a result of this case, Tacitus says, "This alarmed Piso and gave rise to a great number of unsuc-cessful conspiracies against Nero" (14.65.2). By mentioning the seeds of the Pisonian conspiracy on the heels of death and prosecution, Tacitus suggests reasons for the discontent that drove the conspirators: endless bloodshed and pernicious litigation.

Three years later, in 65, soldiers, senators, and equestrians banded together out of hatred for Nero and agreed to assassinate the emperor and give their support to Piso. It was a powerful alliance of senate and soldiery. The ring-leaders were Subrius Flavus, a tribune of a praetorian cohort, and Sulpicius Asper, a centurion. Their prominence and commitment to the cause in Taci-tus' eyes were proved by their perseverance in death once the conspiracy was revealed (*constantia exitus*, 15.49.2). They were joined by Gavius Silvanus and Statius Proxumus, tribunes of the praetorian cohorts; the centurions Maximus Scaurus and Venetus Paulus; and Faenius Rufus, commander of the guard. Tacitus names four senators. Lucan joined the conspiracy because Nero disparaged his poetry and forbade its publication;[19] Afranius Quin-tianus joined because Nero had insulted him; Flavius Scaevinus also joined for personal revenge. Only Plautius Lateranus was driven by the noble motive, *amor rei publicae* ("love of the republic"). The extensive list of equestrians has been likened to a cast of characters for a theatrical performance:[20] Claudius Senecio, Cervarius Proculus, Vulcacius Araricus, Julius Augurinus, Munatius Gratus, Antonius Natalis, and Marcius Festus.

They formed a conspiracy but could not agree on a risk-free plan of at-tack. While they delayed, a certain Epicharis grew impatient and tried to in-cite action (15.51). While in Campania, she met with Volusius Proculus, the captain of the fleet at Misenum, to try to shake the loyalty of the officers.

When Proculus complained to Epicharis about the way Nero overlooked him, she sensed he was ripe for conspiracy. She told him of the plot but withheld names. But Proculus would not be drawn in, and her plan backfired. He reported her story to Nero; without the names of the conspirators, however, his information was useless.

This bought the conspirators more time. Frightened by the near miss, they were compelled to act. A scheme to kill Nero at Baiae was rejected (15.52); at last they agreed to act while the emperor was in Rome at the games (15.53). Scaevinus claimed the first blow; however, his unusual preparations on the night before the attack prompted his freedman Milichus to inform Nero.[21] Several conspirators were arrested on the information of Milichus and his wife. Panic set in, conspirators betrayed one another, and Piso committed suicide. The rest of the account is taken up with the seemingly endless stream of suicides and deaths. Those not killed were banished, while the informers were rewarded and thanks decreed to the Sun for its power to reveal the secrets of the conspiracy.

No other account of an event in the *Annales* is as long, as detailed, and as convoluted as the story of the Pisonian conspiracy. It occupies the last half of Book 15 in which it is the premier event of the consular year 65. The beginning of Book 16 is taken up with the aftermath of the conspiracy, suggesting that the horror of Nero's suppression could not be contained in one book alone. Thus, the structure signals a design imposed by Tacitus that favors its consideration as a distinct piece within the larger context of the *Annales*.[22] The conspiracy against Nero provides ample opportunity to develop the theme of disguise in a principate characterized by theatricality.[23] Yet beyond such structural and thematic formalities, this episode also betrays an anxiety that the representation of the events will fall short of the reality it attempts to portray. The consul Postumius, in his speech to the people about the Bacchanalian conspiracy, eloquently stated the historian's problem: "Whatever I shall have said, be sure that my words are less than the dreadfulness and gravity of the situation" (Liv. 39.15.5).

The unusual introduction to the account of the conspiracy is the first clue to the difficulty that the subject matter presents to the historian. Tacitus begins the narrative of the Pisonian conspiracy twice. First, he announces the subject with the names of the consuls for 65:

> Entering (*ineunt*) thereupon into the consulship were Silius Nerva and Atticus Vestinus, when at the same time a conspiracy rose up and gained strength, in which senators, equestrians, soldiers, even women enlisted eagerly both out of hatred for Nero and because of favor toward Piso.[24]

He continues with a character sketch of Piso, whose qualities and qualifications are suspect. Like Sallust's portrait of Catiline (*Cat.* 5), Tacitus begins with Piso's illustrious family background. Piso was eloquent and good-looking, but he lacked the physical stamina that distinguished Catiline. Thus, Piso does not measure up to the villainous conspirator.[25] The first word of paragraph 48, *ineunt*, is etymologically equivalent to the first word of the next paragraph, *initium*. Again we read the beginning of the conspiracy:

> The origin (*initium*) of the conspiracy did not rest with the desire of [Piso] himself. Nor would I easily recount who first started it and by whose impetus there rose up that which so many later joined.[26]

This sort of duplication serves several purposes. By narrating the beginning of the conspiracy twice, Tacitus emphasizes the year 65 as the beginning of the conspiracy. In fact, it is not clear when the conspiracy actually began. Tacitus reports that Subrius Flavus was once tempted to kill Nero when he was singing on the stage and again during the great fire of 64 (15.50.4). In effect, the repetition of the origin of the conspiracy downplays any earlier tendencies toward revolution that had been growing for at least three years (since the dismissal of Seneca), so as to consolidate the conspiracies into one narrative piece. The repetition also delays the events; the intervening character sketch of Piso does not advance the action of the conspiracy but rather raises the reader's expectation for a narrative along the same lines as Sallust's *Bellum Catilinae*.

Furthermore, the two separate beginnings of the conspiracy bespeak the tension manifest throughout the *Annales* between republican and imperial history. First, Tacitus opens in the traditional manner with the naming of the consuls and the events at Rome.[27] But unlike republican historians, he does not continue to narrate *res externae* (foreign affairs), but fills the rest of the account of the year in Books 15 with *res internae* (domestic events), namely, the conspiracy. The political change from republic to empire hindered historiography; in Dio's estimation:

> Events occurring after this time [i.e., after the Augustan settlement of 27 B.C.E.] cannot be recorded in the same manner as those of previous times. Formerly, as we know, all matters were reported to the senate and to the people, even if they happened at a distance. . . . But after this time, most things that happened began to be kept secret and concealed, and even though some things are perchance made public, they are distrusted just because they cannot be verified.[28]

Tacitus responds to the change by departing from the traditional annalistic format and narrating only *res internae*. The doublet underscores this departure.

Finally, the dual beginnings of the Pisonian conspiracy recapitulate the trouble that lurks at the beginning of any historical work, and the *Annales* especially. *Urbem Romam a principio reges habuere* ("From the beginning, kings ruled the city of Rome") announces the topic of the *Annales* with a prepositional phrase denoting inauguration. But Tacitus starts again: *Primum facinus novi principatus fuit Postumi Agrippae caedes* ("The first crime of the new regime was the murder of Agrippa Postumus," 1.6.1).[29] So commences the reign of Tiberius, famously echoed at the beginning of the reign of Nero: *prima novo principatu mors Iunii Silani* ("The death of Junius Silanus was the first under the new regime," 13.1). Likewise, the beginning of the *Histories* is marked by a series of "false starts."[30] *Initium* is the first word of the *Histories,* but Tacitus hesitates, and at 1.4.1, he postpones the narrative proper in order to dispense with preliminaries: *ceterum antequam destinata componam.* Repeated beginnings such as these bespeak a frustration with the problem of how much prior information is necessary to understand the issue at hand.[31]

The beginning of a new topic, namely, the Pisonian conspiracy, is a narrative threshold. With the mention of the eponymous consuls, the historian crosses a boundary into the new year 65 and into a new subject. He crosses this boundary twice, betraying a degree of hesitation. The first sentence of paragraph 48 states the subject of the ensuing paragraphs definitively. But the first sentence of paragraph 49 reveals that specific knowledge of the conspiracy needed to construct a coherent narrative is lacking. When the time comes to narrate the actual conspiracy, the facts are so elusive that he admits the deficit openly. Yet he does not say the task is impossible, only that it is difficult, *nec tamen facile.* He makes it clear that it is necessary to proceed with caution. A similar technique is at work in Kutler's transcription of the eighteen-and-a-half-minute gap in the Nixon tapes for June 20, 1972. Where information is lacking, the historian conjectures as best he can, *quam verissume potero* ("as truthfully as I am able"), in the words of Sallust.

Tacitus' second admission of uncertainty about the events comes with the introduction of Epicharis, one of the most fascinating characters of the *Annales:*

> Meanwhile, as they were delaying and deferring hope and fear, a certain Epicharis provoked and blamed the conspirators; it is uncertain (*incertum*) how she became actively informed, nor had she a care for any decent matter before.[32]

Twice already in the *Annales,* Tacitus used *incertum* to introduce alternate explanations at the end of a sentence. In Book 1, Tacitus reported that Augustus advised against extending the borders of the empire; it was uncertain whether he did so out of fear or jealousy (*incertum metu an per invidiam,* 1.11.4). In Book 14, Burrus died, whether from illness or poison was a question (*incertum valetudine an veneno,* 14.51.1). When Tacitus gives two reasons for a statement, the second is usually meant to be considered more seriously than the first. Indeed, when presented with an excess of inconsistent information, readers tend to trust the last. Loaded alternatives are but one venue for innuendo and insinuation in the *Annales.*[33] But in the case of Epicharis, *incertum* does not introduce alternatives. Tacitus offers no explanation. *Incertum* does not lead the reader to a particular interpretation. Instead, it is an expression of ignorance about the impetus for her involvement.

In addition to admitting his ignorance of the facts, Tacitus also casts doubt upon his sources for the conspiracy. He relates the conspirators' plan and includes a peculiar detail: while Lateranus and the others attacked and killed Nero, Piso was to wait in the sanctuary of Ceres until summoned by Faenius, commander of the guard. Piso would be accompanied by Antonia, daughter of Claudius,

> as Pliny recounts. It was not my intention to withhold that which has been handed down to us in any way (*quoquo modo*), although it seems strange, either that Antonia would lend her name and risk to a worthless cause, or that Piso, known to love his wife, would obligate himself to the marriage of another, unless the desire to rule is more inflammatory than all emotions.[34]

The adverbial phrase *quoquo modo* flags the difficulty of narrating conspiracy and casts a degree of suspicion on the story. The one-upmanship allows Tacitus to present himself as a more reliable, more critical historian than Pliny. Tacitus closed his account of the death of Germanicus and the trial of Piso using the same phrase. By repeating *quoquo modo* in the Neronian conspiracy, Tacitus reminds us of the earlier context and the difficulties of narrating secrets.

Tacitus admits that his source, Pliny, is far-fetched, but with little else except his own common sense to verify the story, he must report what he has at his disposal. In fact, he exposes Pliny's account rather than hide it (*non occultare*) and so unmasks its absurdity.[35] But while he unmasks Pliny, he disguises his own ignorance of the facts. He displaces the responsibility for the veracity of the story onto Pliny and thereby occludes his own uncertainty of Piso's relationship (if any) to Antonia. Tacitus exonerates himself. The appeal to common sense, as expressed in the phrase *quamvis absurdum videretur* ("although it seems strange"), hides one inadequacy but reveals another. Brushing aside the problem, Tacitus avoids the difficulty and assumes an air of superiority meant to suffice in place of direct evidence contrary to Pliny's information. Thus, by demanding that the reader accept his version according to his common sense, he actually perpetuates that which he seeks to destroy, namely, unquestioned assumptions.[36] The *quamvis absurdum videretur* clause merely gives the impression of advancing historical understanding beyond Pliny's explanation.

Finally, at the end of Book 15, Tacitus admits one last time that the events of the Pisonian conspiracy may seem dubious to the reader. Popular rumor accused Nero of indiscriminately murdering citizens out of jealousy or fear and not because of any organized attempt to overthrow him (15.73.1). It makes the historian's task quite difficult if facts are shrouded in uncertainty or are obscured by hostility toward Nero. Therefore, he adds the statement:

> But they for whom it mattered to ascertain the truth did not doubt in those days that a conspiracy was begun, matured, and checked, and they who returned to the city after the death of Nero confirm it.[37]

After twenty-six chapters on the subject, Tacitus still feels the need to assert that the conspiracy actually happened. Ironically, his best evidence is a group of exiles—rather biased individuals who could assert the truth only after the death of Nero ensured their personal safety. If the very occurrence of the Pisonian conspiracy can be questioned, then representing it is no less confounded.

By admitting his ignorance or by calling his sources into question, Tacitus renders the factual underpinnings of the account of the Pisonian conspiracy suspect. Yet, he continues the story in spite of the suspicion that taints his attempts. The intractable is not left unnarrated.

## TORTURED SILENCE

Tacitus has no explanation for the involvement of a woman like Epicharis, which, to him, makes her noble actions even more surprising.[38] Tacitus states that she had no care for any decent matter before (*neque illi ante ulla rerum honestarum cura fuerat*, 15.51.1). Indifference to honorable undertakings seems to be an attribute of the sexually promiscuous woman, for Tacitus described the notorious Messalina in similar terms. Having grown bored with the usual adulteries, she craved to marry Silius, who hoped to replace Claudius as emperor. The calculating imperial freedman Narcissus did not tell Claudius himself but enlisted two of the emperor's regular prostitutes to reveal the attempted coup d'état. Calpurnia told Claudius that Messalina married Silius; Cleopatra corroborated the story. Their fortuitous names allow Tacitus to hint at the eponymous wife and mistress of Julius Caesar and the conspiracy that was no doubt deeply embedded in collective memory.[39] These two prostitutes fit the pattern, that women (often lower class), privy to information otherwise inaccessible, channel secrets to those in power, thereby bringing down conspiracies and preserving the status quo.

Once Claudius was informed, several equestrians confessed, and Narcissus saw to their swift punishment. The death of Messalina was inevitable. As she waited in the Gardens of Lucullus, her mother Lepida tried to convince her that suicide was the only decent way out. But Messalina was too overcome by her passions, and nothing noble remained, *nihil honestum inerat* (11.37.4). Thus, Tacitus casts the noble heroine of the Pisonian conspiracy in terms that call to mind an empress both villainous and scandalous. By casting Epicharis and Messalina in similar terms, he emphasizes the extent to which each woman thwarted expectations of her status. A woman of Messalina's standing was supposed to care about *res honestae*, but she did not. On the other hand, very little was expected of a woman like Epicharis, who in the end turned out to die more nobly than the empress.

Intent on conspiracy, Epicharis tried to determine in a private meeting whether Proculus was likely to join:

> Volusius Proculus was captain of that fleet. . . . Having known the woman for some time, or else because of a recently developing affair (*amicitia*), he divulged his services to Nero, and how they had lapsed to no effect, and added complaints and his determination for vengeance, if the opportunity arose. He thus inspired the hope that he could be persuaded and could secure many others.[40]

Tacitus alludes to the amorous nature of the relationship (*amicitia*); by now the scenario is familiar. The secrets of conspiracy were traded between lovers in a private venue.

Epicharis was so capable of winning the trust of Proculus that he felt comfortable complaining to her about Nero. His attitude convinced her that he was a potential conspirator. Once she ascertained Proculus' hostility toward Nero, their conversation turned to the incipient conspiracy:

Epicharis accordingly said more and listed all the emperor's crimes, saying that the senate had no power left. Yet, means had been provided, whereby Nero might pay the penalty for having ruined the state. Only let Proculus gird himself to do his part and bring over to their side his bravest soldiers, and then look for an adequate recompense.[41]

Tacitus goes so far as to report the substance of Epicharis' conversation with Proculus, even though the exchange took place behind closed doors, with no witnesses. The substance of their communication, the senate's loss of freedom and its enslavement to the emperor, is a familiar theme of the *Annales*. By enhancing the conversation between the lovers and relying on its probability, Tacitus ventriloquizes Epicharis, who speaks of a criminal *princeps* and an impotent senate.

Epicharis, however, was circumspect with Proculus; she withheld the names of the conspirators. Her caution paid. In reporting her information to Nero, Proculus made the substance of the private conversation public. His disloyalty to Epicharis brought her secrets to light and allowed their meeting to be narrated. But her silence was a potent force, protecting the conspiracy and discrediting the traitor. Without names, Proculus was powerless, and Nero's hands were tied. Epicharis was summoned and confronted, but she easily silenced Proculus, unsupported as he was by a single witness. Her silence bought the conspirators time, but it could not prevail against another woman's speech.

Although tortured for her information Epicharis remained silent. She is contrasted with the cowardly senator Scaevinus and equestrian Natalis, both of whom paled at the mere threat of torture. In his speech on the punishment of the Catilinarians, Caesar appealed to the notion of the inviolability of the citizen body, the bedrock of citizenship. Likewise, the Bacchanalian conspiracy betrayed an anxiety over the transgression of the boundary between citizen and slave. But the tyrant tortures at will, regardless of status.[42] The senator Scaevinus and the equestrian Natalis remained untouched, as they should, but not because they were respected as citizens. Rather than submit to torture, they simply denounced the conspiracy.

Tacitus sets the image of Epicharis' ordeal before our eyes in excruciating detail. Whips and firebrands did not move her, and on the second day of interrogation she sat in a chair because her limbs were too dislocated to support her standing; nevertheless, she remained silent. Rather than prolong her torment, she committed suicide by fashioning a noose from her undergarment. The scene elicits a feeling of heightened sympathy because the wounds of her broken body nearly prevent her from accomplishing the deed (15.57).[43]

Tacitus' grim account of the torture of Epicharis has antecedents in Seneca's *Controversiae* 2.5: "A wife, tortured by a tyrant to find out if she knew anything about her husband's plot to kill him, persisted in saying she did not. Later her husband killed the tyrant. He divorced her on the grounds of her barrenness when she bore no child within five years of marriage. She sues him for ingratitude." The collection of arguments proceeds for and against the wife's suit, but of special interest are the explicit descriptions of the torture she suffered:

> The apparatus of cruelty is deployed against a miserable woman; the instruments that break the spirit even of men by their very look are set forth to extract the secrets in a woman's breast. The tyrant attacks with intimidation before torture, racks her with threats: she is silent. She sees the tyrant's set face, his threatening eyes: she is silent. . . . Her limbs are cut by whips, her body broken by lashings, the blood forced out of her very vitals: she is silent.[44]

> Now I come to describe the torments, the extraordinary physical endurance she showed amid the raging of the tortures the tyrant applied. Fires that her blood had put out kept being rekindled; her tortures were halted occasionally, just so that they could be reapplied the more often. They used whips, plates, the rack, whatever ancient cruelty had invented, and whatever modern cruelty had invented in addition. . . . She kept silent.[45]

Such dismembered bodies litter the pages of Lucan and the tragedies of Seneca the Younger, evidence of a distinctly "Silver Latin" penchant for excessive carnage.[46] These passages bear witness to the institutionalization of the violence of torture. Seneca's rhetorical handbook provides stock—acceptable—ways of describing the physical mutilation of the human body.[47] I suspect that Tacitus' depiction of Epicharis had its origins in such literature.

Beyond creative imitation and erudite engagement with the tastes of his age, Tacitus uses this opportunity to moralize. He compares Epicharis' willingness to die on behalf of strangers to the indifference of freedmen, equestrians, and senators toward their own cause:

> With a more outstanding example (*clariore exemplo*), a woman—a freedwoman (*libertina mulier*), died by defending others and those practically unknown to her under such terrible compulsion, when free men and noble men, both Roman senators and equestrians (*ingenui et viri equites Romani senatoresque*), untouched by torture each betrayed the dearest of his relatives.[48]

This female *clarius exemplum* has a precedent in Tacitus' *Histories* 2.13.[49] As the army of Otho marched through Italy, they came to the province of the Maritime Alps, where an indecisive conflict exasperated the soldiers. Unable to secure plunder, they vented their greed on the innocent people of Albintimilius. There, a Ligurian woman aggravated the horror by her outstanding example (*praeclaro exemplo*). She had hidden her son in safety. But the soldiers believed she was hiding money too, and so they tortured her (*per cruciatus interrogarent*). She did not betray her son. In spite of the terrors and even the threat of death, she maintained her silence. As the example of the Ligurian woman shows how depraved the soldiers of Otho were, so the example of Epicharis damns the Pisonian conspirators. When citizens turn on fellow citizens, whether in civil war or conspiracy, humble women provide the moral compass. Exceptional times require exceptional means.

Carefully constructed pleonasms, playing off each other with apposition (*libertina mulier*) and polysyndeton (*ingenui et viri et equites Romani senatoresque*) heavily weigh Tacitus' moralizing statement against the Pisonian conspirators. They are shamed, and by a woman: is this not the worst humiliation, to be bested by a woman, and one of such low social standing at that? Often Epicharis is adduced as evidence that although Tacitus has a very low opinion of the masses, still he is capable of giving credit where it is due.[50] Yet perhaps he is not motivated so much by admiration of the lowly woman as by a willingness to exploit her to promote his own interest from a safe vantage point.[51] In her silence, she delivers his moral lesson, so he can comfortably condemn his fellow members of the senatorial order. Then, conveniently, she dies.

Her lesson was not lost on Nero, who comprehended the possible dangers of lovers' prattle in the aftermath of the conspiracy. Tigellinus, out of jealousy (so Tacitus says), plotted the destruction of Petronius by implicating him in the conspiracy and by bribing a slave to betray him (16.18). Petronius saw the writing on the wall and, taking matters into his own hands, staged his memorable death. He opened and closed his veins at will, reciting light poetry and playful verses. Mocking Stoic suicides modeled on the death of Socrates, Petronius conversed with friends on topics most unsocratic. Rather than flatter the emperor and his minions, Petronius' will described in detail Nero's shameful behavior, including the names of his partners, young boys and women, as well as their innovative sexual practices (16.19). Nero was in doubt as to how his escapades had become common knowledge, until he remembered that one of his women, the infamous senatorial Silia, was also intimate with Petronius. Once again, a woman channels information from the private to the public sphere because of her intimate relations with those in power. Silia was banished for not keeping quiet about what she had seen and done (16.20).

Epicharis may be contrasted with the women who informed on the Catilinarian and Bacchanalian conspiracies. Fulvia heard about the Catilinarian conspiracy from her paramour and betrayed the conspirators. Although she withheld the name of her source, her information convinced everyone to entrust matters to Cicero. Livy's Hispala was the lover of Aebutius, to whom she told the secrets of the Bacchanalia. This information reached the consul, who called upon her to testify and then dismantled the cult. Thanks to Fulvia and Hispala, the republic was saved from the internal threats of the Catilinarian and Bacchanalian conspiracies. By their intimate contact with men, they served as conduits for the secret information that was transferred to the appropriate authorities.

Fulvia, Hispala, and Epicharis were all privy to the secrets of the conspiracies, but the similarities dwindle rapidly. Curius held a sword to Fulvia; Hispala feared for her life, threatened by both the conspirators and the consul. But Epicharis alone was actually tortured in an attempt to extract the information perceived as residing in her body. Fulvia received information from her lover Curius; Epicharis transmitted information to her lover Proculus. Fulvia betrayed the Catilinarians; Epicharis protected the Pisonians. Fulvia and Hispala spoke out to save the state; Epicharis kept quiet to save the conspiracy. The cowardly Hispala surrendered to the pressure of the consul for the good of the republic; the brave Epicharis remained steadfast to the end for the good of the conspiracy. Epicharis subverted the republican model of the conspiratorial bedfellow. She was no informant. The downfall of the Pisonian conspiracy rested instead upon the hollow greediness of Milichus, the former slave.

### GIVING IT UP

Plutarch recounts the downfall of the Pisonians in his essay *De Garrulitate* (*Mor.* 505c–d). The details of his abbreviated version differ from Tacitus in every way. Yet Plutarch preserves the tension between silence and speech, secrecy and revelation, that lies at the core of conspiracy. On the night before the assassination, the man who was to kill Nero (Plutarch does not name him) encountered a prisoner who was about to be led before Nero. The unnamed assassin approached the prisoner and whispered, "Pray that today passes by, and tomorrow you will be thankful to me." The prisoner inferred the assassin's intentions and told Nero what he had heard. We are not told whether the prisoner was rewarded for betraying the conspiracy, but his calculated risk must have paid off. Uncertain as to whether the conspiracy would actually succeed, the prisoner chose instead to betray the conspiracy to save his life. Immediately the assassin was arrested and tortured. According to Plutarch, "he denied in the face of constraint what he had revealed without constraint." The assassin's eager speech to the prisoner was more potent than his tortured silence before the emperor. Likewise in the *Annales,* Epicharis' brave endurance was useless against the powers of speech.

With Epicharis in custody and Nero's suspicions aroused, the conspirators were forced to action. Tacitus elaborates in great detail a plan that was never realized. He specifies that Nero was to be attacked at the games held in honor of Ceres; Lateranus was to overwhelm the emperor; Scaevinus was to claim the first blow; Piso was to wait in the sanctuary of Ceres (15.53). Such details Tacitus gleaned from his sources.[52] But how did they come to light? "It was amazing," says Tacitus, "how everything remained cloaked in silence among people of different class, rank, age, and sex, among rich and poor, until betrayal emerged from the house of Scaevinus" (15.54.1).

The day before the assassination attempt, Scaevinus met with Natalis in long conversation. Returning home, he sealed his will. He turned his attention to a knife he kept, according to Tacitus, as though dedicated to some noble deed. He decided it needed to be sharpened and polished; he assigned this task to his freedman Milichus. After a sumptuous meal, he manumitted his favorite slaves. In a fit of depression he ordered Milichus to prepare bandages for wounds. Scaevinus is portrayed as a beneficent master and Milichus as a loyal servant: "Either he [Milichus] knew of the conspiracy and was faithful up to this point, or he was in complete ignorance and then first caught suspicions, as most sources have inferred from what followed" (*ut plerique tradidere de consequentibus,* 15.54.3). As a former slave, Milichus had access to the private words and deeds of Scaevinus. Because he was manumitted, he owed his former master his loyalty. Yet manumission destroyed the direct motivation and domination of Milichus' actions because the master could no longer hold out the promise of freedom in exchange for obedience. Milichus had no reason to protect his former master and was free to decide for himself how to act on his information. Driven by thoughts of his own preservation and even possible reward, he chose to betray the conspiracy. Tacitus' language is revealing:

> For when his servile imagination (*servilis animus*) contemplated the rewards
> of betrayal, and he saw before him at the same time boundless wealth and

power, conscience and care for his patron's life (together with the remembrance of the freedom he had received) fled from him.[53]

Servile thoughts alone did not convince Milichus to inform. He did not betray the conspiracy until his wife reminded him of the many witnesses—both slave and freedmen—to Scaevinus' conspiratorial preparations. Milichus' silence not only would be useless, it would be dangerous, she argued, if another should inform on the conspiracy before him. Convinced, Milichus went to Nero, showing him the weapon that had been prepared for his murder.

Scaevinus was arrested and interrogated. He cunningly discredited the evidence as circumstantial: the dagger held religious significance for his ancestors, and the freedman had simply stolen it from his bedchamber. It was his custom on occasion to sign his will, free his slaves, and dine sumptuously. He denied the order for the preparation of bandages. Scaevinus' self-confidence was convincing, and he was about to walk out, when "Milichus was reminded by his wife (*nisi Milichum uxor admonuisset*) that Antonius Natalis had had a long secret conversation with Scaevinus, and that both were Piso's intimate friends" (15.55.4). Until now it had appeared that Milichus went to Nero on his own; the subjects and verbs are singular (*pergit, dictitans deductusque, urgens, audiverat, coniectaverat, docet, ostendit,* 15.55.1), implying he acted alone. But, in the nick of time, his wife appeared. Her crucial piece of information brought down the entire conspiracy. Because of the exchange between husband and wife, the information needed to unravel the conspiracy finally reached the emperor. Scaevinus and Natalis gave in under the threat of torture and revealed the other conspirators.

The collapse of the soldiery gives final witness to the power of speech and silence for the conspiracy. Faenius Rufus, commander of the guard, maintained a posture of innocence and was given charge over punishing Scaevinus. When Scaevinus mocked him as an accomplice, Faenius was dumbstruck, defenseless against the charge: *non vox adversum ea Faenio, non silentium* (15.66.2). The fallen conspiracy confounded the power of both speech and silence, but it was a familiar condition of the principate: *crimen ex silentio, ex voce* (4.60.2).[54]

For the tribune Subrius Flavus, there was nothing left to lose. He was incriminated in the conspiracy, and his first impulse was to defend himself on the basis of his moral rectitude. An honorable soldier would not consort with unarmed, effeminate associates. When his case appeared futile, he "embraced the glory of confession" (*confessionis gloriam amplexus,* 15.67.1). He spoke out and openly admitted his hatred to Nero's face: "I hated you, nor was any soldier more faithful to you, while you deserved to be loved. I began to hate you after you killed your mother and your wife, and you paraded yourself as a charioteer, an actor, and an arsonist" (15.67.2). Tacitus presents the quote in *oratio recta*, verifying it as the soldier's *ipsa verba*.[55] Regardless of the veracity of the words, their verisimilitude allows the message to be heard loud and clear.

The outspokenness of Subrius Flavus is an excellent example of what I call a "distant voice of freedom."[56] His words exemplify the technique used throughout the *Annales*: that bold opposition is often expressed by those who are scarcely able to cause any real distress to the *princeps*. The undertone of resistance in the *Annales* is a result of the candid characters who nevertheless pose no threat, for example, the eloquent, yet doomed historian Cremutius Cordus. To maintain a safe distance from what is easily construed as a criticism of his own situation, Tacitus nullifies the last words of Cremutius before they are ever spoken: "certain that his life must end" (*relinquendae vitae certus*, 4.34.2). He reverses the natural order of the events. Normally in a trial, the defendant speaks before the verdict is handed down. But Cremutius is convicted before he even speaks, and he sentences himself to death. Thus, Tacitus deploys a brilliant example of *hysteron proteron* (the reversal of natural or rational order) to emphasize the death, and so the futility, of Cremutius. In this way, he can compose for the noble—yet already dead—Cremutius the most remarkable defense of freedom in the entire corpus. Tacitus puts words of ardent opposition in the mouth of a senator condemned to death. Similarly, the force of Subrius Flavus' strident animosity is attenuated by his dire circumstances. With no hope of survival, he might as well be as candid as possible.[57]

Some could doubt whether there was a Pisonian conspiracy or whether Nero perpetrated an elaborate counterconspiracy whereby he eliminated his personal and political rivals and foes.[58] The Catilinarian conspiracy also has its skeptics; Waters ambitiously asserts that "the whole affair was largely invented by Cicero," to rid Rome of his enemy Catiline.[59] One scholar asserts that the Bacchanalian affair was no conspiracy at all but merely a bid for power by the Roman senate.[60] Livy, however, presents the actions of the consul Postumius as a sort of counterconspiracy intent on the destruction of the foreign, servile Bacchic worshippers.

Debates about the existence of conspiracies and counterconspiracies arise because the events themselves are secret and because the sources are necessarily muddled, unclear, and incomplete. It is difficult to prove the unrealized intentions of conspirators. The Catilinarians, Bacchanalians, and Pisonians failed and were punished at the hands of the consuls or the emperor; therefore, we will never know what they might have achieved. The assassinations of Caligula and Julius Caesar, on the other hand, prove that the charge of conspiracy cannot be confirmed until it is too late.[61]

## TYPOLOGY OF CONSPIRACY NARRATIVE

Before turning to the assassinations of Caligula and Julius Caesar, it will be useful to collate our findings from these three conspiracies. The detailed analyses of the narratives in the preceding chapters allow us to identify several elements common to the narratives of Sallust, Livy, and Tacitus. First of all, they share formal features. The topic of conspiracy is announced with the word *coniuratio*.[62] The conspirators are listed by name.[63] The end of each narrative is signaled by the intervention of the senate, suggesting that the threat of conspiracy has been successfully crushed.[64]

In addition to these formalities, the narratives also resemble each other in content. In each narrative, crucial information about the conspiracy is shared between women and men in private, amorous settings. Fulvia receives information from her lover Curius (Sal. *Cat.* 23.3); Hispala gives information to her lover Aebutius (Liv. 39.9.6, 39.13.2); Epicharis gives information to her lover Volusius Proculus (Tac. *Ann.* 15.51.2). In each narrative, women are exposed to the threat of physical violence. Curius draws a sword on Fulvia and treats her more roughly than usual (Sal. *Cat.* 23.3); Postumius becomes enraged with Hispala who begs mercy because she fears the retribution of the Bacchantes (Liv. 39.13.63, 39.13.5); Epicharis is tortured (Tac. *Ann.* 15.57). The authors object to the participation of all types of people in the conspiracy, thus expressing a concern over the violation of the social boundaries of gender, age, and status.[65] Each conspiracy is betrayed and so revealed; the revelation of the secrets allows the conspiracy to be narrated.[66] Each narrative details the punishment of the conspirators. Caesar and Cato debate the capital punishment of the five Catilinarians held in custody (Sal. *Cat.* 51–53.1). The consuls condemned to capital punishment the Bacchantes guilty of *stuprum,* murder, false testimony, counterfeited seals, substitution of wills, and other acts of fraud (Liv. 39.18.4). Tacitus remarks that the city was filled with funerals, and then he lists those who were banished (Tac. *Ann.* 15.71.1). Informants are recognized and rewarded.[67]

I submit that among these shared traits is a typology of conspiracy narrative. The continuous narrative of a secret event depends upon the transmittal of information from a private setting to the public sphere. Women are ideal conduits for this information, and their pillow talk is an ideal medium for the transfer of sensitive information. Because of their proximity to the conspirators, they are vulnerable to physical harm.

Furthermore, we can reach general conclusions about the strategy of containment by examining the ways the historians confront the limits of knowledge about conspiracy. Each author suggests at least once that he is unable to give a straightforward account of the conspiracy and that the details are uncertain.[68] When knowledge about a conspiracy is weak, when the narrative approaches an epistemological gap, then the Roman historian signals the difficulty in order to achieve continuity of the narrative. Such a self-proclaimed loss for words can lend a degree of innocence to the narrative. It can also serve to inoculate the statements that follow. By admitting the accidental gap in knowledge beyond his control, the historian acknowledges a principal gap and actually asserts his control over the uncertainty. He immunizes the less-than-trustworthy contents of the ensuing narrative from a debilitating loss of credibility by means of a small injection of openly acknowledged ignorance.[69] Each author transmits information from unnamed sources about the conspiracy, in a sentence whose subject is unnamed.[70] When a historian introduces a statement in this way, he can both exculpate himself and mitigate the effect of what follows. Such inoculation is central to the strategy of containment.

Yet we must not discount the possibility that such self-proclaimed statements of uncertainty serve another concurrent function in the narrative. An admission that "I am not sure," while it signals a lack of knowledge, may be the only thing the historian can say with any certainty, and in this sense, such a statement may be the only "fact" in the narrative. Such statements thus raise the reader's awareness to the possibility that information not marked with such first-person qualifiers may be suspect. Such admissions establish the reader's confidence that he is in the hands of a sensible narrator, one who is prepared to admit the limits of his knowledge. The historian is most trustworthy at precisely those moments when he openly admits his inability: the one thing we know for certain is that *the historian does not know what happened.* While such statements may appear at any point in a historical narrative, they are more heavily freighted in conspiracy narratives, where the facts are deliberately kept secret and hidden and the stakes of containment are higher.

The historian, however, does not always openly acknowledge his uncertainty. The less-transparent moments of dubiety are signaled with more subtlety and in a variety of ways. For instance, an element of doubt can be introduced into the narrative by adverbial phrases or clauses or by reference to unnamed, anonymous sources. Adverbs like "perhaps," and phrases like "in whatever way," cast doubt over a statement while at the same time they permit the narrative to advance, in spite of the uncertainty of the facts they proclaim. Moreover, the historian can exonerate himself by saying, "There are those who say," or "Tradition has it that." Sometimes the historian discredits a source but fails to offer an alternate explanation. In his study of authority and tradition in ancient historiography, Marincola surveys rhetorical devices of this sort from the immense body of extant Greek and Latin historical writings. He shows how the historian will manipulate these traditional ways of establishing authority, thereby redefining the borders of the genre while simultaneously working within them. It is a thoroughgoing study of the dialectic of tradition and originality at work in the genre of history writing.[71]

My concern is the historian's patent *in*ability to claim authority over what he is narrating and the ways in which Roman historians produce narratives of historical events that, at their core, resist telling. Conspiracy requires silence. Often authors must negotiate silence because of ideological restrictions on what can be said safely.[72] But silence hinders a conspiracy narrative not only because of strictures imposed by a dominant ideology but also because of the limits imposed by the knowability of events. The symptomatic points in the text reveal a dialectic between the uncertainty of the event and the historian's attempt to gain control over the uncertainty in order to narrate it. Such instances of uncertainty and indeterminacy provide opportunity to see how the author negotiates the difficulty, how he exerts rhetorical control over the text at the moment it becomes epistemologically intractable.

It is no coincidence that the chronologies of the Catilinarian, Bacchanalian, and Pisonian conspiracies are difficult to establish. The year 63 B.C.E. becomes synonymous with the Catilinarian conspiracy, but there is evidence that trouble began the year before. The cult of Bacchus was surely well established in Rome before the year it was suppressed by the *senatus consultum,* but Livy's annalistic history pinpoints the conspiracy to the year 186 B.C.E. Likewise, Tacitus telescopes the Pisonian conspiracy under the rubric of the year 65 C.E. The formal structure of annalistic history demands that the historians place the beginnings of these conspiracies under a particular year. Thus, the dates 63 B.C.E., 186 B.C.E., and 65 C.E. are somewhat artificial. But the overall effect is to lend the narratives a greater degree of authority. The annalistic format harnesses the potential for temporal uncertainty to arouse fear.

Such rhetorical control translates to social control; the silence and secrecy of conspiracies, both incipient and patent, is appropriated and disarmed. By openly admitting his uncertainty, by pointing directly to the moments of *aporia* (literally, difficulty), the historian reclaims the force of silence for his own purpose. Failure to observe this phenomenon is to miss out on one of the most powerful lessons that history teaches: that between the occurrence of an event and the production of its representation lies the opportunity for the historian to interpret, to judge, to shape his reader's opinion, and to express his own.[73]

The emphasis on reward and punishment also works to alleviate fear of further uprising. A conspiracy narrative is careful to confirm the complete suppression of the internal threat and to guarantee a return to normalcy. In this sense, a conspiracy narrative serves to contain fear and deter future unrest. Narrative is the revelation of events in a particular mode for the purpose of storing knowledge and maintaining identity. What is so striking about conspiracy narratives, then, is their ability to contain and deter, in spite of the mode in which they are cast. For conspiracy narratives are cast in a mode of indeterminacy. Sallust's Fulvia gathers information *quoque modo* (23.4). Livy recounts how the Bacchanalian conspiracy was disclosed *hoc maxime modo* (39.9.1). Tacitus tempers his narrative with the phrase *quoquo modo* (15.53.3). "In whatever way": this register of uncertainty signals the difficulty posed by events shrouded in secrecy and silence. In whatever way necessary, in spite of the uncertainty that shrouds the events, the narrative attempts, with varying degrees of success, to contain fear and deter unrest.

From these three narratives it is possible to draw conclusions about the meaning of conspiracy in its social context. Each conspiracy failed in its immediate goals, but in the larger picture, each conspiracy heralds the brink of radical social and political change. The Catilinarian conspiracy is only one episode in the gradual erosion of the institutions of the late republic. Although Catiline effected no lasting change, the events of the year 63 were to have serious repercussions for the republic. Cicero would be exiled for his illegal execution of the conspirators; Pompey would return to a Rome weakened by the internal threat; Caesar would cross the Rubicon in a march on Rome anticipated by Catiline and Manlius. The suppression of the Bacchanalian cult and the capital punishment of more than seven thousand persons occurred at a cusp in the history of Rome. According to Livy, this period marks the beginning of foreign luxury introduced into the city by the veteran soldiers returning from Asia. Rome was on the brink of moral disaster. The Pisonian conspiracy stands at the end of the Julio-Claudian principate, when all claims to power were ultimately challenged—three times—throughout the long year 69. Conspiracy ferments in the vats of great social and political upheaval, as a taste of great social and political change to come.

We are now prepared to see how these elements, both rhetorical and social, are received and transformed in Josephus' and Appian's Hellenistic narratives of the successful conspiracies to assassinate Caligula and Julius Caesar.

# PART TWO

# SUCCESSFUL CONSPIRACIES

# FOUR

# JOSEPHUS

## *The Assassination of Caligula*

$S$allust, Livy, and Tacitus could narrate the Catilinarian, Bacchanalian, and Pisonian conspiracies in spite of the veil of secrecy and silence that shrouded the events. In each case, women (and in one case, foreigners) betrayed the conspiracy and saved Rome from the internal threats posed by Catiline and his forces, by the foreign worshipers of Bacchus, and by those backing Piso. But what happens when no one betrays a conspiracy? The conspirators are free to carry out their plans and bring their secret plot into full view. To appreciate the difficulty that Sallust, Livy, and Tacitus faced when writing about conspiracies, it is now time to examine a narrative of a successful conspiracy. We turn to the account of the assassination of the emperor Gaius Caligula in the *Jewish Antiquities* by the Flavian historian Josephus.

A Jewish priest of royal descent born in 37 C.E. (the year Tiberius Caesar died and Gaius Caligula became emperor), Josephus was a leader in the Jewish revolt of 66–73 against Rome. He commanded forces in Galilee against Vespasian and survived the forty-seven-day siege of Jotapata in Northwestern Galilee and was taken prisoner. Because his prophecy that Vespasian would become emperor was fulfilled, Josephus was released and granted freedom. He followed Vespasian to Rome where he was given a villa and a generous pension.

Under these circumstances, he produced an immense literary corpus. The *Jewish War* was originally composed in Aramaic but translated into Greek to reach a broader audience (*B.J.* 1.3).[1] After the successful publication of the *Jewish War,* Josephus undertook the ambitious task of writing a history of the Jews. The voluminous *Jewish Antiquities* was written in Greek under Domitian and published in 93 (*A.J.* 20.267). It begins with the story of his people from the creation to the administration of the last procurators before the war with Rome. It falls into two halves, the first of which records Jewish history until the time of the first destruction of Jerusalem, concluding with the prophecy of Daniel. These first ten books paraphrase and embellish Scripture. The second half of the work includes the post-exilic and Hellenistic periods, the rise and fall of the Herodian kingdom, and three final books on Roman imperial history that bear loosely on Jewish affairs. More than half of Book 19 is taken up with the assassination of Caligula and the accession of Claudius, an event that occurred fifty-two years before.[2]

This chapter begins with the conspiracies against Caligula that remain shrouded in mystery. Then, my analysis of the narrative of the assassination takes its cue from Josephus himself, who promises "an exact account" of the events. He states his purpose for including the episode in his history at the outset: the death of Caligula illustrates the power of God to overcome all evil foes. Josephus uses the story to reassure his readership that morality cannot be overrun by tyranny, and in that sense, he contains fear of the Romans by affirming the power of faith. The third part of the chapter considers the roles of slaves, foreigners, and especially women in the assassination narrative. Once again we see that the exceptional behavior of a woman underscores the exceptional nature of the conspiracy.

## ABORTED ATTEMPTS

Any attempt to discuss the reign of Caligula is hampered by the problem of the biased sources. Two major contemporary sources survive: Seneca the Younger refers to Caligula often but provides little by way of political analysis; Philo of Alexandria makes no effort to conceal his hostility toward Caligula. Suetonius and Dio provide the most continuous narratives, but both embellish and exaggerate. Yet, even the most cautious assessment yields an unfavorable impression of the emperor.

Caligula's brief reign of three years, ten months, and eight days was riddled with intrigue from the outset, and not without good reason, according to Suetonius. His reckless behavior alienated both the senate and the imperial *domus*. He committed incest (*Cal.* 25.1). He flogged a quaestor suspected of conspiracy (26.3). On occasion, he would close the granaries, thereby starving the urban populace (26.5). He burned a poet alive for writing verses with a hidden meaning (27.4). He called for the disembowelment of a senator (28). He ordered especially painful executions, saying, "Strike so that he may feel he is dying" (30.1). He respected the chastity of none and engaged in novel sexual practices with men and women of all social ranks (36.1). He squandered the entire sum of money that Tiberius had amassed, and then to replace it, he auctioned off the treasures of Rome and levied burdensome taxes (37–40). It was said that Caligula planned to make his horse Incitatus a consul (55.3). In short, Suetonius finds Caligula mentally weak (51) and finally mad (55). It is no surprise that the emperor became the target of several conspiracies.

The sources hint at two conspiracies before the third, and successful, attempt on the emperor's life.[3] The conspiracy of Lepidus and Gaeticulus in 39, like the so-called first Catilinarian conspiracy, is a perfect example of the great difficulty of uncovering the facts about an event intended to be kept secret. The evidence is so sketchy that modern historians have debated whether there was a conspiracy at all. Ferrill affirms "a genuine conspiracy," while Simpson, on the other hand, argues that "there is no support in our ancient sources." Barrett, taking the middle ground, prudently observes that the conspiracy was "shrouded in obscurity, and, given the nature of a conspiracy, this is not surprising." Faur argues that there was indeed a conspiracy, but the sources downplay it to emphasize the final, successful assassination.[4]

Suetonius is the only source to refer specifically to a *Lepidi et Gaeticuli coniuratio* (*Cl.* 9.1), linking both names together in one plot. An entry in the *Acta Fratrum Arvalium* (the records of the priestly college of the Arval Brothers in Rome) dated 27 October 39 records the suppression of a "wicked conspiracy of Cn. Lentulus Gaeticulus" against Caligula.[5] And in 39, the senator and future emperor Vespasian recommended that as an additional punishment the conspirators be cast out unburied, but Suetonius does not specify the names of these conspirators (*Vesp.* 2.4). Dio relates that Caligula had Lentulus Gaeticulus, governor of Germany for ten years, put to death because he was too popular with his soldiers. In the very next sentence, Dio names Aemilius Lepidus as another of Caligula's victims.[6] Yet Dio does not connect them together in a common cause.

Tacitus provides an interesting story about Gaeticulus that lets us apprehend something of his character. After the fall of Sejanus (the praetorian prefect under Tiberius), Gaeticulus was accused of having attempted to forge an alliance with him.[7] Gaeticulus responded to the charge by sending Tiberius a letter, the substance of which Tacitus reproduces: "His alliance with Sejanus had not originated in his own choice but in the advice of Tiberius; he could be deceived as easily as Tiberius, so that the same mistake ought not be considered innocent in the *princeps* but a source of ruin to others. His loyalty was still untainted and would so remain" (*Ann.* 6.30.3). Tacitus appends a note that Gaeticulus, of all those connected with Sejanus, was the only man to survive and to retain imperial favor (*Ann.* 6.30.4). Suetonius tells of Gaeticulus' memoirs in which he flattered Caligula outright (*Cal.* 8.2). He also gained the favor of his soldiers. Clearly Gaeticulus knew how to steer a middle course in the treacherous political waters of the Julio-Claudian principate. Exactly why he was executed is not readily apparent.

Marcus Aemilius Lepidus is even more intriguing. According to Dio, he enjoyed special status as Caligula's lover and as husband of Drusilla, Caligula's favorite sister. Lepidus was publicly marked by Caligula to succeed him. A statue group of the imperial family from the Carian city of Aphrodisias includes a base reserved for the figure of Marcus Lepidus.[8] He belonged to a resplendent family. In the estimation of Syme, the father of Marcus Aemilius Lepidus, by the same name, was the most distinguished senator in the reign of Tiberius. He was consul in the year 6 C.E., and it is said that Augustus considered him a potential successor—*capax imperii* (Tac. *Ann.* 1.13.2).[9] It seems apparent that Marcus Lepidus was able to survive safely in the dangerous milieu of the Tiberian age.

In the year 24, the woman Sosia was banished for a trumped-up charge of treason; half of her estate was confiscated. Lepidus made a proposal in the senate, neither bold nor servile. He simply suggested that the prosecutors confiscate her property in accordance with the law, which was incidentally, only one quarter of her estate (*Ann.* 4.20). This seemingly simple act, related in just one sentence, evokes fulsome praise from the generally reserved Tacitus: "This Lepidus, I am satisfied, was for that age a wise and highly principled man, for many cruel suggestions made by the flattery of others he bent for the better."[10] Here was a man who exhibited the Roman virtue of *gravitas* and the virtues of a Stoic *sapiens*, a word that escapes Tacitus' pen but twice in the *Annales*.[11] Lepidus' success rested in his ability to bend but not break. This was an ability that he acquired and developed to perfection, setting him apart as an extraordinary example. He learned to walk the fine line between disruptive (and futile) defiance and disgraceful servitude. His son, however, appears not to have inherited his father's political finesse, and he was to be the last of the Aemilii Lepidi.[12] He fell from Caligula's grace and was brought to trial, according to Suetonius. Caligula accused his other two sisters, Agrippina and Livilla, of sleeping with Lepidus and sharing in his secret conspiracies (*Cal.* 24.3).[13]

The conspiracy of 39 is linked with the fantastic tale about a military campaign in Gaul, when Caligula ordered his troops to collect seashells on the beach and then praised them as though they were gathering precious booty (Suet. *Cal.* 46.1; Dio 59.25.3). On this expedition, Caligula discovered a plot against himself. It is not clear whether the emperor undertook the campaign to collect a large army in Gaul, and without suspicion, to suppress the conspiracy, or whether he actually planned an invasion of Britain, during which he learned of the designs against his life. Whether Lepidus and Gaeticulus, in collusion with the imperial sisters, conspired against Caligula, or whether the deluded emperor sought a pretext for their individual destruction, the result was the same. Gaeticulus was executed in Germany; Lepidus was tried and executed somewhere outside Rome. Three daggers were dedicated at the Temple of Mars Ultor. The sisters Agrippina and Livilla were exiled, and their goods were confiscated (Dio 59.22.5–8).[14]

Harsh punishment did not deter the discontented. The following year, Caligula discovered another conspiracy and ordered Betilinius Bassus to death. The man's father, Betilinius Capito, was compelled to witness the execution. When he begged permission to close his eyes, Caligula ordered his death as well. To save his life, Capito then pretended to have been one of the conspirators and promised to disclose the names of the rest. He listed those whose influence over Caligula was most harmful and brought several to destruction. But when he went so far as to name the prefects, the powerful freedman Callistus, and Caligula's own wife Caesonia, he aroused the emperor's distrust and was put to death (Dio 59.25.7). Overall, one gets the impression that Caligula did not hesitate to act on his paranoid suspicions of conspiracies.

Coins and inscriptions attest the emphasis Caligula constantly placed on his descent from Augustus.[15] While Caligula may have promoted such an Augustan image, in practice he was nothing like Augustus. Caligula did not wait for evidence of a conspiracy but executed at will. In contrast, Augustus was not always so quick to act. Sometimes he chose to spare conspirators, preferring to capitalize on the opportunity to display his *clementia*. Perhaps nowhere is the evidence more difficult to ascertain than in such cases of generous pardon granted to would-be conspirators. Conspiracies are difficult enough to narrate when proven and punished. But suspects who were exonerated were open to embellishment by the sources, as Dio attests:

> It is not possible, of course, for those on the outside to have certain knowledge of such matters; for whatever measures a ruler takes, either personally or through the Senate, for the punishment of men for alleged plots against himself, are generally looked upon with suspicion as having been done out of spite, no matter how just such measures may be.[16]

In the *De Clementia*, a treatise on mercy addressed to the young emperor Nero, Seneca portrays an elaborate vignette in which Augustus learned that Cinna conspired against him. The distraught *princeps* consulted his advisors and pondered the dilemma long into the night. The solution came from none other than his wife, Livia. Severity had not deterred men from conspiring against him: Salvidienus, Lepidus, Murena, Caepio, Egnatius. Therefore, she recommended the opposite of punishment: pardon. According to Seneca, it worked; no one ever plotted against him again (Sen. *Clem.* 9). According to Dio, Augustus heeded the suggestions of Livia and released the accused with warnings only. No one dared plot against him after that (Dio 55.14–22). Both Seneca and Dio record this conspiracy to showcase Augustus' capacity for forgiveness and mercy. The amnesty granted to Cinna obfuscates the memory of the other conspirators, all of whom were executed. But because he pardoned the last conspirator, Augustus is remembered for his *clementia*.[17]

Tiberius did not always choose such a course of action. Like Tacitus, Josephus tells of the vast conspiracy led by Sejanus. The praetorian prefect was joined by senators, freedmen, and the army. Indeed, Sejanus would have succeeded if not for the daring of Antonia, Tiberius' sister-in-law. Antonia was raising her young grandson Gaius Caligula in her house, and he had every reason to benefit from the downfall of the powerful Sejanus. She was informed of the plot against Tiberius and sent him a letter at Capri. With this information, Tiberius put Sejanus and his fellow-conspirators to death.[18] Tiberius' punishment was cruel and relentless according to Tacitus, who records the brutal murders of the children of Sejanus; there was no precedent for the capital punishment of a virgin, and so the executioner raped the girl before strangling her (Tac. *Ann.* 5.9). Gaeticulus alone escaped with his life, only to die at the hands of Caligula, under the suspicion of conspiracy.

## "AN EXACT ACCOUNT"

Finally, in 41, Caligula's suspicions of conspiracy were confirmed to all. Josephus begins by enumerating the abominations of Caligula's madness as a pretext for recounting the death of the emperor, whose fate teaches that good fortune without virtue is disastrous:

> I wish to give an exact account of that man, especially since it proves well the power of God; it provides encouragement for those (i.e., Jews) in misfortune, and a lesson in self-control for those (i.e., Romans) who think good fortune is everlasting and do not know that it changes for the worse if virtue does not accompany it.[19]

This is an explicit statement of the strategy of containment and deterrence at work in conspiracy narratives. The story will comfort the Jews who suffer at the hands of the Romans; in this sense, it is intended to assuage their apprehensions about Roman rule. The story will also serve to deter the Romans from further tyrannical abominations. Future rulers will learn from the fate of Caligula that it is better to behave nobly. The story thus contains the fear of the Jewish readers and deters further tyranny on the part of the Roman readership.

Josephus introduces three conspirators—Aemilius Regulus, Cassius Chaerea, and Annius Vinicianus[20]—and their motives against Caligula.[21] But throughout Josephus' account, Cassius Chaerea, tribune of a cohort of the praetorian guard, is the undisputed ringleader. Chaerea hated the emperor because of his repeated insults against his manliness, for Caligula daily taunted the tribune by giving an obscene password, much to the amusement of the other soldiers.[22] Josephus adds that Chaerea took the lead because as a praetorian tribune with freer access to the emperor, he could more easily find an opportunity to kill him. Chaerea next sought the support of Clemens, commander of the guard, and Papinius, a military tribune. At first, Clemens did not openly support Chaerea but urged him to keep his intentions secret to avoid discovery. Chaerea next approached Sabinus, a fellow tribune, who welcomed the plan and begged him not to waste time. They turned to Annius Vinicianus, who wished to avenge the death of his friend Aemilius Lepidus, the conspirator of 39. Vinicianus encouraged the plot, which had reached senators, equestrians, soldiers, even the freedman Callistus.

In spite of the many opportunities to kill Caligula, the conspirators delayed. Finally, Chaerea convinced them to strike the emperor at the games on the Palatine. Caligula had been in the habit of leaving the show at midday, and the conspirators hoped to use the opportunity to isolate the emperor from his guards. Caligula arrived, sacrificed, and proceeded to his seat. As the morning progressed, he could not decide whether to go and bathe, eat, and then return to the theater or to stay through the conclusion of the games, since it was the last day. Caligula showed no signs of leaving, and Chaerea, growing impatient, began to leave. Vinicianus rose from his seat to urge Chaerea, but Caligula, tugging at his toga, asked where he was going. Vinicianus was obliged to sit back down. Finally, Nonius Asprenas persuaded Caligula to leave. He departed the theater, intending to go to the baths and to inspect some dancing boys recently arrived from Asia. In a narrow passageway, Chaerea struck the first blow, and in the turmoil, Caligula was murdered at the hands of the conspirators.

The soldiers of the emperor's German bodyguard were the first to discover the murder, and they stormed the palace in search of the assassins, killing three men. When news reached the spectators in the theater, the reaction was mixed. Some were glad but were afraid to show it; others, who benefited from

Caligula's whims, refused to elieve that anyone had the courage to kill him. Senators feigned their respon e, afraid that if Caligula were still alive, they would be punished for their remature joy. The German troops stormed the theater but were deterred fro further vengeance. In what appeared to be a restoration of the republic, a p pular assembly was called, and the senate met. The consul Sentius Saturnin delivered a resounding oration defending the tyrannicide and proposing re ards to Chaerea.[23] That evening Chaerea saw to the death of Caligula's wif and daughter.

Throughout the confusion f the assassination and its aftermath, Claudius kept to the shadows, suspecti g he was in danger by virtue of his relation to Caligula. Terrified by the viol nce of the German guard and alarmed for his own safety, he hid in an alcov . One of the praetorians, a man named Gratus, discovered Claudius and bro ght him forth; the soldiers hailed him as emperor. Thus, a clear difference emerged between those who simply wanted to replace Caligula and those w o wanted to revert to the republican system of government. The senate sent n embassy to Claudius, and his reply made it clear that he intended not to estore the republic but to continue the principate as emperor. With dwin ing resolve and diminishing momentum, the senate was paralyzed by fatal ndecision. Claudius summoned the senate to meet on the Palatine and calle for the death of Chaerea, whose deed had been honorable but whose loyalty as questionable. Josephus closes the account with the deaths of the conspi ators.

Chaerea requested he be illed by the sword used against Caligula. The conspirator Sabinus, however was exonerated by Claudius and was even allowed to keep his commissio as an officer. Wracked with guilt for deserting his comrades, he commit ed suicide, falling on his sword until the hilt touched the wound. These d tails recall the deaths of Brutus and Cassius, for Brutus committed suicide nd Cassius slew himself with the same dagger he had used against Caesar.[24] Indeed, the conspiracy of Brutus and Cassius looms large in Josephus' imagination.[25] When Chaerea met with Vinicianus, the senator asked Chaerea for the daily password. "Liberty," he said, "is the password you give me." Upon the brief restoration of the republic, the consuls gave the same watchword. *Libertas* was of course Brutus' password at Philippi.[26] Furthermore, the consul Sentius calls for rewards to Chaerea, since "he is beyond comparison with Cassius and Brutus, the slayers of Julius Caesar."[27] A subtle irony lurks behind the proposal. The honors proposed to the assassins of Caesar in 44 B.C.E. were vetoed by Antony, the great-grandfather of Caligula.[28] Finally, Josephus notes that Caligula was murdered one hundred years after Rome first fell under tyranny, reckoning from 59 B.C.E., the first consulship of Julius Caesar.[29] Thus, throughout his account, Josephus aligns the tyrannicides of Gaius Caligula with those of Julius Caesar.

In comparison to the other conspiracy narratives, Josephus' account is marked by a high degree of self-confidence. Unlike Sallust, who uses the first person thirty-one times in the *Bellum Catilinae*, Josephus uses a first-person verb to enter the narrative only five times.[30] Moreover, unlike Sallust, who cross-references his account eight times, Josephus uses the first person only once to give direction in the narrative.[31] Once he voices his own opinion: "It seems (to me) that Callistus invented this story."[32] Once he differs with his source: Chaerea struck the first blow, and although it was severe, it was not mortal. Some say Chaerea deliberately held back his force so that Caligula would have to suffer a more violent death. "This account, however, I cannot believe," says Josephus. "If Chaerea did entertain such a thought, I consider it foolish to indulge anger rather than assure the safety of the conspirators."[33] The most self-assured use of the first person occurs at beginning, when he states his desire "to give an exact account of everything that happened." His wish (βουλόμαι) to relate an exact account, δι' ἀκριβείας, is bold—a claim Sallust pledges only to the best of his ability—and reveals his confidence in his sources to narrate the conspiracy and assassination. Thus, unlike Sallust and Tacitus who use the first person to express the difficulty of narrating conspiracy, Josephus displays confidence in his ability to tell the story fully and accurately.

In the preface to the *Jewish War,* Josephus states even more emphatically, "I shall accurately report (διέξειμι) the actions of both sides."[34] He acknowledges, however, that he may not always fulfill this claim, since he will at times lament the fate of his people. He attempts to distinguish between the facts of history and the lamentations of the historian. In this statement, Josephus indicates his knowledge of the conventions of classical historiography and appears to provide a veneer of rational analysis while in fact conveying partisan ideology.[35] But this is a programmatic statement at the beginning of a work, best aligned with other such statements of impartiality that characterize historical prose prefaces. Whatever bias emerges in the account of the assassination of Caligula is surely inherited as much from the Roman sources Josephus followed as from Josephus' own pro-Flavian inclinations.

It is evident that Josephus consulted various sources to construct his narrative. Six times he uses third-person verbs with unnamed subjects to relate information gleaned from earlier historians.[36] The first use occurs at the beginning of Josephus' account, in the catalogue of Caligula's tyrannical behavior. The emperor dared to order the Phidian statue of Zeus at Olympia be brought to Rome, but the architect Memmius Regulus outwitted the mad command. "It is said (λέγεται) that Memmius postponed removing the statue not only for this reason but because of certain portents too serious to disregard" (*A.J.* 19.9). Josephus' second use relates that according to another unnamed source, when Chaerea entered the senate house, a voice from the crowd urged him to maintain his courage.[37] As his third use, Josephus writes that on the day of his death, Caligula was said to have been in a very good mood.[38] These three references simply indicate that Josephus consulted and drew from his sources. Twice the sources are said to agree (ὁμολογεῖται, 19.95, 19.110), and only once does Josephus say his sources disagree. The last words of Caligula's wife, Caesonia, "I warned you," spoken to her husband's corpse, were interpreted differently. According to Josephus, some saw the words as a warning to the emperor to desist from his barbarity; others thought she meant to warn him of the conspiracy.[39] Thus, the only explicit controversy between sources occurs with the possibility of a woman's involvement in the conspiracy.

Josephus shows that he carefully checked his sources, and he places reliability squarely on their shoulders. Indeed, one of the sources may have been an eyewitness to the assassination. Josephus relates an anecdote that a senator of praetorian rank was sitting next to Cluvius, an ex-consul. Taking care not to be overheard, the senator asked whether he had heard anything about revolution. Cluvius denied it. "Well, then, Cluvius, the program for today will include the assassination of a tyrant." To which Cluvius replied, with a paraphrase of Homer, "Quiet, lest one of the Achaeans should hear your word."[40] Such repartee would only be preserved by the actual speaker, so Mommsen argued, suggesting that the Cluvius of Josephus' anecdote is none other than the historian Cluvius Rufus. Cluvius' *Historiae* would have been replete with first-hand information about the events of the day. The hypothesis has demanded much attention, with some accepting and others rejecting the notion.[41] Regardless of whether Cluvius Rufus was Josephus' source for this particular detail of the narrative, it is certain that he consulted his Roman sources and constructed his narrative from among the different accounts available to him.

Throughout the account, the dual capacity of silence both to impede and to propel the conspiracy simultaneously lends the narrative a palpable hermeneutic tension. Silence is the very substance of conspiracy that makes it difficult to narrate. On the other hand, the same silence ensured the success of the conspirators. Aemilius Regulus joined the conspiracy out of indignation; he had such a bold spirit that he was against keeping the plots secret (*A.J.* 19.19). Chaerea is credited with having the boldness to speak openly of the plot and thereby bring the conspirators together (*A.J.* 19.112).

The exchange between Clemens and Chaerea, however, clarifies the need for secrecy. Clemens told Chaerea to keep silent, so that the secret that should be properly concealed might not leak, and the plot be discovered before completed, resulting in their punishment.[42] Sabinus was glad to join the conspiracy and would have broken his silence sooner if he had known whom to trust (*A.J.* 19.48). Likewise, when the conspirators approached Vinicianus, he too refrained from speaking out because of fear of danger (*A.J.* 19.51). In the end, so many conspirators knew about the plot that Chaerea was afraid it had been betrayed (*A.J.* 19.62). Care was taken to keep the secret especially on the day of the assassination (*A.J.* 19.91). Even after the murder was perpetrated, many senators consigned their joy to silence, and those who did know about the plot were still more secretive, since they did not know how many were actually involved (*A.J.* 19.132–133). Thus, silence hindered the progress of the conspiracy from gaining momentum. But silence was also necessary to ensure the success of the conspiracy. Thus, the fulfillment—not the betrayal—of the plans brought the secrets to light, enabling the conspiracy to be narrated.

While secrecy gagged the conspiracy on the human level, on the divine level, omens and portents announced the conspiracy loud and clear. When Caligula sacrificed to Augustus Caesar, the blood of one of the victims splattered the toga of Asprenas. Caligula burst out laughing, but to Asprenas, Josephus tells us, it turned out to be a manifest omen, for he was one of the three whom the German bodyguard struck down that day (*A.J.* 19.87). The games themselves portended great bloodshed, for they included a mime in which an officer was caught and crucified and a performance of the myth of Cinyras and Myrrha, both slaughtered.[43] More blood than usual was spilled that day. Furthermore, it was also the same day on which Philip II, king of Macedon, had been killed by Pausanias as he entered the theater.[44] Conspiracy is a secret. Couched in divine omens, the knowledge of the conspiracy is protected but still permitted to those who are careful enough to observe the signs. Proper attention to the portents would have been a better indicator than any mere human informant. The tyrant should have known better; he should have been more attentive to the signs he was given. But Caligula was hated in part because he considered himself divine. His tyrannical hubris cost him.

### SENTINELS OF SECRECY

None of the conspirators were slaves, but perhaps more surprising is that no slave betrayed the conspiracy. According to Suetonius, Caligula announced upon his accession that, unlike his predecessor, he would not listen to informants (*delatores*, Suet. *Cal.* 15.4). The promise was short lived. For according to Josephus, Caligula permitted slaves to bring accusations against their masters on whatever charges they pleased, and the historian attributes the conspiracies against Caligula in part to the elevated status he bestowed on the many slaves who informed on their masters. Because of their intimate contact with the masters, the slaves were easily believed. In the current climate of suspicion, anything reported was bound to have serious consequences. As a result, a contingent of slaves supported the emperor because they stood to gain their freedom. Accusation allowed slaves to obtain satisfaction for the ill-treatment suffered at the hands of harsh masters, and many took advantage of the opportunity.[45] With so many incentives to inform, it is remarkable that the conspiracy was not betrayed by a slave. Although slaves might have contributed to the causes of dissatisfaction under Caligula, nevertheless in the final analysis, the conspiracy and its aftermath belonged to freeborn citizens alone.

Passing references to slaves add little to the sequence of cause and effect in the narrative. For example, contrary to custom, seating at the games on the day of the murder was indiscriminate—women and men, free and slave mixed together.[46] When Caligula finally left his seat in the theater, he is said to have avoided the direct route that was lined on both sides with slaves who were in attendance. These slaves later blocked the escape route for the perpetrators (*A.J.* 19.103, 116). When the senators learned that the guard favored Claudius, they were prepared to enlist slaves in a force against him if necessary (*A.J.* 19.232, 242). Thus, slaves were at the disposal of the senate, which never did resort to using them.

Metaphorical references to slaves, on the other hand, reveal the pro-republican, anti-Caligulan sentiment that pervades the sources Josephus used.[47] Chaerea explained to Clemens and Papinius that they must stop acting on behalf of "one who makes them slaves in body and mind."[48] Speaking to Vinicianus, Chaerea lamented that his country had been reduced from freedom to slavery.[49] The assassin Sabinus threatened to kill himself rather than establish Claudius as yet another monarch and revert to a "doulocracy," a government of slaves.[50]

The death of Caligula gave the senators the chance to escape the slavery they had become accustomed to (*A.J.* 19.181, 227, 248). These passages recall the attitude of Sallust in the *Bellum Catilinae* and adumbrate the theme that runs deep in the *Annales* of Tacitus, in which freedom is contrasted with the servitude of the senatorial class toward the *princeps*.[51] Unlike Tacitus, Josephus does not berate the senate for its cowardly adulation. It appears that the pro-republican underpinnings of his narrative were part of a received tradition.[52]

So although slaves did not actually participate in the conspiracy, attitudes toward slavery definitively shape the narrative's ideology.

Like slaves, the role of foreigners in the conspiracy is also negligible, and the attitude toward them is similarly negative. Chaerea, weary of delay, addressed the conspirators: "Suppose some Egyptian found his [i.e., Caligula's] insolence more than freeborn men could stand and killed him—what would we think of ourselves if *that* humiliation happened?"[53] The conspirators needed to act before some foreign power stepped in. The memory of the influence of the wicked Queen Cleopatra on Caesar and Antony inspired the conspirators to emulate Brutus and Cassius. The only other foreign presence in the narrative is Caligula's German bodyguard, the first to realize that Caligula was dead. The stereotypical description does not flatter; the unit was recruited from a Celtic nation, whose people were known for their hot temper and physical prowess, and their loyalty was easily purchased.[54]

No conspiracy narrative is complete without a woman, and Josephus' account is no exception. He attributes Chaerea's growing resolve against Caligula to an episode involving an actress. Pompedius was a senator who had held nearly all the offices, although he espoused Epicurean philosophy with its well-known dictum to avoid politics. Perhaps this aloof attitude made him an easy target, for his enemy Timidius accused him of "uttering disgraceful slanders against Gaius."[55] The charge fits the description of *maiestas*, defined under the early principate as slander of the *princeps* or his family.[56] Deeper motives often lurked behind the claim of *maiestas*, conveniently invoked when a prosecutor wished to ruin someone against whom evidence of any other crime was lacking. The prosecution called as a witness the actress Quintilia, a beautiful, promiscuous woman. She knew the charge was false and refused to bear witness against her lover. So Timidius called for her torture. Caligula leapt at the opportunity and ordered Chaerea to the task. Then Josephus relates a curious detail:

> Quintilia, when brought in for torture, trod on the foot of one of those privy to the conspiracy as a sign that he should keep cool and have no fear of her yielding to torture, for she would hold out bravely.[57]

Gleason has explored the significance of body language in the *Jewish War* of Josephus, and her remarks on the difficulties of defining "body language" illuminate our passage: "Any use of the body to convey a message, from highly stylized gestures to one-of-a-kind improvisatory tableaux, will count as 'body language'. . . . The metaphor of 'body language' prompts us to ask, of any given gesture both 'How was it meant?' and 'How was it understood?'"[58]

Quintilia uses her foot to convey a rather complicated message. She must trust that the silent communication of her body language will be interpreted properly. Josephus interprets her communication for us; treading on the foot of someone means, "I will keep silent." What Josephus does not tell us, however, is whether that message was received. There is no indication that the trodden conspirator understood Quintilia's message, except that, unlike the Pisonian conspiracy, panic did not set in. No one reacted as she was dragged off for torture; no one objected; no one cheered. She faced the torture alone.

Apparently, Quintilia knew something about a conspiracy. Presumably, she learned about it from her lover Pompedius. Once again the phenomenon of conspiratorial pillow talk is at work. But was it the same conspiracy that Chaerea headed? Barrett assumes that Quintilia stepped on Chaerea's foot, making this episode an earlier phase of the conspiracy.[59] But the indefinite pronoun is not so specific. She may have been privy to a different conspiracy altogether, giving her signal to someone other than Chaerea. Furthermore, Josephus cites this episode as galvanizing Chaerea's resolve to embark on a conspiracy. How could Quintilia be privy to a plan that had not yet been formulated?[60] Regardless, Quintilia had information about a conspiracy, and Chaerea was forced by his position to torture her cruelly.

When Quintilia showed no weakness, Chaerea brought her back to Caligula in so sorry a state that even the emperor was affected. He acquitted both her and Pompedius of the charge and generously rewarded her as a consolation for her agony and the abuse that marred her beauty. Permanently scarred, her mutilated body bore witness to the cruelty of Caligula. But the scars also spoke of the incipient conspiracy. Extracted from the depths by means of torture, a conspiracy was brought to the surface for all to see. She may have kept silent, but her disfigured body spoke volumes. Presumably, all who beheld her saw what she endured to protect her lover and the conspiracy. Caligula, too, must have been able to read the signs, but he chose to ignore this visible evidence of the conspiracy and to release and reward her instead.

Quintilia was privy to secrets by virtue of her involvement with a conspirator. As a lower-class woman, she was unprotected from torture; she refused to betray a conspiracy. The obdurate Quintilia is an example of determination and bravery in the face of tyrannical brutality, and she is the predecessor of Tacitus' Epicharis. It is possible that Tacitus had heard of the trial of Pompedius and the torture of Quintilia (it may have figured in the lost portion of his *Annales*) and incorporated its general framework into the ordeal of Epicharis.

Other authors treated Quintilia's story. Dio's epitomator condensed it, and with notable differences. In the first place, rather than prove the goodness of

Quintilia or the resolve of Chaerea, it demonstrates that Gaius in fact was capable, "with youthful impetuosity, of doing a few excellent things" (Dio 59.26.4). Second, the defendant is Pomponius, not Pompedius, and his unnamed prosecutor is actually called a friend. Third, this Pomponius is charged with plotting against Caligula. Both Dio and Josephus agree that the tortured mistress kept silent, and then to prove the point of the story, Caligula released and rewarded her.[61]

Suetonius also recounts the incident, although he does not mention Quintilia by name either:

> To make it known that he encouraged every kind of noble action, he gave 800,000 sesterces to a freedwoman because she had kept silent about the guilt of her patron although subjected to the cruelest torture.[62]

Suetonius removes the anecdote from the context of the conspiracy altogether and places it instead at the end of a list of virtuous acts for which Caligula earned a *clipeus aureus* (a golden shield to be carried in a procession of honor). Only Suetonius imputes guilt to the defendant; both Josephus and Dio imply that the tortured woman was protecting an innocent man.

The accounts of Josephus and Dio cannot be reconciled on the most fundamental levels; they do not agree on the name of the defendant (Pompedius versus Pomponius), nor do they state the same accusation. For Dio's epitomator (as for Suetonius), the tortured woman serves as an example of the emperor's intermittent bouts of human decency. For Josephus, Quintilia serves as a pretext for Chaerea's growing resolve against Caligula. In both accounts, she serves as an *exemplum*, illustrating a particular moral: to protect one's patron by silently enduring physical torture is admirable.[63] In both accounts, she protects a conspiracy. Moreover, she is privy to the secrets of the conspirator because of her intimate relationship with him. It is not clear whether she was a willful participant, but she was a conduit for sensitive information. Like Fulvia and the wife of Milichus, Quintilia received information about a conspiracy from a lover; like Hispala and Epicharis, she was physically harmed for that information.

It is now evident that Roman attitudes towards conspiracy are largely concerned with the violation of boundaries (between public and private, male and female, free and slave). Yet, as the Pisonian conspiracy and the assassination of Caligula show, these attitudes are not always negative. While some conspiracies are indicative of failing morality, certain conspiracies are, morally speaking, good. Sometimes good citizens must join in secret with like-minded fellows to overthrow an oppressive government. There is no question as to the honorable motives of Chaerea and his fellow conspirators. Claudius admits as much; he sentences the assassins to death not because they were wrong but because conspirators—even when right—are never to be trusted. As conspiracy always raises the possibility of counterconspiracy, so conspiracy can be either reprehensible or honorable. The assassination of Julius Caesar, however, was not so easy to label; consensus remained in the distance. Sorting out the morality of a conspiracy (and thereby disengaging alternative moral interpretations) is the historian's job; however, when it comes to judging the actions of Brutus and Cassius, the reader finds no leisure.

# FIVE

# APPIAN

## *The Assassination of Julius Caesar*

Wе come at last to perhaps the most renowned event in Roman history, and certainly the most commemorated assassination of a Roman statesman in Western thought. Caesar's death had been contrived by the most upstanding citizens of the day, men whose lives were measured by their belief in, and their adherence to, an intangible *mos maiorum* (ancestral custom). Leading the conspirators were Brutus, his brother-in-law Cassius, and Caesar's former legates Decimus Brutus and Gaius Trebonius. Not one woman, slave, or foreigner betrayed the conspiracy. The successful assassination of the dictator belonged solely to Rome's most élite citizens.

A conspiracy narrative is characterized by an epistemological gap caused by the secrecy and silence that shroud the event. But the successfully executed assassination of Julius Caesar revealed the secrets, brought the conspiracy to light, and enabled it to be narrated. Nicolaus of Damascus, Suetonius, and Plutarch recount the details in biographical form; the epitomes of Livy and Florus outline the major events of the Ides of March; the historians Velleius Paterculus and Dio also recount the events. Valerius Maximus includes certain peculiarities of the conspiracy under various rubrics in his *Facta et Dicta Memorabilia*. Of all the ancient testimonia, however, we shall concentrate on the account given by the Antonine historian Appian in his *Civil Wars*, since he offers the longest connected narrative of the event in a historical work.

Born in 96 C.E. in Alexandria, Appian enjoyed a distinguished career as an advocate. His forensic skills earned him notoriety among his compatriots. He spent some time in Rome pleading cases before emperors, evidence that he was fluent in Latin as well as Greek.[1] He flourished in the reign of Antoninus Pius and began his *Roman History* in 150. He was the first historian to organize material geographically and ethnically, according to the nations conquered and not according to the rigid annalistic formula employed since the inception of Roman historiography. Although his writing betrays an admiration for the Romans, nevertheless, like Josephus, he cannot escape his position as an outsider. He thereby proffers the unique perspective of history from the standpoint of the provincial.

The recent revival of interest in Appian is a welcome trend with several driving forces behind it. First, Barbu's monumental study of Appian's sources effectively demonstrated the principle that Appian used contemporary sources for an event whenever possible. For example, he used Sallust for the Catilinarian conspiracy and Nicolaus of Damascus for the assassination of Julius Caesar.[2] Gabba attempted to establish that the lost work of Asinius Pollio was the principal source for the whole of Appian's *Civil Wars*.[3] Thus, regardless of how one judges his methods, whether he is regarded as an inept compiler or a faithful copier, Appian brings us as close as possible to the events he narrates and as close as possible to some otherwise irretrievable sources. Second, scholarship on the second sophistic, and especially Plutarch, has provided a much needed social context for writers such as Appian. We are now in a better position to understand the milieu in which Appian composed his history.[4]

A general shift in modern expectations of ancient historiography has opened new avenues to explore Appian. Rather than expect objective history in the nineteenth-century sense of the word, instead we appreciate the worldviews that such an author projects in his representations of the past.[5] As with Josephus, Appian is an extremely valuable source, and sometimes he is the only source for a period. He offers the best surviving connected narrative of the years 133–35 B.C.E., and his is the sole connected narrative for the years 133–70. Naturally, he should merit attention for this reason alone. But recent scholarship has also made fruitful advances by comparing Appian with Dio and Florus.[6] All these factors make it easy to incorporate Appian into this study of conspiracy narratives in the Roman historians.

This final chapter proceeds along the two main avenues of inquiry that have guided this study throughout, namely, the historiographical issue of narrative form and function and the historical role of women in conspiracies. In the first part, I examine the narrative strategies deployed by Appian in his account of the assassination. Appian's narrative of the assassination of Julius Caesar bears few of the marks of epistemological uncertainty or hesitancy that characterize especially the conspiracy narratives of Sallust and Tacitus. Third-person impersonal verbs are used sparingly throughout Books 1 and 2 of the *Civil Wars*, and use of the first person is no more prevalent than at other points.[7] Instead, Appian presents the assassination quite matter of factly, in a manner that is consistent with his overall approach to history writing. Therefore, we shall concentrate on the mode of revelation that Appian deploys in his narrative, in particular, the suspense, mimesis, and causality that create narrative continuity. The second part of the chapter compares the role of Porcia, the wife of Brutus, in the conspiracy with our other conspiratorial bedfellows.

## THE HERMENEUTICS OF ASSASSINATION

Just as Josephus lists Caligula's abominations as the reason for his assassination, so Appian lists the unparalleled honors that had been awarded to Caesar upon his return to Rome in October 45 B.C.E. as goading the conspirators. Proclaimed *pater patriae,* Caesar was chosen dictator for life and consul for ten years. The senate granted that he conduct all business on a chair of ivory and gold; that he should always sacrifice in triumphal dress; that the magistrates, immediately upon inauguration, should swear not to oppose any of Caesar's decrees. The month of July was named after him and many temples were dedicated to him (2.106).

As Caligula suspected and punished the conspirators Lepidus and Gaeticulus, so Caesar suspected the tribunes Epidius Marullus and Caesetius Flavus of conspiring to degrade his *dignitas.* Someone had put a laurel crown with a white fillet, a symbol of royalty, on a statue of Caesar. The tribunes ordered the crown to be removed and the perpetrator to be taken to prison. Later, someone else greeted Caesar as king, but Marullus discovered who had spoken and brought him before trial. Apparently the tribunes overreacted to the recognition of Caesar's popularity, and their responses called too much attention to his unprecedented status. So Caesar accused Marullus before the senate of conspiring to cast upon him the slanderous name of tyrant. Although the tribunes deserved death, he found it sufficient that they be deposed from office and expelled from the senate (2.108).[8] Appian reports that Caesar was immediately sorry for his impulsive reaction; as a result, Caesar then dismissed his bodyguard in a show of confidence and trust.

Royal honors were thrust upon Caesar again at the festival of the Lupercal. As Caesar was sitting in the forum before the rostra, Antony leapt up and put a crown on his head. Caesar threw it down, but Antony replaced it. Caesar rejected it again, and the crowd rejoiced for two entirely different reasons. On the one hand, Caesar prevailed over Antony, demonstrating his superiority, but on the other hand, he did not accept the crown, demonstrating his humility (2.109). Finally, the potential for Caesar to become monarch was manifest to all. He planned a campaign against the Parthians, hoping to recover the lost standards of Crassus. A rumor went about that the Sibylline oracle predicted that the Parthians would be subdued by the Romans only if Rome were ruled by a king. Although some suggested that Caesar should be called king, he declined (2.110). He was assassinated four days before he planned to depart for Parthia.

Appian begins the account of the conspiracy against Julius Caesar with the statement, "Four days before his intended departure, his enemies killed him in the senate house." Thus, the conclusion of the narrative is announced at the beginning. There is no suspense as to whether Caesar will escape the attempt on his life, no question as to the success of the conspirators. The deed is accomplished before it is even narrated. Why, then, should the reader continue? In a monograph on the modern phenomenon of assassination, Cooper offers a compelling reason:

> Assassination carries with it an all-pervading sense of mystery and intrigue. The central event may have been a matter of public record, reported and analyzed in the greatest detail. Yet the continuing fascination of the matter, its hold over the minds of the people, often resides in what is thought to lie behind it all; the unknown, and the unknowable. Some assassinations are, on their face, deceptively simple. The what, when, where, who, why, and how are seemingly answered convincingly and conclusively by the historical record. Yet, even in these relatively clear-cut cases, many remain unpersuaded that the full story has been truthfully told. Skepticism is part of the folklore of assassination. In particular, there is always a tendency to wonder why and to feel a nagging dissatisfaction with the answers to this part of the interrogatory. Assassination makes its own kind of mystery and the nature of man's curiosity tends to deepen it; therein lies much of the power of the crime.[9]

By the time Appian came to narrate the events surrounding the Ides of March, 44 B.C.E., dozens of writers had already covered the material in histories and biographies alike. The interpretations of the assassination were by no means unanimous; according to Tacitus, some regarded the murder of Caesar as the worst crime, others as the best.[10] For Appian, there was no question but that the murder was a terrible crime, although he reserved his judgment of the deed until the obituary of Brutus (4.134).

Appian's hostile judgment of the conspirators is closely tied to the aim as stated in his preface to the *Civil Wars* (1.6), to show how the Roman state evolved from violent civil unrest to a harmonious monarchy. The history of the civil wars demonstrates measureless ambition, dreadful lust for power, and countless forms of evil; in other words, it serves as a negative example of behavior. Thus, the assassination of Caesar fulfills the didactic purpose and maintains the overarching theme of harmony from stasis that infuses the *Civil Wars*. Appian delivers a convincing and conclusive account of the assassination. But an undertone of mystery and intrigue is manifested in the many suspenseful delays posted along the way between the beginning and the end. Repeated delays in the progress of the conspiracy give the impression that Caesar might actually escape his fate, even though the reader is assured from the outset that he did not.

A common means of delaying narrative in historiography is digression. According to Cicero, digressions are regarded as a source of pleasure and entertainment for the reader.[11] In addition to the varieties of fortune and the vicissitudes of circumstance that delight the reader, ancient historiographers also include topographical and ethnographical descriptions for the purpose of entertainment.[12] Although digression is a common feature of historiography, Appian formally digresses only once in Books 1 and 2 of the *Civil Wars*. At 2.39, he begins his account of Pompey's campaign against Caesar at Dyrrhachium in 48 B.C.E. Seeking to clarify the name of the place, he launches into an explanation for the confusion, concluding, "Nevertheless, the former name prevailed finally, and it is now called Dyrrhachium." Thus, the topographical digression is clearly signaled to the reader; the material contained within it has no bearing on the outcome of the campaign at Dyrrhachium. The narrative is suspended; the action between the armies of Caesar and Pompey does not advance, although suspense builds as the outcome is kept in the balance.

Appian employs no such formal digression in his account of the assassination of Caesar, and yet the action of the conspirators is repeatedly impeded in other ways. At 2.112, we are told that Brutus and Cassius, praetors at the time, quarreled over who should hold the more prestigious post of urban praetor. Caesar mediated the dispute in favor of Brutus. Appian then comments on the preference Caesar habitually showed Brutus; it was thought ($\dot{\epsilon}\nu o\mu\acute{\iota}\zeta\epsilon\tau o$) that Brutus was his son.[13] Then we are given a list of reasons why Brutus, so beloved by Caesar, would still choose to conspire against him. This list, which interrupts the action of the narrative, is in turn interrupted by evidence of the people's expectations of Brutus:

> Whether Brutus was ungrateful, or ignorant of his mother's fault, or disbelieved it, or was ashamed of it; whether he was such an ardent lover of liberty that he preferred his country to everything, or whether, because he was a descendant of that Brutus of the olden time who expelled the kings, he was aroused and shamed to this deed principally by the people, (for there

were secretly affixed to the statues of the elder Brutus and also to Brutus' own tribunal such writings as, "Brutus, are you bribed?" "Brutus, are you dead?" "Would that you were living now!" "Your posterity is unworthy of you," or "You are not *his* descendant"). At any rate, these and many like incentives fired the young man to a deed like that of his ancestor.[14]

This extended discussion of Brutus' relationship to Caesar and of his possible motives both personal and public is indicative of Appian's abiding interest in character over politics.[15] If the task of the historian is to assign causality, it would seem that here Appian declines, in a sentence that offers no fewer than six alternative explanations, capped by the indefinite "these and many like incentives." Embedded in the final explanation is the evidence from the graffiti on the tribunal of Brutus and the statues of his ancestor, intended no doubt to strengthen the claim, that of all the reasons Brutus was induced to act, it was his connection to his ancestor that moved him the most. Suetonius records just one of the graffiti on the base of the elder Brutus' statue; Plutarch ascribes Brutus' motive to the popular sentiment and records several of the same slogans.[16] Clearly Appian cannot escape the positive, pro-liberator tradition of Brutus found in the sources.[17] Yet the allusion to events that happened centuries ago derails the forward temporal progress of the narrative.

The next paragraph restores the sequence of events and returns the reader to the year 44, for we are told that "while the talk about the kingship was at its height, and just before there was to be a meeting of the senate, Cassius met Brutus" (2.113). At this point, Appian changes the mode of presentation, from straightforward description in the third person to direct speech. He shifts to *oratio recta* in the first person, from the narrator's voice to the characters' voices. Instead of descriptive revelation, Appian uses dramatic revelation, and perhaps in this part of the story, he draws on a dramatic representation of the conspiracy.[18]

The conversation exchanged between Brutus and Cassius, given in direct discourse, manifests and externalizes the conspirators' inner secrets. We are given a glimpse of the private thoughts of both Cassius and Brutus, uniformly illuminated. Their conversation is situated temporally and spatially; it took place just before a meeting of the senate. Appian even includes a few gestures for vividness:

> Seizing him by the hand, he said, "What shall we do in the Senate if Caesar's flatterers propose a decree making him king?" Brutus replied that he would not be there. Then Cassius asked him further, "What if we are summoned there as praetors, what shall we do then?" "I will defend my country to the

death," he replied. Cassius embraced him, saying, "If this is your mind, whom of the nobility will you not rally to your standard?"[19]

This conversation is not reported in any of the other sources. If it is not derived from some dramatic performance, it may well be the work of Appian himself. Appian embellishes the meeting with a high level of detail; Cassius took Brutus by the hand and embraced him. The shift of voice, from the narrator to the characters, forces the reader to shift his perception of authority in the text. Rather than simply repeat the content of the conversation, Appian lets the characters speak for themselves. The conspiracy is laid out for the reader: "Thus did they disclose to each other what they had been privately thinking about for a long time" (2.113). Brutus and Cassius conversed in unveiled language. Nothing was left to inference, as Fulvia had to infer the conspiracy from Curius; nothing was withheld, as Epicharis kept names from Proculus; no one hesitated, as Hispala hesitated to relate the secrets of the Bacchanalia. The shift to dramatic mimesis is a highly effective means of revelation.

Immediately following this scene, Appian lists some of the other conspirators by name (2.113). He had already named the chief conspirators, Brutus, Cassius, and Decimus Brutus, at the beginning of the account (2.111). Therefore, the continuation of the list of conspirators effectively retards the progress of the narrative. He admits as much when he names Decimus Brutus a second time, "whom I have already mentioned" (2.113). He names Caecilius, Bucolianus, Rubrius Ruga, Quintus Ligarius, Marcus Spurius, Servilius Galba, Sextius Naso, Pontius Aquila, Gaius Casca, Trebonius, Tillius Cimber, and Minucius Basilus. Of all our sources for the assassination, Appian is the only one to identify more than four conspirators by name.[20] In contrast to his predecessors, his deliberate choice to list twelve names stalls the action of the conspiracy.

Suspense derives from the tension between delay and progress in a narrative. After these diversions, Appian impels the narrative forward by using internal focalization. As we saw in Sallust's *Bellum Catilinae*, the shift in point of view allows the narrator to attribute cause and effect, and so Appian explains three motivations for the plot (2.114). First, the conspirators decided to act when they did because "they thought they had sufficient numbers and that it would not be wise to divulge the plot any more." The more who knew of the plot, the more likely it was to be discovered; the need for secrecy dominated the conspirators' actions. It is interesting to note that the conspirators did not swear oaths or perform sacrifices. Perhaps they could rely on a gentleman's code of honor to bind them together in their common goal. Perhaps in their arrogant self-assurance, the conspirators did not feel the need for divine sanction. Perhaps because the conspiracy was not led by any military faction, there was no sense that a common oath of allegiance was necessary. Surely the absence of any oath or sacrifice distinguished this conspiracy from the dire Catilinarian conspiracy, with its grim oath reputedly sealed with human blood.[21]

Then Appian explains why they chose the senate house for the attack, "believing that, even though the senators did not know of it beforehand, they would join readily when they saw the deed" (2.114). Further focalization allows Appian to align the assassination of Caesar with the death of Romulus, for the senators "thought that this deed, like that one of old, taking place in the open senate, would seem not to be a private conspiracy, but in the public interest" (2.114). Caesar is thus equated with the eponymous founder of Rome, thereby revealing yet again the pro-monarchical sentiments of the narrator.

Finally, some thought Antony should also be killed, but Brutus argued that the death of the tyrant alone would bring them glory; to kill Antony too would debase the deed as merely factional. Thus, the opinion of many (οἱ μέν) is juxtaposed with the opinion of one (ὁ δέ), and the character of Brutus is thrown into ever sharper relief. So while internal focalization asserts the causality that impels the narrative forward, it also allows the narrator to develop characters and to infuse the narrative with opinion.

The day before the assassination, Caesar dined with Lepidus and Decimus Brutus (2.115). After the meal, they debated the best kind of death. Various opinions were given, but Caesar alone expressed preference for a sudden death, inadvertently foretelling his own demise. That night, his wife Calpurnia dreamed she saw him streaming with blood, and she begged him not to leave the house the next morning. When he offered sacrifice, there were many unfavorable signs. What is the effect of such concentrated omens? What does Appian gain by such overdrawn foreshadowing?

To answer this question, it is useful to consider the possible ways an author can manipulate representations of time, past, present, and future, in narrative. In his seminal essay, "Forms of Time and of the Chronotope in the Novel," Bakhtin awakens us to the problem of representing novelistic time as open and unrestricted. He poses, but does not answer, the question of how an author can ultimately achieve freedom in a narrative in which time is always a constraining factor. Bakhtin's initial steps toward a theory of time begin with a chronological history of the novel, from antiquity to Rabelais, and the result is a crude framework for understanding the relationship between time and space.[22]

Gary Morson refines Bakhtin's ideas of time, and in *Narrative and Freedom,* he constructs a theory of time built on more formal methods of argumentation than Bakhtin's loosely construed survey. Morson begins by examining the familiar trope of foreshadowing, a device that imposes order on causality. Most importantly, "foreshadowing seems utterly to preclude the possibility of options." This trope, more than any, robs narrative of its sense of freedom. Characters have no choice, or if they do, it is merely illusory. Then, in an analysis of nineteenth-century novels, Morson posits the solution to this dilemma: authors use what he calls "sideshadowing," in which "two or more alternative presents, the actual and the possible, are made simultaneously visible."

Sideshadowing opens up possibilities in narrative; what emerges is not one single linear narrative but a network of possible outcomes and conclusions. Sideshadowing allows us to see *what might have been;* this is the essential ingredient of the novels of Dostoevsky and Tolstoy. Thus, sideshadowing allows for a degree of freedom from the constraints of time.[23] Such open possibilities are precisely what history denies; the genre demands that historians resist the temptation to narrate what might have been and instead reduce the narrative to a single strand of what indeed happened. Such reduction is a fundamental feature of the strategy of containment. Alternative narrative outcomes are disengaged; there is no fear of possibility.

Thus Michael Bernstein, in *Foregone Conclusions,* takes the final step in developing Bakhtin's theory of freedom and time by applying the concept of temporal shadowing to historical texts. He explores the concept of what he calls "backshadowing":

> Backshadowing is a kind of retroactive foreshadowing in which the shared knowledge of the outcome of a series of events by narrator and listener is used to judge the participants in those events *as though they too should have known what was to come.*[24]

Foreshadowing provides knowledge of future events to the reader but denies it to the characters; it is a trope of fiction. Sideshadowing opens up possibilities of future events to the reader; this is also a fictive move. Backshadowing, however, assumes prior knowledge of the outcome of events and freights this knowledge with a moral judgment of the characters and their ignorance. Backshadowing is the essential characteristic of history, in which both author and reader know full well the singular outcome of events, and confident in this knowledge, both despise the characters who stumble in the darkness of their ignorance toward foregone conclusions. By manipulating the narrative, by casting temporal shadows forward and back, the narrator can drain events of their immediacy, so that they seem either inevitable, as in the case of foreshadowing, or obvious, as with backshadowing.

Through a tacit acknowledgement of the outcome of events, as yet unknown to the characters at the time, both narrator and reader can pass judgment on the characters. From this omniscient vantage point, the impact of the event is tamed. Thus Lepidus' portentous symposium, Calpurnia's prophetic dream, and Caesar's unfavorable sacrifices weaken the impact of the assassination while simultaneously granting the reader power over the characters. We know better than the great Caesar himself what was about to happen.

As if to counter this inevitability, Appian proceeds with one of the most suspenseful moments in the entire narrative. The senators gathered at the Curia behind the theater of Pompey and awaited Caesar's arrival. Rumors spread of the bad omens and the possible dismissal of the senate, and the conspirators were worried. Just then, a certain person took Casca by the hand and said, "You kept the secret from me, although I am your friend, but Brutus has reported to me." There is no clue who this mysterious, informed person is, and immediately Casca is terrified that the conspiracy is at risk. If this stranger knows, then others must know too. Perhaps even Caesar himself ascertained the plot and will punish the conspirators. It would seem that at this moment the conspiracy was about to collapse. Then the stranger continued to explain his cryptic remark: "Where shall you get the money to stand for the aedileship?"[25] A sense of relief washed over Casca, and the reader is assured, yet again, of the inevitability of the outcome of events.

Suspense is further maintained when Appian reports that three people knew of the conspiracy and tried to warn Caesar (2.116). The first, an unnamed friend, ran to Caesar's house to inform him but found only Calpurnia. Ignorant of the details, the informant waited in vain for Caesar to return from the senate. The second informant was a friend named Artemidorus, who arrived at the senate too late. Finally, someone gave Caesar a telltale tablet, but Caesar did not read it in time; it was found in his hand after his death.[26] The tablet became a matter of public record after the assassination, as if it were necessary to verify the conspiracy in writing.

The final moment of suspense occurred when Caesar finally reached the senate house and Popilius Laena engaged him in conversation at the entrance. The conspirators, unable to hear the conversation, feared that Popilius would betray them. But he did not, and according to custom, Caesar proceeded to offer sacrifices at the entrance of the senate house. Again the auspices were bad. Repeated sacrifices yielded the same results. At last, Caesar entered in spite of the omens. At this point, the actions follow in swift succession: Trebonius distracts Antony, while Cimber approaches Caesar. Casca strikes the first blow. As Caesar attempts to recover, another stabs him. Cassius attacks his face, Brutus his thigh, Bucolianus the back. Crying out, Caesar finally composes himself for death and falls at the foot of Pompey's statue. He had received twenty-three wounds.

This brief but close reading of chapters 111–117 reveals several techniques by which Appian sustains the narrative of the conspiracy to assassinate Julius Caesar. Most importantly, the narrative is composed of a tension between progress and delay. The outcome of the conspiracy, stated at the beginning, is a foregone conclusion toward which the narrative strives. But artfully placed detours assert causality and maintain suspense. Mention of the slogans on the statue of Brutus is incidental; inserted parenthetically, it interrupts the flow of the narrative, but it also serves to explain why Brutus undertook the murder. The names of the conspirators are repeated, and repetition negates progress.[27] The constant threats of betrayal also retard the progress of the conspiracy and its inevitable conclusion.

When the narrative does advance, Appian uses different methods to reveal knowledge to the reader. The shift from description to dramatic mimesis allows characters to speak for themselves, while the less-overt shift to internal focalization explains motives and defines characters. Unlike Josephus, who promises an exact account of the assassination of Caligula, Appian does not preface his account of the assassination of Julius Caesar with such a statement. In the end, Appian seeks to explain not so much what happened on the Ides of March but why it happened; he tries to account for the reasons the conspirators undertook the murder. Either they were jealous or they desired to restore the republic, "as they themselves alleged" (2.111, ὡς ἔφασκον αὐτοί). Appian then ventures his opinion as to why the conspirators decided to act when they did: "On mature consideration, I conclude that they did actually find an excuse for the plot in the prospect of this additional title."[28] Appian needs neither the first-person disclaimers of Sallust nor the first-person assurances of Josephus. Instead, his expert use of suspense, mimesis, and causality ensure the continuity of the narrative.

## THE NOBLE PORCIA

The Catilinarian, Bacchanalian, and Pisonian conspiracies were all betrayed by an exceptional woman. Fulvia, Hispala, and the wife of Milichus were all responsible for bringing the secrets of the conspiracy to light and causing the downfall of the conspirators. Quintilia, on the other hand, did not divulge the secrets of conspiracy against Caligula, even under torture, and so the emperor did not escape his assassins. Only one woman knew of the plan to assassinate Caesar. Porcia, the wife of Brutus and the daughter of Cato, Caesar's most bitter political enemy, did not reveal the plot. She does not appear in Appian's account of the conspiracy; he relates only her extraordinary death.[29] Plutarch, Dio, and Valerius Maximus recount anecdotes about her involvement in the conspiracy that illustrate, one final time, the principle of the conspiratorial female body of knowledge, that is, the close relationship between a woman's intimate contact with a conspirator and her knowledge of the conspiracy.

Let us begin with the earliest evidence of Porcia's knowledge of the conspiracy to assassinate Caesar. According to Valerius Maximus,

> Learning of her husband Brutus' design to kill Caesar, on the night before the day of that foul deed, Brutus having left the bedroom, she asked for a barber's knife to trim her nails and wounded herself with it, pretending that it had slipped by accident. Called back to the bedroom by the cries of the maidservants, Brutus started to scold her for forestalling the barber's function. Porcia said to him in private: "What I did was no accident; in the plight we are in, it was the surest token of my love for you. I wanted to try out how coolly I could kill myself with steel, if your plan did not turn out as you hope."[30]

The episode is an example of fortitude, and Porcia is one of only two women (the other is Cloelia) among the distinguished company of Roman men who displayed physical bravery: Horatius Cocles, Romulus, Scipio Aemilianus, Scipio Metellus, Mucius Scaevola, to name a few. Porcia's self-mutilation with manicure scissors seems out of place next to the story of Scaeva, legendary Caesarian soldier at Dyrrhachium, who withstood no fewer than one hundred and twenty wounds.[31] But Porcia's place in the annals of bravery is secured by her father, Cato the Younger, who fell on his sword rather than surrender to Caesar in Africa.[32] Valerius does not specify how Porcia learned about the conspiracy; instead, he focuses on the result of her knowledge. She was not as worried about her own ability to keep the secret as she was concerned about the success of the plot. Knowing that if the conspirators failed, they would die, she too was resolved to die with her husband.

The story of Porcia's self-mutilation does not surface in the ancient sources again until Plutarch's *Life of Brutus*, with much greater detail.[33] According to Valerius, Porcia learned about the conspiracy first, then subjected herself to mutilation. But according to Plutarch, Porcia did not even try to question Brutus about his secrets until she put herself through a physical ordeal first. With a manicure tool, she was able to inflict a deep gash in her thigh that produced much blood and eventually became infected. Seeing Brutus' great emotional distress in the days before the assassination, she approached him, saying,

> Brutus, I am Cato's daughter, and I was brought into your house, not, like a mere concubine, to share your bed and board merely, but to be a partner in all your joys and troubles. You are faultless as a husband; but how can I show you grateful service if I am to share neither your secret suffering nor the anxiety that craves a loyal confidant? I know that woman's nature is thought too weak to endure a script; but good rearing and excellent companionship go far towards strengthening the character, and it is my happy lot to be both the daughter of Cato and the wife of Brutus. Before this I put less confidence in these advantages, but now I know that I am superior even to pain.[34]

In Valerius' account, Porcia tested her ability to commit suicide; in Plutarch's account, she tests her ability to endure pain. She acknowledges that she is merely a woman, even if she is the daughter and husband of noble men. She distances herself from the stereotypical weak woman and approximates male virtue by her tolerance of physical pain. Mere concubines—like Fulvia and Hispala—reveal secrets when threatened with pain, while the properly wed Porcia demonstrates to Brutus that she is capable of distancing her body from her mind. Although her body may be broken, her mind is intact; therefore, if he should reveal his secrets to her, they would also remain intact, regardless of her physical state.

Conspiracy threatens to violate the citizen body. But Porcia's mental and physical integrity proves her worthiness to be the wife of a leading citizen. There is no sense of torture in her actions; she wounds herself merely to show her strength and manliness and therefore her worthiness to be her husband's confidant. Her story is recounted as what Parker calls a "tale of loyalty," a comforting story intended to reassure husbands in general that despite the inherently dangerous nature of women, at least *his* wife will be loyal.[35] She is another example of women's heroism in protecting the menfolk.[36]

Finally, Dio recounts the anecdote of Porcia's self-mutilation, this time in the explicit language of torture. Porcia was worried about her husband's sullen, withdrawn mood. When he refused to confide in her, she thought he distrusted her because of her physical weakness, "lest having heard something she might reveal it under torture" (ἐκ βασάνων).[37] Although the torture of women who were not slaves was obviously practiced by the tyrants Caligula and Nero, it is unthinkable that anyone would threaten to torture a woman of such high social standing as Porcia. I suggest that Dio overlays the circumstances of women like Quintilia and Epicharis onto his version of the story of Porcia.

Unlike Quintilia and Epicharis, who are tortured at the command of the emperor, however, Porcia inflicts the wound upon herself, testing her own tolerance. Convinced that she could endure pain, she went to Brutus. "You, my husband, trusting my spirit would not betray you, nevertheless distrusted my body. But I have found that my body can also keep silence."[38] She showed him her wounded thigh and explained her trial. Brutus, amazed at her forbearance, thereupon disclosed the conspiracy to her. Porcia had to prove that her body was capable of containing a secret. She also proved that her body was inviolate; in spite of a wound, a secret could still remain intact. Torture was the means of extracting the knowledge that lay hidden in the body, and it was presumed that a woman, like a slave, would be unequal to the pain. But it was safe for Brutus to fill Porcia with his secrets. No one would be able to extract them from her. Her nobility raised her to a level above slaves and other women; in her ability to keep a secret, she approximated the virtue of her husband and her father.

To a certain extent, Porcia's legendary fortitude in the face of conspiracy survived in the imaginations of Sallust, Livy, Tacitus, and Josephus, as they recreated the women of the Catilinarian, Bacchanalian, Pisonian, and Caligulan conspiracies. Porcia was the ideal female conspirator. As the daughter of Cato, she did not squander the inheritance of her father's nobility and dignity. As the wife of Brutus, she displayed the bravery worthy of such a bold husband. Against her, Fulvia, Hispala, and the wife of Milichus fell woefully short. They were not daughters or wives of leading citizens. They were not capable of keeping secrets. Fulvia leaked the Catilinarian conspiracy to Cicero. Hispala buckled at the slightest hint of physical pain. The motives of the wife of Milichus were anything but noble.

By maintaining silence in the face of physical pain, Porcia set the example that Epicharis and Quintilia followed; she proved her ability to keep a secret under physical duress. For Tacitus and Josephus, who held the Julio-Claudians in limited esteem, the silence of Epicharis and Quintilia, a prostitute and an actress, was as praiseworthy as the actions of a woman like the noble, senatorial-class Porcia. All three exceeded the commonly held expectations of women. Perhaps this is why Porcia finds no home in Appian; the historian who placed such a high premium on monarchy had no need of an exceptional woman who was willing to protect a conspiracy against the founder of the first dynasty of imperial Rome.

# CONCLUSION

*I brought myself down. I gave them a sword. And they stuck
it in. . . . And, I guess, if I'd been in their position,
I'd have done the same thing.*

— RICHARD M. NIXON[1]

The prevalence of conspiracy in the Roman literary imagination is testimony
to the fear that it generated and the need to assuage that fear by retelling the
stories of how conspiracies were detected, suppressed, and punished. We have
examined five conspiracy narratives with a view to the mode of presentation,
the hermeneutic principle, and narrative continuity. Naturally, each narrative
demonstrates these three principles to a greater or lesser degree, and each is
a unique assemblage of stylistic and substantive elements. Any conclusions
drawn must acknowledge the vast differences in time and place, political and
social circumstance.

As the only extant monograph devoted solely to conspiracy, Sallust's *Bellum Catilinae* serves as a sort of model text against which the others are compared. In it, we see evidence of Sallust's attempts to maintain narrative continuity, his manipulation of suspense, and the importance of Fulvia and the
Allobroges to the revelation of the conspiracy and so the salvation of the *res
publica*. Although the Bacchanalian affair is not technically a political conspiracy involving threats of assassination and political revolution, nevertheless
Livy's account (as well as the inscription of the *senatus consultum*) casts the
affair as a *coniuratio*, thereby imbuing the events with all the moral and political weight that conspiracy bears. Perhaps more than any other narrative
examined here, Livy's account seeks to contain the fear that such a conspiracy
engenders. Tacitus' account of the Pisonian conspiracy forces the reader to
admit that the return to a republic is in no way a viable solution to the ills
that plague the principate. Although the assassination of Nero could restore
a sense of political order, the conspirators are not up to the task of govern-

ing, and so—with characteristic Tacitean irony—there are no heroes. Only Epicharis comes shining through, however, and in this respect she approximates her republican forbears, Fulvia and Hispala, whose actions in the face of treacherous conspiracy can be considered praiseworthy.

Narratives of successful conspiracies are noticeably different from the narratives of betrayed conspiracies. While one might dismiss Josephus' account for any number of reasons (e.g., historical unreliability or ideological bias[2]), still one cannot discount the high degree of self-confidence with which he narrates the assassination of Caligula. His anecdote about the torture of Quintilia points us to the recurring phenomenon, that women's bodies are often conduits for the transfer of sensitive information about conspiracies. Finally, Appian rounds out this investigation quite neatly, allowing us to conclude with the most famous conspiracy in Roman history from the most distant vantage point. Of all the historians considered, Appian receives the most layered and most nuanced tradition about his topic—and manages to create from it one of our most suspenseful and engaging narratives.

It has been the aim of this book to show that the specific phenomenon of conspiracy provides a unique opportunity for us to observe the ways historians handle the more general difficulties faced when attempting to achieve narrative continuity. Sallust, Livy, and Tacitus had to contend with the veil of secrecy that obscured the conspiracies they tried to narrate. By admitting their uncertainty in the first person, by shifting responsibility to unnamed sources, by employing internal focalization and indefinite pronouns, these authors negotiated an epistemological gap and created a rhetoric of conspiracy by which to persuade the reader that their version of the events was credible, so as to create narratives that dispelled fear and deterred further thoughts of uprising. Josephus and Appian, on the other hand, were able to narrate assassination with a much greater degree of confidence because the conspiracies succeeded and the shroud of secrecy and silence was thrown off. Both authors worked diligently to maintain suspense throughout their narratives.

Furthermore, this study has examined conspiracies through the lenses of social status, gender, and ethnicity. Conspiracy effaces the boundaries between free and slave, male and female, Roman and foreigner. Sallust tells that Catiline attracted to his cause different kinds of men and even women (*Cat.* 24.3). Tacitus marvels that the secrets of the Pisonian conspiracy were guarded by men and women, young and old, rich and poor alike (*Ann.* 15.54.1). Livy reports that the Bacchic rites tainted both men and women (39.8.5). His narrative of the Bacchanalian conspiracy, with its intimations of xenophobia, betrays a preoccupation with the violation of the male citizen body that rendered it servile and effeminate. Sallust, Tacitus, and Josephus cast the conspiracies as battles for freedom over slavery; fear of servile behavior colors all five of the narratives. Conspiracy inevitably involves transgressing the boundaries between public and private; as a result, those who are excluded from public life—slaves and women especially—play a disproportionately large role.

Such a preoccupation with boundary violation gives conspiracy narratives their characteristically moralizing tone. Such transgressions of the boundaries of status, gender, and sexuality are symptomatic of an unease with the unequal relations of power that define Roman society. Catiline, Caligula, and Nero were all reported to have engaged in perverted sexual behavior, but it was easier to find fault with their excessive sexual behavior than with the underlying socioeconomic tensions that caused the political crises in the first place.[3] Under the Julio-Claudians, the morality of conspiracy is reversed. For Tacitus, the Pisonian conspiracy exposes the utter lack of integrity among the senatorial class. Both Tacitus and Josephus capitalize on conspiracy to demonstrate that the state was so corrupt that those who ought to behave properly, namely, the senators, have instead become the conspirators. In contrast to republican conspiracies, the morality of speech and silence is inverted under the Julio-Claudians. Conspirators who stay silent are virtuous, while squealers are contemptible.

Make no mistake, conspiracy was regarded as morally reprehensible, an act in which no decent statesman ought to engage. Thus, Brutus and Cassius remained problematic for the historians. They belonged to the highest class of citizen but engaged in the lowest form of political behavior. They were tyrannicides and therefore heroes; at the same time, they were assassins and therefore villains. When Tacitus says that the assassination of the dictator Caesar seemed to some to be the best of crimes, to some the worst, he states the two opinions using artfully balanced language and then discards them both. When the scale refuses to tip in favor of one opinion over the other, Tacitus (and his reader) can walk away from the dilemma. Both alternatives are dismissed because it is impossible (or embarrassing, or dangerous, or finally meaningless) to choose between them. In such an interpretive situation, according to Barthes, "one no longer needs to choose, but only to endorse."[4] This unresolved dilemma transforms Brutus and Cassius into mythological figures, giving them a powerful hold over the imagination. No doubt, they paid with their lives for their actions; regardless of opinion, their fate set a precedent. No matter how praiseworthy tyrannicides can be, assassins must be punished, for while their motives may be good, no state can tolerate unchecked violence.

## READING CONSPIRACY

In a society like ancient Rome, based on large-scale slave ownership, unequal relations of power and status, and the unequal distribution of wealth, conspiracy was doubtless never far from the surface. By exaggerating the exceptionality of conspiracy, the historians were able to circumscribe its effects. The exceptional presence of women and slaves in conspiracy narratives serves to underscore the singular nature of conspiracy. The dual subjectivity of women and slaves, as beings who are not only necessary and beneficial to society but also unpredictable and dangerous, makes them ideal participants in the duplicitous act of conspiracy. Therefore, it is especially important to celebrate them in written word when they behave in ways that are advantageous, so as to assure a male citizen readership that the presence of women and slaves in society can be salutary. Although women are regularly denigrated for their inability to keep secrets,[5] conspiracy renders this flaw a virtue. The transfer of information to women in their capacity as sexual partners inscribes their bodies with knowledge both physically and metaphorically. Instead of leaky vessels, women become tablets to be read. It is a powerful metaphor that drives the story of the assassination of Domitian and persists well beyond his death. Therefore, before closing, I offer one final Roman conspiracy.

Domitian fell victim to a plot in the year 96 C.E.[6] According to the epitome of Dio, "The plot was not unknown to Domitia, the emperor's wife . . . for Domitia was ever an object of Domitian's hatred and consequently she stood in terror of her life." The next part of the narrative is qualified by a statement in the first person: "For my part, I have heard also the following account." Thus, the historian feels it necessary to exonerate himself for the story he is about to tell:

> Domitian, having become suspicious of those persons, conceived the desire to kill them all at the same time and wrote their names on a two-leafed tablet of lindenwood, which he placed under his pillow on the couch on which he was wont to take his rest; and one of the naked "whispering" boys filched it away while the emperor was asleep in the daytime and kept it without knowing what it contained. Domitia then chanced upon it, and reading what was written, gave information of the matter to those concerned. Accordingly, they hastened the plot that they already were forming.[7]

Like the other conspiratorial women, Domitia is a link in the chain of causality but with an important difference. The women of the Catilinarian,

Bacchanalian, and Pisonian conspiracies had direct physical contact with conspirators. Domitia, on the other hand, is physically removed from the evidence and kept at a distance from the conspiracy. The boy, not the empress, found the tablets in the emperor's bed. As wife of the emperor, Domitia remains inviolate. The secrets are not hidden in her body, to be physically extracted; rather, they are openly inscribed on the tablets to be read.

The whispering boy who filched the tablet is a peculiar detail. It was apparently customary for the members of court to keep attractive little boys for their amusement and their prattle.[8] Dio describes such a boy at the wedding feast of Augustus and Livia:

> One of the whispering boys, such as the women keep about them for their amusement, naked as a rule, on seeing Livia reclining in one place with Augustus, and Nero in another with a man, asked, "What are you doing here, when your husband is over there?"[9]

Livia's whispering boy asks a very impertinent question that strikes at the legality of Augustus' marriage. For she was six months pregnant by Tiberius Claudius Nero when she divorced him to marry Augustus, who obtained the permission of the priests for the unusual circumstances.

A whisper is a tone reserved for conveying something that ought not be spoken at all; words for whispering in Greek also connote slander.[10] By whispering, one has a certain latitude to say things not otherwise permitted. Whispering is a breach of silence that acknowledges the strictures placed on speech. It is the medium that transmits the secrets of conspiracy not meant to be spoken.[11] Domitian's whispering boy substitutes for the pillow talk that eventually unravels conspiracy.

One last peculiarity of Dio's account of the conspiracy against Domitian deserves attention. Domitian made a list of those he intended to kill; the list proved his undoing. The story is familiar. Caligula kept similar lists and even named them "Sword," and "Dagger," indicating the intended weapon of destruction.[12] Long after the Flavian dynasty, the story repeats itself: a slave of Commodus found a tablet in the emperor's bedroom on which the he recorded his intended victims.[13] Syme believes that Dio imposed contemporary events surrounding the death of Commodus on his account of the death of Domitian.[14] It could also be the case that the slanderous anecdote was handed down from tyrant to tyrant with diminishing detail. Caligula's tablets had names; Domitian's tablets passed from a whispering boy to the empress to the conspirators; Commodus' tablets merely betrayed his intentions. In all three cases, written evidence discloses the tyrant's paranoid counterconspiracy.[15] The rich metahistorical contexts of assassination demonstrate the continued engagement with the past in the present, the tradition and originality, of conspiracy narratives.

In each conspiracy, crucial information resides with women, and possession of knowledge puts the women at risk. The degree of peril they face depends upon their social status. The high-born Porcia and Domitia are removed from direct physical contact with the conspirators. Porcia, not Brutus, inflicts a wound on herself. Only then does Brutus reveal the conspiracy to her. She was not harmed because she knew about the conspiracy of Brutus and Cassius; she could choose the manner of her death: suicide (Plu. *Brut.* 53.4). Domitia, despite her involvement in her husband's assassination, lived well into the second century, honored for her father's reputation more than harmed by her husband's scandal.[16]

On the other hand, women in direct contact with conspirators are more susceptible to physical danger. Curius' sexual behavior with Fulvia, more rough than usual, leads her to deduce the Catilinarian conspiracy. Hispala's attendance on her mistress at the Bacchic rituals inscribes her with knowledge of the secrets of the Bacchantes; she in turn transfers this knowledge to Aebutius via their love affair. Quintilia, mistress of Pompedius, is privy to a conspiracy. Milichus shares the secrets of the Pisonian conspiracy with his wife. Epicharis, fully involved in the Pisonian conspiracy, uses her sexual charms to try to enlist Volusius Proculus. Fulvia and Hispala were threatened with physical harm but did not suffer at the hands of the men who desired to know their secrets. The Julio-Claudian regime offered no such protection to women who were unfortunate enough to possess knowledge of a conspiracy. The actress Quintilia and the prostitute Epicharis faced the gravest consequences of all: torture.

Normally, only slaves were subject to torture. The severity of the Julio-Claudian tyranny, however, is measured by the ease with which Caligula and Nero ordered the torture of persons without regard for their status as slave or free. Torture is the regulated infliction of pain upon a subject by a higher authority. When practiced against Roman citizens, it is a ritual that deprives subjects of their previous status as inviolate persons and confers them with a new status as legible property. The victim is separated from the rest of society. Soldiers face death on the battlefield in a highly structured social order. But torture is inflicted upon the individual, and it confounds social order. Soldiers are reintegrated into society in the ceremonial triumphal parade, while the tortured victim cannot return to society as before. Epicharis must forfeit her life; Quintilia, forever scarred, is compensated beyond her previous status. Torture effects this profound and permanent change.

The tortures of Epicharis and Quintilia conflate the investigation of the conspiracies with the punishment of the suspected conspirators. Detection of the conspiracies is confused with deterrence. Thus, the most extreme treatment of Quintilia and Epicharis again manifests deep confusion of categories and a disturbing violation of boundaries. Such a reading of the role of women in conspiracy narratives attempts to keep bodily practices from being assimilated into discourse and to recognize the materiality of bodily experience, in particular, women's bodily experience. Our picture of women in conspiracy narratives is therefore as physical as it is rhetorical, and we must avoid any interpretation that denies or ignores this duality.[17]

## RIGHTING CONSPIRACY

For every conspiracy, it is possible to detect a counterconspiracy. Cicero could be seen as plotting to bring down Catiline because of his radical economic proposals and the threats he posed to the dominant optimate party. Livy portrays the consul Postumius as engaging in an elaborate counterconspiracy to disband the Bacchic worshipers. Tacitus asserts that there was a Pisonian conspiracy, but he also registers contemporary rumors alleging Nero simply needed a pretext for eliminating his enemies. Josephus records the consul's sentiment that Caligula was a victim of his own treachery.

The direction of the conspiracy, who conspires against whom, depends on one's point of view, determined and shaped by the historian for a distinct purpose. The villainization of Catiline was but a fraction of the propaganda of the late republic pitting optimates against populists. More than the reputation of Cicero's consulship rode on the suppression of the Catilinarian conspiracy; the very fabric of the republic was unraveling. Livy hints that the uncontrolled sexuality of the Bacchantes was a cause of moral decline, rather than admit the possibility that Rome was ill equipped for the upheavals caused by post-Hannibalic imperial expansion. Despite his initial claim to write history *sine ira et studio* ("without animus or eagerness"), Tacitus builds his *Annales* on a solid foundation of anti-Julio-Claudian propaganda. His portrayal of the harsh treatment of the Pisonian conspirators and the bloody aftermath adds to his cause.

Even the two modern American conspiracies that have provided a backdrop for this study are subject to diametric interpretations. The report of the

Warren Commission on the assassination of President Kennedy was anything but definitive. Rather than solve the question of who killed JFK, it became fodder for those who wished to accuse the government of a vast counter-conspiracy. Close scrutiny revealed the many inconsistencies and omissions of evidence and testimony, leading many to believe that the president was killed by forces from within the U.S. government. As for Watergate, several questions remain unanswered. What was the content of the eighteen-and-a-half-minute gap in the recording? Who was "Deep Throat"? And most puzzling, why did Nixon not simply destroy all the White House tapes? According to Kutler,

> Nixon believed that carefully selected excerpts from the tapes could exonerate him in the Watergate matter. . . . Nixon thought his tapes would insure his control of his own history. In a tantalizing passage in his memoirs, Nixon revealed the most deep-seated of his motives. The tapes, he wrote, "were my best insurance against the unforeseeable future. I was prepared to believe that others, even people close to me, would turn against me just as Dean had done, and in that case the tapes would give me at least some protection."[18]

The elaborate conspiracy to cover up his crimes backfired, and all the evidence meant to support him in the end brought him down. Like Caligula, Nixon unwittingly conspired against himself.

The Januslike quality of conspiracy is inescapable, although narrative attempts to disengage the possibilities of counterconspiracy. Each author chooses a side and tells the story accordingly. But the continuity of the historical narrative is, in the final analysis, contrived. As conspiracy disrupts society, so conspiracy narratives are discontinuous in the historical record. Sallust's monograph (as Cicero advises Lucceius) separates the Catilinarian conspiracy from the rest of Roman history. The conventional, annalistic format permits Livy and Tacitus to detach the Bacchanalian and Pisonian conspiracies from the rest of their works, lodging them under distinct rubrics of consular years. In Josephus' work devoted to Jewish history, the assassination of a Roman emperor discretely stands apart. For Appian, the assassination of Caesar is a removable link in a seemingly never-ending chain of civil stasis.

Yet once these historians embark on narrating conspiracy, they complete the journey by disconnecting the possibilities of alternative narrative outcomes and by assigning causality, even where it is tenuous. They succeed only to the extent that the reader is persuaded by the seamless continuity of their narrative. I have tried to show that for the Roman historians, narrating conspiracies that were deliberately shrouded in secrecy and silence was no mean feat. Once we acknowledge that epistemological uncertainty is a fundamental feature of conspiracy narrative, no author escapes censure, no reader finds comfort. Perhaps this, more than anything, explains the lasting fascination of conspiracy for both authors and readers, ancient and modern alike.

# ABBREVIATIONS

Abbreviations for journals and series follow those in *L'Année philologique* 63 (1992), xvii–xxxix. Abbreviations for ancient authors and works and modern collections of ancient sources follow those in H. G. Liddell, R. Scott, and H. S. Jones, *A Greek-English Lexicon* (Oxford 1968) xv–xxxviii; P. G. W. Glare, ed., *Oxford Latin Dictionary* (Oxford 1982) ix–xxi; and S. Hornblower and A. Spawforth, eds., *The Oxford Classical Dictionary*, 3rd edition (Oxford 1996) xxix–liv. Translations (verbatim or adapted) from the Loeb Classical Series are noted. All other translations are my own.

# NOTES

## INTRODUCTION

1. Nixon (1978) 631.

2. Kutler (1990) 429–430; Hoff (1994) 104–105.

3. Kutler (1997) vii.

4. Kutler (1997) 47. Alexander Butterfield was a presidential aide; John Ehrlichman, counsel to the president and chair of the domestic council; John Mitchell, attorney general and chair of the Committee to Re-elect the President; and John Dean, counsel to the president.

5. Thompson (1967); Marrs (1989) 64–72.

6. For the history and reception of the Zapruder film, see Trask (1994) 57–153; Sturken (1997) 26–33.

7. Arist. *Poetica* 1451a36–38: φανερὸν δὲ ἐκ τῶν εἰρημένων καὶ ὅτι οὐ τὸ τὰ γενόμενα λέγειν, τοῦτο ποιητοῦ ἔργον ἐστίν, ἀλλ᾽ οἷα ἂν γένοιτο καὶ τὰ δυνατὰ κατὰ τὸ εἰκὸς ἢ τὸ ἀναγκαῖον. ("It is clear from what has been said that it is the task of the poet not to relate particular events but what might be expected to happen and the possibilities according to probability or necessity.")

8. Herodotus begins his history of the Persian wars by calling his work an ἱστορίης ἀπόδεξις, a display or revelation of knowledge gained through inquiry, and visual perception in particular. On the importance of autopsy in Herodotus, see Hartog (1988) 265; seeing is more reliable than hearing, see Woodman and Martin (1996) 169; autopsy in ancient historiography, see Marincola (1997) 63–86.

9. See Martin (1955) esp. 127.

10. On the date of composition of Nicolaus of Damascus' biography of Augustus, see Wacholder (1962) 25–26.

11. Beesly (1878); Last (1948) 363–364, 366–367; Kaplan (1968); and Wilkins (1994) attempt to rehabilitate Catiline and rescue his character from the blackening effects of the biased sources by reevaluating the evidence.

12. Verg. *A.* 8.668–670; cf. the allusion to the *gens Sergia* at *A.* 5.121. Catiline's crimes were exemplary in Sen. *Dial.* 5.18.2, 6.20.5. See also August. *Conf.* 2.5.11.

13. Hor. *Epod.* 16.6, so Syme (1964) 285, *contra* Mankin (1995) *ad loc.;* Luc. 7.64, 6.793; Mart. 9.70.

14. Liv. 8.18, *contra* Oakley (1998) 595.

15. Juv. 10.286–288; see also 2.27, 8.231–244, 14.41.

16. HA *V. Avidius Cassius* 3.5: *nec defuerunt qui illum Catilinam vocarent;* HA *V. Clodius Albinus* 13.2: *ut non male sui temporis Catilina diceretur.*

17. Sen. *Suas.* 6.26.5–7; for commentary, see Homeyer (1961) 329.

18. Sen. *Suas.* 7.14; Tac. *Dial.* 37.6; Mart. 9.70, cf. 5.69.

19. According to Paul (1966) 96, Sallust's *Bellum Catilinae* was an immediate success. Vergil was familiar with it, so Syme (1964) 286; Woodman (1989) 145 n. 61; Harrison (1997) 74; Ash (2002) 257. It was also read by Fronto *Ad Caesarem et Invicem* 3.12.2, *Ad Antonium* 3.1.2, and is quoted by Gellius 3.1.1, 4.15.1, 6.17.7, 12.9.2, 20.6.14; Serv. *A.* 1.6, 1.195, 1.298, 1.378, 1.488, *G.* 2.499. The epitome of Florus (2.12) follows it quite closely.

20. V. Max. 5.8.5 (cf. Sal. *Cat.* 39.5); 9.1.9; see Bloomer (1992) 111.

21. Quint. *Inst.* 5.10.3 (cf. Sal. *Cat.* 47.2; Cic. *Catil.* 3.9); Ampelius 27.5.

22. Orosius 6.6.5: *interea coniuratio Catilinae adversus patriam per eosdem dies in urbe habita et prodita . . . sed hanc historiam agente Cicerone et describente Sallustio satis omnibus notam nunc a nobis breviter fuisse perstrictam sat est.* ("Meanwhile, in those same days in the city the conspiracy of Catiline against the state was conducted and betrayed . . . but because Cicero wrote an account and Sallust's description is well known enough to everybody, now it is enough for me to have kept the mention brief.")

23. Cf. Eutropius 6.15.

24. Suet. *Aug.* 94.5: *quo natus est die, cum de Catilinae coniuratione ageretur in curia.* Augustus was born in the infamous year 63 but not on October 21. At the beginning of the biography (5.1), Suetonius correctly records the birthday as September 23: *natus est Augustus M. Tullio Cicerone C. Antonio coss. IX Kal. Octob.*

25. *Men.* 835; *Mil.* 857–858, also 1016; *Aul.* 408; *Am.* 703–704; *Cas.* 978–982; *Bac.* 371–372. The Plautine references predate the conspiracy but reveal that the cult was well known to the Romans. Bruhl (1953) 111–113; Tarditi (1954) 273; Nilsson (1957) 12–14; Toynbee (1965) 391; Gallini (1970) 12, 13, 42; Stockert (1972) 402; North (1979) 88; Pailler (1988) 230–231; Bömer (1990) 132; Gruen (1990) 50; Walsh (1994) 4; Nippel (1997) 71; Beard, North, and Price (1998) 93. On the general influence of the contemporary Roman comic theater for this episode of Livy, see Walsh (1996); Wiseman (1998) 48. Arcellaschi (1990) esp. 39 argues that the *Bacchides* was produced in 188 B.C.E. and is a parody of the Bacchic rites described in Livy.

26. Verg. *A.* 4.301–303, 469–470; Luc. 1.674–675; Sil. 4.774–777; Stat. *Theb.* 5.92–94. Cf. Prop. 1.3.5–6; Sen. *Tro.* 672–677. Bacchic imagery was a commonplace in Latin literature, which, according to Henrichs (1978), is ultimately traced to Euripides. See also Hershkowitz (1998) 35–48.

27. *qui Curios simulant et Bacchanalia vivunt;* see Braund (1996) *ad loc.*

28. Pliny, *Ep.* 10.96.8: *quo magis necessarium credidi ex duabus ancillis, quae ministrae dicebantur, quid esset veri, et per tormenta quaerere.* ("Wherefore I believed it was more necessary to extract the truth by torture from two slave women, whom they call deaconesses.")

See Cova (1974) 107–108; Pailler (1988) 759–770; Bauman (1990) 343; North (1992) 181–182; Nippel (1997) 71–72. Sherwin-White (1966) 692 and esp. 705 discredits the notion that Pliny's terminology is drawn from Livy's account of the Bacchanalian affair.

29. August. *C.D.* 6.9; see also Tertullian *Apol.* 6.7. Robin (1979) 70–71; Burkert (1998) 380–381.

30. Petronius: Connors (1994). Lucan: O'Gorman (2000) 155–156. See also Griffin (1986) 65 on Seneca, and Laird (2000) 153–161 on Seneca, Lucan, and Petronius in the *Annales.*

31. HA *V. Clodius Albinus* 12.10: *non eam gratiam mihi redditis quam maiores vestri contra Pisonianam factionem, quam item pro Traiano, quam nuper contra Avidium Cassium praestiterunt.* Piso is also mentioned in a statement on the difficulties of writing biography: HA *V. Pescennius Niger* 9.1–2: *non enim facile, ut in principio libri diximus, quisquam vitas eorum mittit in libros, qui aut principes in re publica non fuerunt aut a senatu appellati non sunt imperatores, aut occisi citius ad famam venire nequiverunt. inde quod latet Vindex, quod Piso nescitur.* ("For it is not easy, as I said at the outset of this chapter, for anyone to record the lives of those who were not leading men in the state, or who were not declared emperors by the senate, or who were not able to achieve fame because they were killed too soon. Hence Vindex is obscure and Piso unknown.")

32. Dio 60.4.5–6; Barrett (1989) 178–180; Varner (2000) 96–113.

33. Wiseman (1998) 60–63 suggests that the momentous crossing of the Rubicon may have been the subject of a satyr play at Rome.

34. Verg. *G.* 1.463–497 with Thomas (1988) *ad loc.*; Plut. *Caes* 63.1–6; Suet. *Caes.* 81.1–2; Dio 44.17.1, 18.4; App. *B.C.* 2.116; V. Max. 1.6.13, 8.11.2; Vell. 2.57.2; Obsequ. 67; Schol. Horace *Carm.* 1.2.1–2: *post occisum C. Caesarem quem Cassius et Brutus aliique coniurati interfecerunt multa portenta sunt visa.*

35. App. *B.C.* 2.117; Suet. *Jul.* 82; Liv. *Per.* 116; Florus 2.13.95; Zonaras 10.11.D; Eutropius 6.25; V. Max. 4.5.6; Plut. *Caes.* 66. Dio 44.19.5 records "many wounds" πολλοῖς τραύμασι. Nic. Dam. 24 alone records thirty-five.

36. Tac. *Ann.* 4.35.3: *nec derunt, si damnatio ingruit, qui non modo Cassii et Bruti, sed etiam mei meminerint,* with Rawson (1986). See also Ampelius 19.5.

37. Although the manuscripts transmit the title *Bellum Catilinae* or variants of this title, Sallust clearly announces his subject matter at 4.3: *de Catilinae coniuratione.* Ramsey (1984) 5 n. 9 suggests that by emphasizing the event as a *bellum,* Sallust responds to Cicero's claims in the orations to have delivered the republic from the threat of war; see also Vretska (1976) *ad loc.* Both Livy and the senatorial inscription refer to a Bacchanalian conspiracy (*ad intestinae coniurationis vindictam* ["for the purpose of punishing an internal conspiracy"], 39.8.1; *coniourase neve comvovise neve conspondise* ["not to conspire or make vows or make promises together"], *ILS* 18.13), and Tacitus opens the year 65 C.E. with the announcement of the Pisonian conspiracy (*aucta coniuratione,* 15.48.1).

38. Trojan War: Verg. *A.* 4.426: *Aulide iuravi,* "having sworn an oath at Aulis" (and Serv. *A. ad loc.: Aulis insula est in qua coniurarunt Graeci se non ante reversuros quam Troia caperetur* ["Aulis is the island where the Greeks swore a communal oath not to return until Troy was captured"]); Hor. *Carm.* 1.15.7; Man. 3.7; Ov. *Met.* 12.6; Stat. *Ach.* 1.36; see also

Quint. *Decl.* 306.13.1; Mela 2.45.5; Serv. *A.* 11.279; Hyg. *Fab.* 95. Lemnos: Stat. *Theb.* 5. 162–163; Hyg. *Fab.* 15; Liv. 34.2.3: *virorum omne genus in aliqua insula coniuratione muliebri ab stirpe sublatum esse.* ("Every kind of man on a certain island was utterly destroyed by a women's conspiracy.")

39. See Nicolet (1980) 102–105; Campbell (1984) 19–23; Weinstock (1971) 223–227.

40. Liv. 22.38.2–4: *Tum quod nunquam antea factum erat, iure iurando ab tribunis militum adacti milites; nam ad eam diem nihil praeter sacramentum fuerat iussu consulum conventuros neque iniussu abituros; et ubi ad decuriandum aut centuriandum convenissent, sua voluntate ipsi inter sese decuriati equites, centuriati pedites coniurabant sese fugae atque formidinis ergo non abituros neque ex ordine recessuros nisi teli sumendi aut petendi et aut hostis feriendi aut civis servandi causa.* ("An oath was then administered to the soldiers by their tribunes, something they had never done before. For until that day there had only been the general oath to assemble at the bidding of the consuls and not depart without their orders; then after assembling, they would exchange a voluntary pledge amongst themselves, the cavalrymen in their decuries and the infantry in their centuries, that they would not quit their ranks for flight or fear, but only to take up or seek a weapon, either to strike an enemy or save a comrade." tr. Loeb, adapted.) Cf. Frontinus *Str.* 4.1.4: *ceterum ipse inter se coniurabant se fugae atque formidinis causa non abituros neque ex ordine recessuros nisi teli petendi feriendive hostis aut civis servandi causa.* ("But they swore an oath among themselves that they would not depart for flight or fear nor quit ranks unless to seek a weapon either to strike an enemy or to save a comrade.")

41. Serv. *A.* 8.1: *aut certe si esset tumultus, id est bellum Italicum vel Gallicum, in quibus ex periculi vicinitate erat timor multus, quia singulos interrogare non vacabat, qui fuerat ducturus exercitum ibat ad Capitolium et exinde proferens duo vexilla, unum russeum, quod pedites evocabat, et unum caeruleum, quod erat equitum—nam caeruleus color maris est, a cuius deo equum constat inventum-dicebat 'qui rem publicam salvam esse vult, me sequatur,' et qui convenissent, simul iurabant: et dicebatur ista militia coniuratio.* Cf. Serv. *A.* 7.614: *coniuratio, quae fit in tumultu, id est Italico bello et Gallico, quando vicinum urbis periculum singulos iurare non patitur, ut inter Fabios fuit.* ("Conspiracy, which occurs in cases of sudden tumult like the Italian or Gallic war, refers to when the nearness of danger to the city does not allow for individual oaths of allegiance, as occurred among the Fabii.")

42. According to Linderski (1984) 77, the joint oath or *coniuratio* was the characteristic element of the calling out of the troops, or the *evocatio*.

43. *ILS* 6087.106. The colony was established in the months just before Caesar's assassination; Hardy (1912) 9.

44. Stockton (1971) 43.

45. Cic. *Ver.* 2.5.10–14. For other slave *coniurationes*, see 2.3.68 and 2.5.17.

46. Cic. *Font.* 21.3: *potest igitur testibus iudex non credere? cupidis et iratis et coniuratis et ab religione remotis non solum potest, sed etiam debet.* ("Therefore is the judge able to mistrust witnesses who are covetous, rash, conspiratorial, and devoid of any sense of obligation? Not only is he able to mistrust them, indeed he is obliged to.") See Vasaly (1993) 194.

47. On the characterization of Gauls in Polybius and Cato, see Williams (2001) 68–99.

48. Cic. *Catil.* 2.11: *omnia sunt externa unius virtute terra marique pacata: domesticum*

*bellum manet, intus insidiae sunt, intus inclusum periculum est, intus est hostis.* ("By the courage of one man, all affairs at home and abroad are settled: the war is waged at home, the plots are laid within, the danger is enclosed within, the enemy is within.")

49. Serv. *A.* 8.5: *nota de re bona coniurationem dici posse: nam coniuratio τῶν μέσων est;* on the concept of neutral words in Greek and Latin, see Wheeler (1988) 93–110.

50. Habinek (1998) 76–78.

51. See Bleicken (1963), esp. 60–61; Kent (1978) 11 with pl. 7.

52. Holland (1961) 305.

53. *RGDA* 25.2: *iuravit in mea verba tota Italia sponte sua et me belli quo vici ad Actium ducem depoposcit. iuraverunt in eadem verba provinciae Galliae Hispainiae Africa Sicilia Sardinia.* On the oath, see Syme (1939) 284; Premerstein (1937) 36; Herrmann (1968) 78–89; Linderski (1984) 79.

54. E.g., M. Livius Drusus (91 B.C.E.): D.S. 37.11. Cinna's oath to Sulla (88 B.C.E.): Plu. *Sull.* 10.6. Catiline (63 B.C.E.): Sal. *Cat.* 22.1. Antony (44 B.C.E.): App. *B.C.* 3.46, 58; cf. Dio 45.13.5. See Premerstein (1937) 26–36; Herrmann (1968) 54–66.

55. E.g., Tiberius: Tac. *Ann.* 1.7; Dio 57.3.2; cf. Mitford (1960). Caligula: *ILS* 190. See Premerstein (1937) 36–60; Bauman (1967) 222–229; Herrmann (1968) 99–115.

56. Macherey (1978) theorizes the relationship between the circumstances of production and the literature produced.

57. I.e., a reversal of the usual anxiety of influence that dominates the production of Latin literature; see Braund (2002) 242–264.

58. E.g., for Tacitus, see Rutland (1978); Kaplan (1979); Syme (1981) 50; Santoro-L'hoir (1994); Joshel (1997) 227.

59. Archer, Fischler, and Wyke (1994) xvii; Skinner (1997) 8.

60. Richlin (1992); Edwards (1993) 35–36, 57.

61. Braund (2002) 152–175 skillfully explores the problems that different types of evidence present for our understanding of "real" lives.

62. Skinner (1997) 5.

63. A similar strategy is at work in Roman *exemplum* literature; see Parker (1998).

64. Paul (1985) 17. The generalization persists well beyond antiquity, e.g., *The Complaynt of Scotlande*, an early English text written in 1549, records that "sometimes conspiracy is revealed through the ease of the conspirators who show their secret to a woman or a friend whom they love." Murray (1872) XV.132. The urge to implicate a woman in a conspiracy is irresistible; Marilyn Monroe has been repeatedly accused of involvement in conspiracies surrounding the Kennedys; see Baty (1995).

65. A category from New Comedy: Scafuro (1989) 125; Santoro-L'hoir (1992) 91, 135; McGinn (1998) 89.

66. Cf. Belsey (1980) esp. 4; this is the approach to morality taken by Edwards (1993) esp. 12, and to literary allusion by Hinds (1998) esp. 40.

67. McCarthy (2000) 24–25.

68. On barbers, see Fitzgerald (2000) 49; messengers, 59. Bradley (1984) 31–45 and (1994) 107–131 outlines the major ways slaves demonstrated resistance, ranging from open revolt to deliberate idleness.

69. Plin. *Ep.* 3.14.5: *vides quot periculis quot contumeliis quot ludibriis simus obnoxii; nec est quod quisquam possit esse securus, quia sit remissus et mitis; non enim iudicio domini sed scelere perimuntur.* Cf. the remarks of Cassius Longinus as recorded by Tac. *Ann.* 14.43–44 on the murder of Pedanius Secundus; see Nörr (1983), Wolf (1988), Ginsburg (1993) 96–103.

70. On the obligation of the slave's silence in the presence of his master, cf. Bömer (1990) 134; on broken silence as a betrayal of the master, cf. Fitzgerald (2000) 59; on torture, see Brunt (1980).

71. Buckland (1969) 86–91; Finley (1980) 93–94; Brunt (1980); Watson (1987) 84; Bradley (1994) 165–170.

72. For the ancient arguments for and against the efficacy of slave torture, see Berry (1996) 290.

73. For this notion, see duBois (1991) 90. Coleman (1993) registers serious reservations about duBois' project, notably the lack of a precise definition that distinguishes between torture for interrogation (as in ancient slave torture), for ordeal, and for punishment.

74. Edwards (1993) 140; moralizing discourse reflects anxieties about status, gender, and the nature of power itself. On institutionalized violence, see Bradley (1984) 118–124; Wiseman (1985) 5–10.

75. Cic. *Clu.* 177: *cum iam tortor atque essent tormenta ipsa defessa neque tamen illa finem facere vellet, quidam ex advocatis, homo et honoribus populi ornatus et summa virtute praeditus, intellegere se dixit non id agi ut verum inveniretur sed ut aliquid falsi dicere cogerentur.* ("Although the torturer and even the tortures were already worn out and still she did not want to stop, one of the counsellors, a man distinguished by public office and possessed of great virtue said that he thought it was done not to find the truth but to compel [the slave] to say something false.") Curt. 6.11.21: *Philotas verone an mendacio liberare se a cruciatu voluerit anceps coniectura est, quoniam et vera confessis et falsa dicentibus idem doloris finis ostenditur.* ("It is difficult to conclude whether Philotas wanted to free himself from torture by truth or by lies, since the same painful result was held out to those who confess the truth as to those who simply lie.")

76. Tac. *Ann.* 14.60.3: *ex quibus una instanti Tigillino castiora esse muliebria Octaviae respondit quam os eius.* Richlin (1992) 93–94 contextualizes the insult in the Roman discourse of the *os impurum* (impure mouth).

77. Garnsey (1970) 145; see also 214. Garnsey lists the victims of the emperors' caprice but fails to mention two women who figure prominently in conspiracies: Quintilia, tortured by the order of Caligula, and Epicharis, tortured by the order of Nero. Their stories are treated below, Chapters 4 and 3.

78. *Bellum Catilinae:* On structure, see the different schema of Vretska (1970), who argues for unity, and Giancotti (1971) 15–84, who believes the monograph is composed of two principal sections built around the central chapter 31. See also Tiffou (1973) 354–361; Drexler (1976) 316–326. For the characterizations of Catiline, Caesar, and Crassus, see, e.g., Beesly (1878); Hardy (1917); Last (1948); Earl (1966) 308–309; for Sempronia, see Paul (1985). For the debt to Thucydides, see esp. the review of scholarship in Scanlon (1980)

11–19; see also Patzer (1970); Bringmann (1972) 107; Syme (1964) 51–56; Paul (1966) 95; Drexler (1976) 314–315. Livy's Bacchanalian affair: Scafuro (1989); Walsh (1996) 188, 192 (dramatic form), 196–198 ("Acts" I–V); Wiseman (1998) 48. On the Pisonian conspiracy in the context of Tacitus' works, see Walker (1952) 131–137; Syme (1958) 407; Baldwin (1967); Corsi Zoli (1972); Martin (1981) 183–184; Rudich (1993) 87–131.

79. I follow Prince (1982), who outlines the characteristics and significance of the narrator, the narration, and the narratee for interpretation of a text.

80. Cobley (2001).

81. See esp. McHale (1978) 250; Laird (1999) 79–115.

82. McHale (1978) 262.

83. Genette (1980) 189–211. According to Fowler (1990) 45 and Laird (1999) 99, the distinction between free indirect discourse and shift in focalization is not rigid and is often indistinguishable.

84. Pagán (1999).

85. Hor. *Ars* 343–344: *omne tulit punctum qui miscuit utile dulci, / lectorem delectando pariterque monendo.* ("He has born every point who mixes usefulness and pleasure by simultaneously delighting and advising the reader.") On pleasure, see Barthes (1975).

86. Barthes (1974) 19, 84–88.

87. On beginnings in classical literature, see Dunn and Cole (1992); on endings, see Roberts, Dunn, and Fowler (1997); in general, see Kermode (1967).

88. E.g., Thuc. 1.1.2 on the greatest war; Tac. *Ann.* 1.1.3: *sine ira et studio;* see Marincola (1997) 215–216 on the magnification of theme; Luce (1989) on programmatic statements of impartiality in the ancient historians.

89. For an application of the concept of cohesion and continuity to a New Testament text, see van Neste (2002) 121.

90. On narrative connection, see Carroll (2001) 118–133.


## CHAPTER ONE

1. Cic. *Fam.* 5.12.2: *tu quoque item civilem coniurationem ab hostilibus externisque bellis seiungeres. equidem ad nostram laudem non multum video interesse, sed ad properationem meam quiddam interest non te exspectare dum ad locum venias ac statim causam illam totam et tempus arripere; et simul, si uno in argumento unaque in persona mens tua tota versabitur, cerno iam animo quanto omnia uberiora atque ornatiora futura sint.*

2. Shackleton Bailey (1977) 318.

3. Cic. *Att.* 2.1.3; cf. Sal. *Cat.* 31.6; for bibliography, see Berry (1996) 55 n. 258.

4. Taylor (1966) 13; see also Lintott (1999) 173–174.

5. *Contra* Gruen (1974) 411, for whom the *lex* does not represent general agitation by aliens or Latins; rather, it was meant to counter the political aims of Crassus.

6. Yavetz (1963) 491–492.

7. Magie (1950) vol. 1, 344–345; Sherwin-White (1984) 176–185; *CAH*[2] IX, 242–243.

8. Cic. *Man.*; Plu. *Pomp.* 33-42; Magie (1950) vol. 1, 351-352; Sherwin-White (1984) 188-190. For the political history of Armenia in Roman times from Pompey to the commission of Corbulo, see Debevoise (1938) 70-178; Colledge (1967) 36-50; *CAH²* X, 641-675.

9. The *gens Sergia* claimed to trace its descent from one of the companions of Aeneas, cf. *A.* 5.121.

10. Beesly (1878) 25-26 insists there was no first conspiracy. Hardy (1917) 160-166 argues that (1) it was covered up by the senate, (2) Caesar and Crassus were behind it, and (3) at the very least it ushered in an atmosphere of suspicion and distrust. Frisch (1947) catalogues the sources and surveys the scholarship on the first Catilinarian conspiracy, and upon reevaluating the character of Crassus, he concludes that there was no conspiracy proper; cf. Brunt (1957). The exacting source criticism of Henderson (1950) 13-14 debunks the myth of the first Catilinarian conspiracy. According to Stevens (1963), the sources reveal that a plot was believed to have existed. Earl (1963) 127 and (1966) 309, Seager (1964), Syme (1964) 88-102, Gruen (1969), and Bringmann (1972) 102-108 maintain that the account of Sallust is fundamentally flawed. See also the review in Drexler (1976) 86-106. Berry (1996) 150-154, 265-272 reviews the evidence for the conspiracy from the point of view of the *Pro Sulla*.

11. It is interesting to note, however, that none of these uses denote autopsy of the conspiracy per se. See Earl (1966) 307; Paul (1966) 87; Marincola (1997) 11.

12. Skard (1932) 85; see also Vretska (1976) 137.

13. 14.7: *fuisse nonnullos qui*; 15.2: *pro certo creditur*; 17.7 and 22.1: *fuere item ea tempestate qui*; 22.3: *nonnulli . . . existumabant*; 24.3: *ea tempestate . . . dicitur*; 43.2: *hoc modo dicebantur*; 48.3: *quem ad Catilinam proficiscentem ex itinere retractum aiebant*; 48.7: *erant eo tempore qui*; 59.3: *quam bello Cimbrico C. Marius in exercitu habuisse dicebatur*.

14. 17.7, 22.1, 24.3, 48.7.

15. This is an example of Sallust reporting the views not of contemporaries, but of received tradition. Cf. 15.2, 59.3, and 6.1, *sicuti ego accepi* (of the Roman constitution).

16. Sal. *Cat.* 17.3-7: *eo convenere senatorii ordinis P. Lentulus Sura, P. Autronius, L. Cassius Longinus, C. Cethegus, P. et Ser. Sullae Ser. filii, L. Vargunteius, Q. Annius, M. Porcius Laeca, L. Bestia, Q. Curius; praeterea ex equestri ordine M. Fulvius Nobilior, L. Statilius, P. Gabinius Capito, C. Cornelius; ad hoc multi ex coloniis et municipiis, domi nobiles. erant praeterea complures paulo occultius, consili huiusce participes nobiles, quos magis dominationis spes hortabatur quam inopia aut alia necessitudo. ceterum iuventus pleraque, sed maxume nobilium, Catilinae inceptis favebat: quibus in otio vel magnifice vel molliter vivere copia erat, incerta pro certis, bellum quam pacem malebant. fuere item ea tempestate qui crederent M. Licinium Crassum non ignarum eius consili fuisse.*

17. Cf. Dio 44.14.3: "There is no need to give a full list of the names [of those conspiring against Caesar], for I might thus become wearisome." tr. Loeb.

18. Tacitus follows the practice; see Pauw (1980) 89-90.

19. Cf. Earl (1966) 308-309.

20. See Bal (1985) 100-118; de Jong (1987) 29-31, employed by Ash (1999) 174 n. 23. For a critique of Genette's focalization, see Bal (1991) 75-108; Rood (1998) 11-14. For a refinement, see Fowler (1990).

21. Bal (1991) 83.

22. On the theory of *inventio* in Cicero, see Woodman (1988) 87–94.

23. On the relevance of the prologue to the rest of the *Cat.*, see Rambaud (1946) 120; Leeman (1954) 326; La Penna (1959) 26; Earl (1961) 10; Williams (1968) 619–633; Tiffou (1973); Drexler (1976) 315–317; Hock (1988) 17; Schmal (2001) 110–127.

24. Sal. *Cat.* 1.1–2: *veluti pecora quae natura prona atque ventri oboedientia finxit. sed nostra omnis vis in animo et corpore sita est: animi imperio, corporis servitio magis utimur.*

25. So Roller (2001) 221 argues that freedom is a negatively defined, default category, with no conceptual core except as "the condition of being not-a-slave."

26. Sal. *Cat.* 20.6: *quom considero quae condicio vitae futura sit, nisi nosmet ipsi vindicamus in libertatem.* With the technical phrase *vindicare in libertatem,* Catiline asserts that they are wrongly held in slavery.

27. Sal. *Cat.* 52.6: *libertas et anima nostra in dubio est.* Again, note that *libertas* is not asserted but rather is threatened.

28. Sal. *Cat.* 48.1: *veluti ex servitute erepta.*

29. Barthes (1986) 129.

30. Ramsey (1984) *ad loc.* identifies *sed* (8.1) and *igitur* (9.1) as marking a digression.

31. Cf. Tac. *Ann.* 2.26.2 (Tiberius recalls Germanicus from the Rhine): *satis iam eventuum, satis casuum* ("enough already of successes, enough disasters"). On the tone of impatience in the phrase, see Fraenkel (1957) 243.

32. For studies of the historiography of battles, see Plathner (1934); Gaida (1934); Wellesley (1969); Gowing (1992) 209–223; Ash (1999a). For battles in epic, see Willcock (1983); Bonds (1985); Horsfall (1987); Rossi (1997); Ash (2002). On battle exhortations, see Woodman and Martin (1996) 346. On the motif of the captured city, see Paul (1982); Rossi (2002). On the sacked city, see Ziolkowski (1993). For aftermath, see Pagán (2000a) 425–434. See Gowing (1992) 209–210 for the two schools of thought regarding battle scenes in antiquity: either battles demanded strict attention to detail and accuracy or they were opportunities to arouse pathos through embellished descriptions.

33. Cf. Bauman (1992) 67–69.

34. Cic. *Catil.* 2.7: *quis tota Italia veneficus, quis gladiator, quis latro, quis sicarius, quis parricida, quis testamentorum subiector, quis circumscriptor, quis ganeo, quis nepos, quis adulter, quae mulier infamis, quis corruptor iuventutis, quis corruptus, quis perditus inveniri potest qui se cum Catilina non familiarissime vixisse fateatur?*

35. Cf. the list of upstanding statesmen, mentioned by name, and their contributions at Cic. *Sest.* 101.

36. Sal. *Cat.* 24.3–4: *ea tempestate plurimos quoiusque generis homines adscivisse sibi dicitur, mulieres etiam aliquot, quae primo ingentis sumptus stupro corporis toleraverant, post, ubi aetas tantummodo quaestui neque luxuriae modum fecerat, aes alienum grande conflaverant. per eas se Catilina credebat posse servitia urbana sollicitare, urbem incendere, viros earum vel adiungere sibi vel interficere.*

37. App. *B.C.* 2.1.2: χρήματα δ᾽ ἀγείρων πολλὰ παρὰ πολλῶν γυναικῶν, αἳ τοὺς ἄνδρας ἤλπιζον ἐν τῇ ἐπαναστάσει διαφθερεῖν. On Appian's use of Sallust, see Barbu (1934) 9–18.

38. Williams (1968) 540–541.

39. Cf. Paul (1985).

40. The adverbial phrase *quoque modo* is textually difficult. Vretska (1976), Ramsey (1984), and Reynolds (1991) prefer *quoque modo,* and the two commentators both suggest *quoque* in the distributive sense of "what she had learned and by what means." For double questions, cf. Ovid *Amores* 2.8.27–28: *quoque loco tecum fuerim quotiensque, Cypassi, / narrabo dominae quotque quibusque modis.* ("I shall tell where and how many times I was with you and how often and in how many ways.") McKeown (1998) *ad loc.* provides parallels for such "familiar forensic terms." Liv. 39.14.3 employs a similar juridical line of questioning: *rem ad senatum Postumius defert, omnibus ordine expositis, quae delata primo, quae deinde ab se inquisita forent* ("Postumius laid the information before the senate, everything disclosed in order: what had been laid before him first, and then what he had ascertained"); see Festugière (1954) 87. The variant reading *quoquo modo* is found in inferior manuscripts. *Quoquo modo* is used by Tac., *Ann.* 3.19.2, where Woodman and Martin (1996) *ad loc.* suggest it alludes to our passage. See also *Ann.* 15.53.4, *quoquo modo,* discussed in Chapter 3 below.

41. Sal. *Cat.* 23.3–5: *erat ei cum Fulvia, muliere nobili, stupri vetus consuetudo; quoi cum minus gratus esset quia inopia minus largiri poterat, repente glorians, maria montisque polliceri coepit, et minari interdum ferro, ni sibi obnoxia foret; postremo ferocius agitare quam solitus erat. at Fulvia, insolentiae Curi causa cognita, tale periculum rei publicae haud occultum habuit, sed sublato auctore de Catilinae coniuratione quae quoque modo audierat compluribus narravit. ea res in primis studia hominum adcendit ad consulatum mandandum M. Tullio Ciceroni.* For *consuetudo* as a euphemism for sexual intercourse, cf. Suet. *Cl.* 1.1: *per adulterii consuetudinem* and Hurley (2001) *ad loc.*

42. Hardy (1917) 170–171; Earl (1961) 87; Drexler (1976) 324.

43. Hardy (1917); Syme (1964) 77–79 on Sallust's displacement of the *senatus consultum.*

44. E.g., Cic. *Catil.* 3.1.1: *laboribus, consiliis, periculis meis* ("through my efforts, plans, personal risks"); 3.1.3: *semper vigilavi et providi* ("I was constantly watchful and observant"). On Ciceronian foresight and the effect of the repetition of *sciam* in *Catil.* 1.24, see Batstone (1994) 253.

45. App. *B.C.* 2.3 and D.S. 40.5 call them lovers; see Syme (1964) 77. Plu. *Cic.* 16.2 mentions Fulvia but not in connection with Curius; Suet. *Jul.* 17 mentions Curius as an informant (cf. Sal. *Cat.* 28.2 where Curius warns Cicero *per Fulviam*) but not Fulvia.

46. D. S. 40.5: ἕνα τούτων διακείμενον ἐρωτικῶς πρός τινα παιδίσκην καὶ ὑπὸ ταύτης παραθεωρούμενον πλεονάκις λέγειν φασὶν ὅτι μετ᾽ ὀλίγας ἡμέρας ἔσται τοῦ πνεύματος αὐτῆς κύριος. τῆς δὲ θαυμαζούσης τὸ ῥηθὲν καὶ μὴ δυναμένης νοῆσαι τὴν αἰτίαν τῆς ἀπειλῆς, τὸν μὲν νεανίσκον μένειν ἐπὶ τῆς ἀνατάσεως, τὴν δὲ κατὰ τὴν συμπεριφορὰν καὶ τὴν μετ᾽ αὐτοῦ μέθην ὑποκρινομένην κεχαρισμένος ὁμιλίας ἀξιοῦν δηλῶσαι τίνα ποτὲ νοῦν ἔχει τὸ ῥηθέν· τὸν δὲ διὰ τὸν ἔρωτα βουλόμενον ταύτῃ χαρίσασθαι πᾶσαν τὴν ἀλήθειαν μηνῦσαι· τὴν δὲ προσποιηθεῖσαν μετ᾽ εὐνοίας καὶ χαρᾶς δεδέχθαι τὸν λόγον σιωπῆσαι, τῇ δὲ ὑστεραίᾳ πρὸς τὴν τοῦ ὑπάτου Κικέρωνος γυναῖκα καταντήσασαν καὶ κατ᾽ ἰδίαν διαλεχθεῖσαν περὶ

τούτων ἀπαγγεῖλαι τοὺς ῥηθέντας λόγους ὑπὸ τοῦ νεανίσκου, καὶ τούτῳ τῷ τρόπῳ φανερὰν γενέσθαι τὴν τούτων συνωμοσίαν. τὸν δὲ τὰ μὲν ἀνατάσει καὶ φόβῳ, τὰ δὲ παρακλήσει φιλανθρώπῳ χρησάμενον μαθεῖν ἀκριβῶς παρ᾽ αὐτῶν τὴν ὅλην ἐπιβουλήν. tr. Loeb.

47. Cicero is outraged that the courtesan Chelidon received matters of business on Verres' behalf, subverting all protocol (*Ver.* 2.1.136–137).

48. Tac. *Ann.* 3.15, 17; *SCPP* 109–120; Caballos, Eck, and Fernández (1996) 193–196.

49. Joshel (1992) 117; see also Jed (1989); Joplin (1990); Vandiver (1999).

50. Even if the genre demanded chronological exposition of events, so Woodman (1988) 85, we know that historians rearranged the order of events to suit their needs.

51. Sanga is mentioned only in App. *B.C.* 2.1.4 and Sallust. Dio 37.33.1 mentions that Cicero has many informants in his employment, but he does not mention Sanga at 37.34.1, although his name may have appeared in this lacunose paragraph.

52. Vretska (1976) *ad loc.*

53. Plu. *Cic.* 18.7: καὶ πολλοὺς μὲν ἔχων ἔξωθεν ἐπισκοποῦντας τὰ πραττόμενα καὶ συνεξιχνεύοντας αὐτῷ, πολλοῖς δὲ τῶν μετέχειν δοκούντων τῆς συνωμοσίας διαλεγόμενος κρύφα καὶ πιστεύων. ("He had many men outside the conspiracy to keep watch on their actions and help track them down; he conferred secretly and gained the trust of many who were supposed to belong to the conspiracy.")

54. Cic. *Catil.* 3.9: *introducti autem Galli ius iurandum sibi et litteras a P. Lentulo, Cethego, Statilio ad suam gentem datas esse dixerunt.* ("Furthermore, upon being led in, the Gauls said they had sworn oaths with each other and that letters had been given to them by Lentulus, Cethegus, and Statilius.")

55. On the historiographical significance of the *Origines*, see Astin (1978) 211–239; for its influence on Sallust, see Schmal (2001) 145–146.

56. Levene (2000).

57. Vretska (1970) 85: "Der Verrat der Allobroger ermöglicht allein die Aufdeckung der Verschwörung."

## CHAPTER TWO

1. Cato, *Orat.* 68 Malcovati; Frank (1927) 130; McDonald (1944) 32; Tarditi (1954) 277; Cova (1974) 89; Astin (1978) 74; Bauman (1990) 336. In his speech on the punishment of the Catilinarians, Cato (as reported by Sallust) might have drawn upon this lost speech of his great-grandfather, especially for the notion that the senate could not afford to wait for the conspirators to perpetrate their crimes before taking harsh, preemptive measures (Sal. *Cat.* 52.4). For further evidence of the influence of Cato the Elder on this speech, see Vretska (1976); Ramsey (1984) *ad* 52.4, 52.7; and the excellent study by Levene (2000).

2. *ILS* 18: (1) *Q. Marcius L. f., Sp. Postumius L. f. cos. senatum consoluerunt nonis Octob. apud aedem | Duelonai. Scribendo arfuerunt M. Claudius M. f., L. Valerius P. f., Q. Minucius C. f.*

*De Bacanalibus, quei foideratei | esent, ita exdeicendum censuere:*

'Neiquis eorum Bacanal habuisse velet; sei ques | esent, quei sibei deicerent necesus ese Bacanal habere, eeis utei ad pr. urbanum | (5) Romam venirent, deque eeis rebus, ubei eorum verba audita esent, utei senatus | noster decerneret, dum ne minus senatoribus C adesent quom ea res cosoleretur. | Bacas vir nequis adiese velet ceivis Romanus neve nominus Latini neve socium | quisquam, nisei pr. urbanum adiessent, isque de senatuos sententiad, dum ne | minus senatoribus C adesent quom ea res cosoleretur, iousiset. Censuere. |

(10) Sacerdos nequis vir eset; magister neque vir neque mulier quisquam eset; | neve pecuniam quisquam eorum comoinem habuise velet; neve magistratum, | neve pro magistratud, neque virum neque mulierem quiquam fecise velet; | neve post hac inter sed coniourase neve comvovise neve conspondise | neve conpromesise velet; neve quisquam fidem inter sed dedise velet. | (15) Sacra in oquoltod ne quisquam fecise velet; neve in poplicod neve in | preivatod neve extrad urbem sacra quisquam fecise velet, nisei | pr. urbanum adieset, isque de senatuos sententiad, dum ne minus | senatoribus C adesent quom ea res cosoleretur, iousiset. Censuere. |

(19) Homines plous V oinvorsei virei atque mulieres sacra ne quisquam | fecise velet, neve inter ibei virei plous duobus, mulieribus plous tribus | arfuise velent, nisei de pr. urbani senatuosque sententiad, utei suprad | scriptum est.'

Haice utei in conventionid exdeicatis ne minus trinum | noundinum, senatuosque sententiam utei scientes esetis eorum | sententia ita fuit: 'sei ques esent, quei arvorsum ead fecisent, quam suprad |

(25) scriptum est, eeis rem caputalem faciendam censuere' atque utei | hoce in tabolam ahenam inceideretis, ita sentatus aiquom censuit, | uteique eam figier ioubeatis, ubei facilumed gnoscier potisit; atque | utei ea Bacanalia, sei qua sunt, extrad quam sei quid ibei sacri est, | ita utei suprad scriptum est, in diebus X, quibus vobeis tabelai datai | (30) erunt, faciatis utei dismota sient. In agro Teurano. tr. Walsh (1994).

3. Liv. 39.8.3: consulibus ambobus quaestio de clandestinis coniurationibus decreta est, and 39.14.3, rem ad senatum Postumius defert. Gelzer (1936), contra Fraenkel (1932).

4. Méautis (1940), esp. 479.

5. McDonald (1944) 26–27; Levi (1969).

6. Tarditi (1954) 284; see also Nilsson (1957) 14; Pailler (1988) 600–612; Wiseman (1998) 47.

7. Tarditi (1954) 287; for a discussion of Livy's sources, see also Pailler (1988) 386–398.

8. North (1979) 91.

9. Toynbee (1965) 390–391.

10. Gruen (1990) 58–65.

11. Lintott (1968) 107–124; Gruen (1974) 224–227; Austin (1988) ad 1.7; Berry (1996) 14–16.

12. Sal. Cat. 31 is the earliest prosecution under this law on record; Ps. Sal. In Cic. 2.3; cf. Cic. Cael. 70.

13. Cf. Nippel (1997) 68.

14. Bruhl (1953) 100.

15. Cf. Cova (1974) 107.

16. See Nippel (1995) 27–29.

17. Bauman (1990) 342–343.

18. Lintott (1999) 89–93. In both the Catilinarian and Bacchanalian conspiracies, the senate opposed the unproven threat of conspiracy with the *senatus consultum*, a vague institution based on custom (*mos*) rather than statute (*lex*) that ignored strict legality. Under the *senatus consultum*, the safety of the republic was entrusted to the consuls or other magistrates to take any measure necessary to counter a violent threat to public security. The enactment of a *senatus consultum* occludes the paradox that conspiracy can only be punished if it is *not* detected.

19. North (1979) 90–91.

20. Cf. Béquignon (1941) 190.

21. Nilsson (1957) 19–20; see also North (1992) 183 and Beard, North, and Price (1998) 95–96 on the destruction of the cult; Bruhl (1953) 116 and Toynbee (1965) 402 on its long-term resilience.

22. Cf. Sal. *Cat.* 12.2: *luxuria atque avaritia*, "indulgence and also greed."

23. Ogilvie (1965) 28–29; Edwards (1993) 176–178.

24. Béquignon (1941) 189; Bruhl (1953) 100.

25. Nilsson (1957) 19.

26. Gruen (1990) 47.

27. Frank (1927) 131.

28. McDonald (1944) 26.

29. Tarditi (1954) 276–277.

30. Bruhl (1953) 107.

31. Gruen (1990) 60–61. Such exceptionality defines the conspiratorial woman.

32. Gruen (1990) 49–50 summarizes.

33. For the terminology, see Robin (1979).

34. Pl. *Am.* 702–704: *quid vis fieri? / non tu scis? Bacchae bacchanti si velis advorsarier, / ex insana insaniorem facies, feriet saepius.*

35. Pl. *Aul.* 408–410: *neque ego umquam nisi hodie ad Bacchas veni in Bacchanal coquinatum, / ita me miserum et meos discipulos fustibus male contuderunt. / totus doleo atque oppido perii, ita me iste habuit senex gymnasium.*

36. Adams (1982) 145–149; Williams (1999) 62–63.

37. Pailler (1988) 233; on dating the plays, see Stockert (1972).

38. Gruen (1990) 50.

39. Liv. 39.8.7, 8: *nec unum genus noxae stupra, promiscua ingenuorum feminarumque erant . . . multa dolo, pleraque per vim audebantur; occulebat vim quod prae ululatibus tympanorumque et cymbalorum strepitu nulla vox quiritantium inter stupra et caedes exaudiri poterat.*

40. Liv. 39.10.7: *ut quisque introductus sit, velut victimam tradi sacerdotibus; eos deducere in locum qui circumsonet ululatibus cantuque symphoniae et cymbalorum et tympanorum pulsu, ne vox quiritantis cum per vim stuprum inferatur exaudiri possit.*

41. Adams (1982) 200–201.

42. Gardner (1991) 121–125.

43. Treggiari (1991) 264.

44. Fantham (1991) 270–273.

45. Williams (1999) 96–124; cf. Walters (1997).

46. During the war against the Cimbri (104 B.C.E.), one of Marius' soldiers killed his superior officer, a man related to Marius, for attempting to inflict an unnatural sexual act upon him. The incident exemplifies Roman intolerance of male-male penetration; see Cic. *Mil.* 9; V. Max. 6.1.12; Plut. *Mar.* 14.3; [Quint.] *Decl.* 3. For an in-depth discussion of this incident, see Gunderson (2003) 153–190.

47. Verstraete (1980) 229 goes one step further, referring to the witch-hunt following the uncovering of the Bacchanalian cult as "anti-homosexual hysteria." Burkert (1998) 380 suggests that the disapproval of homosexuality evident in Livy is influenced by Augustus' attitudes and moral reforms.

48. Redfield (1990) 119–124.

49. Burkert (1998) argues that the mystery cults do not necessarily threaten the *polis;* the Bacchanalian affair was exceptional.

50. Finley (1980) 95; Fantham (1991) 270.

51. Lintott (1968) 92; (1999) 95–99.

52. Sal. *Cat.* 51.22: *an quia lex Porcia vetat?* ("or because the *lex Porcia* forbids it?"). Caesar's sarcastic question may be a jab at his opponent, Cato, whose great-grandfather may have delivered an oration on the *lex de provocatione* (Cato, *Orat.* 117 Malcovati); see Levene (2000) 185 esp. n. 64. See also Cic. *Rab. Perd.* 12; Bleicken (1959) 337–341. Cic. *Rep.* 2.54 is the only evidence that there were three *leges.* See Bleicken (1959) 356–363; Zetzel (1995) *ad loc.*

53. Cic. *Fam.* 10.32.3: *deinde abstractum defodit in ludo et vivum combussit . . . et illi misero quiritanti "c.R. natus sum," responderet "abi nunc, populi fidem implora."*

54. Cic. *Ver.* 2.5.162: *nulla vox alia illius miseri inter dolorem crepitumque plagarum audiebatur nisi haec "civis Romanus sum."*

55. For a discussion of *quiritatio* in the republic, see Lintott (1968) 11–16.

56. Gruen (1990) 60–61.

57. Flower (forthcoming); see also Bauman (1992) 35–40.

58. Cf. Cic. *Leg.* 2.15; V. Max. 6.3.7; August. *C.D.* 6.9, 18.13.

59. Rousselle (1989) 61. Santoro-L'hoir (1992) 91 n. 54 points out that Faecenia, with its root in *faex,* conjures up images of dregs and sediment.

60. Liv. 39.9.5: *scortum nobile libertina Hispala Faecenia, non digna quaestu cui ancillula adsuerat.* ("A noble prostitute, a freedwoman named Hispala Faecenia, although unworthy of the profession she had grown accustomed to as a slave girl.")

61. Scafuro (1989) 140 n. 30. Watson (1974) 338–339 suggests that Aebutius, not as innocent as Livy portrays, served as Hispala's pimp.

62. Scafuro (1989) 128–129; Palmer (1989) [1998] 32–34; on sympathy, see Méautis (1940) 479.

63. Adams (1983) 326 demonstrates that *scortum* is the more pejorative term for prostitute than *meretrix* and attributes the historians' preference for *scortum* to the moralizing tendency of historiography.

64. Liv. 39.11.3: *deinde ex auctoritate eius postero die ad consulem Postumium arbitris remotis rem detulit.*

65. Gruen (1990) 62.

66. For the notion that words are tainted and speaking certain words befouls one's mouth, see Richlin (1992) 26–29.

67. Scafuro (1989).

68. Liv. 39.12.6: *ex quo manumissa sit nihil quid ibi fiat scire.*

69. Liv. 39.13.1–2: *eam primo orare coepit ne mulieris libertinae cum amatore sermonem in rem non seriam modo sed capitalem etiam verti vellet.* ("At first she [Hispala] began to beg her [Sulpicia] to be unwilling to turn a freedwoman's banter with her lover into evidence that was not only significant but indeed punishable by death.")

70. Verg. *A.* 6.46–51: *cui talia fanti / ante fores subito non vultus, non color unus / non comptae mansere comae; sed pectus anhelum, / et rabie fera corda tument maiorque videri / nec mortale sonans, adflata est numine quando iam propriore dei.* ("Saying such things before the gates, suddenly she has no color or expression; her hair is dishevelled; her chest heaves, her heart swells with wild frenzy and she appears larger and her voice of no mortal sound, since now she is inspired with the approaching manifestation of the god.")

Verg. *A.* 6.77–80: *at Phoebi nondum patiens immanis in antro / bacchatur vates magnum si pectore possit / excussisse deum; tanto magis ille fatigat / os rabidum fera corda domans fingitque premendo.* ("But the prophetess, not yet enduring Phoebus, rages wildly in the cave, if so she may shake the great god from her chest; so much the more he tires her raving mouth, tames her wild heart, and molds her by constraint.")

71. Liv. 39.12.2: *postquam lictores in vestibulo turbamque consularem et consulem ipsum conspexit, prope exanimata est.*

72. Liv. 39.12.5: *hoc ubi audivit, tantus pavor tremorque omnium membrorum mulierem cepit ut diu hiscere non posset.*

73. Liv. 39.14.1: *peracto indicio advoluta rursus genibus preces easdem . . . repetivit.* ("When she finished giving the information, again she fell to her knees and repeated the same request.")

74. Liv. 39.19.4–7.

75. Agamben (1999) 158.

76. Sloan and Hill (1992) 101.

77. In the three years after the assassination, thirteen material witnesses died violently from gunfire, automobile accidents, suicides, cut throat, and a blow to the neck. For a list of victims, see Marrs (1989) 555–566; Sloan and Hill (1992) 143–158.


CHAPTER THREE


1. Walker (1952) 131 compares general features of the trial of Piso and the Pisonian conspiracy.

2. See Oakley (2000) for recent bibliography on the inscription.

3. Eck (1993) 201; Caballos, Eck, and Fernández (1996) 127 (line 148); Woodman and Martin (1996) 191 (*ad* 3.18.3).

4. Tac. *Ann.* 3.18.4: *mihi, quanto plura recentium seu veterum revolvo, tanto magis lu-*

*dibria rerum mortalium cunctis in negotiis obversantur: quippe fama, spe, veneratione potius omnes destinabantur imperio quam quem futurum principem fortuna in occulto tenebat.*

5. Tacitus rearranges the sequence of campaigns in the East (*Ann.* 13.8–15.31). On displacement in the trial of Piso (3.10–19), see Eck (1993) 203; Caballos, Eck, and Fernández (1996) 153; Woodman and Martin (1996) 69; Talbert (1999). On the other hand, Griffin (1997) 258–260 and Potter (1998) 452–454 are not convinced that Tacitus rearranged the sequence of events for his own purpose.

6. Tac. *Ann.* 3.16.1: *audire me memini ex senioribus visum saepius inter manus Pisonis libellum, . . . nec illum sponte extinctum, verum inmisso percussore. quorum neutrum adseveraverim, neque tamen occulere debui narratum ab iis, qui nostram ad iuventam duraverunt.*

7. Tac. *Ann.* 3.15.3: *relatus domum, tamquam defensionem in posterum meditaretur, pauca conscribit obsignatque et liberto tradit, tum solita curando corpori exsequitur. dein multam post noctem, egressa cubiculo uxore, operiri fores iussit, et coepta luce perfosso iugulo, iacente humi gladio, repertus est.*

8. The suicides of Seneca (15.64), Lucan (15.70), Petronius (16.19), and Thrasea (16.34), for example, were all conducted before witnesses. Tacitus does not question Otho's suicide (*Hist.* 2.49) because his dying groan was heard by slaves; see Ash (1999) 85–89. According to Appian (*B.C.* 2.99), Cato was also alone when he attempted suicide, but his slaves heard his groan and rushed in (unlike the slaves of Otho) to save him. Cato's second, and successful, suicide attempt was thus carried out in silence.

9. Tacitus does not specify what Piso wrote beyond the indefinite *pauca* ("a few things").

10. As Plass (1995) 134 explains of suicide under the principate: "Uncertainty may itself be a political fact and not solely a matter of historical ignorance, inasmuch as rendering responsibility ambiguous was a major aim of both sides."

11. Wells (1985) 48.

12. Laird (2000) demonstrates how the hidden mechanics of a text cause the reader to form an interpretation that is not explicitly expressed.

13. Tac. *Ann.* 3.19.2: *is finis fuit ulciscenda Germanici morte, non modo apud illos homines qui tum agebant, etiam secutis temporibus vario rumore iactata. adeo maxima quaeque ambigua sunt, dum alii quoquo modo audita pro conpertis habent, alii vera in contrarium vertunt, et gliscit utrumque posteritate.*

14. See White (1973) 37 on the historian's *aporia* and (1978) 244 on Nietzsche's notion of the "incapacity of language to serve the purpose of representation," discussed more fully in (1973) 346–356.

15. Woodman and Martin (1996) 196 (*ad* 3.19.2). Often historians regard their subject matter as *maxima;* Tacitus calls the battle of Idistaviso, for example, *magna ea victoria* (2.18.1) and yet he is the only extant historian to mention the skirmish at all.

16. See Woodman and Martin (1996) 195 on "a sharp distinction between the conclusion of the trial and the continuing inconclusiveness of that which the trial had been intended to settle."

17. When reading Tacitus, it is impossible to concur with Baldwin (1967) 439 that

"there was no sustained terror under Nero." Barthes (1982) is more attuned to the cumulative effect of death in the *Annales.*

18. On the identification of Piso, see Champlin (1989).

19. On Nero's ban of Lucan's poetry, see Ahl (1976) 333-353.

20. Wille (1983) 576; Griffin (1984) 166; Woodman (1993) 105 n. 6.

21. Perhaps there is an irony behind the name of Milichus, who is not at all "propitious" toward Scaevinus. For the possibility of meaningful names in Tacitus, see Sinclair (1995) 30-31; Woodman and Martin (1996) 491-493; Woodman (1998) 221-222; Ash (1999) 59.

22. Woodman (1993) 105.

23. Woodman (1993) explores the theatrical aspects of the conspiracy. On the theatricality of the reign of Nero, see Bartsch (1994) 1-62; Shumate (1997).

24. Tac. *Ann.* 15.48.1: *ineunt deinde consulatum Silius Nerva et Atticus Vestinus, coepta simul et aucta coniuratione, in quam certatim nomina dederant senatores eques miles, feminae etiam, cum odio Neronis, tum favore in C. Pisonem.*

25. Cf. also the sketch of Sejanus, 4.1; see Martin and Woodman (1989) *ad loc.*

26. Tac. *Ann.* 15.49.1: *initium coniurationi non a cupidine ipsius fuit; nec tamen facile memoraverim, quis primus auctor, cuius instinctu concitum sit quod tam multi sumpserunt.*

27. On the pattern, see Ginsburg (1981) 53-56.

28. Dio 53.19.2, 3: πρότερον μὲν γὰρ ἔς τε τὴν βουλὴν καὶ ἐς τὸν δῆμον πάντα, καὶ εἰ πόρρω που συμβαίη, ἐσεφέρετο· ... ἐκ δὲ δὴ τοῦ χρόνου ἐκείνου τὰ μὲν πλείω κρύφα καὶ δι' ἀπορρήτων γίγνεσθαι ἤρξατο, εἰ δέ πού τινα καὶ δημοσιευθείη, ἀλλὰ ἀνεξέλεγκτά γε ὄντα ἀπιστεῖται. If we consider these comments beside Livy's assessment (8.40) of the reliability of early republican evidence, much of which was falsified in funeral eulogies or even mendacious inscriptions to aggrandize family prestige, then the contrast between republican and imperial historiography is set in sharp relief. The veracity of the former was compromised for the sake of noble families; the latter, for the sake of the emperor alone. Cf. Cic. *Brut.* 62. For a recent discussion of Tacitus' concern with the validity and value of imperial historiography, see Clarke (2002).

29. For an analysis of *Ann.* 1.6, see Woodman (1995).

30. On the beginning of the *Histories,* see Haynes (1996) 33; on the problem of beginning a historical text, see Kellner (1989) 61-62.

31. Throughout his scholarship, Syme repeats the refrain that Tacitus had difficulty with his choice of the year 14 C.E. as the beginning of the *Annales;* too much had happened that required explanation, e.g., *Ann.* 3.24.3: *sed aliorum exitus, simul cetera illius aetatis memorabo, si effectis in quae <te>tendi, plures ad curas vitam produxero.* ("But I will recount the deaths of the others as well as the rest of the events of that time, if when my current project is completed I should live on for more works of literature.") Woodman and Martin (1996) *ad loc.* read *si effectis quae intendi.* Syme (1958) 372-374, 427; (1970) 6; (1974) 483-484; (1978) 197-198; (1984) 1027-1028, 1041-1042; (1986) 115, 161, 212, 234, 433. Woodman and Martin (1996) 230 "are skeptical." Cf. Griffin (1995) 33-37; Kraus and Woodman (1997) 91. See also the remarks of Goodyear (1972) 99-100.

32. Tac. *Ann.* 15.51.1: *interim cunctantibus prolatantibusque spem ac metum Epicharis*

*quaedam, incertum quonam modo sciscitata (neque illi ante ulla rerum honestarum cura fuerat), accendere et arguere coniuratos.*

33. On alternative explanations, see Lucas (1974) 105; Whitehead (1979); Develin (1983) 85; "trust the last," Rabinowitz (1987) 154–158. The unsurpassed study by Ryberg (1942) demonstrates that Tacitus uses innuendo in his treatment of Tiberius more than other emperors. For a review of the scholarship on Tacitean innuendo, see Sinclair (1991).

34. Tac. *Ann.* 15.53.3–4: . . . *quod C. Plinius memorat. nobis quoquo modo traditum non occultare in animo fuit, quamvis absurdum videretur aut inanem ad spem Antoniam nomen et periculum commodavisse, aut Pisonem notum amore uxoris alii matrimonio se obstrinxisse, nisi si cupido dominandi cunctis adfectibus flagrantior est.* Furneaux (1907) *ad loc.* and Koestermann (1968) *ad loc.* translate *quoquo modo* as "truly or falsely," comparing 3.19.2. At 6.38, *quoquo modo* denotes the indeterminate origin of insults against Tiberius.

35. Syme (1958) 292 eagerly catalogues Pliny's shortcomings and calls this passage in particular a "silly story." On Tacitus' method of citing his predecessors only in certain details, see Mensching (1967) 460–467.

36. On the reliability of sources, see Wiseman (1993) 135. On the perils of common sense, see Barthes (1972) 154–155; Belsey (1980) 3–4. We should also be wary of the common sense (*scilicet*) that guides Cicero's statement about what constitutes history, *De Orat.* 2.15.62: *nam quis nescit primam esse historiae legem ne quid falsi dicere audeat, deinde ne quid veri non audeat? ne quae suspicio gratiae sit in scribendo, ne quae simultatis? haec scilicet fundamenta nota sunt omnibus.* ("For who does not know that the first law of history is to dare not say anything false, then to dare not say anything not true; that there be no hint of favoritism or pretense in one's writing? Of course everyone knows these basic tenets.")

37. Tac. *Ann.* 15.73.2: *ceterum coeptam adultamque et revictam coniurationem neque tunc dubitavere, quibus verum noscendi cura erat, et fatentur, qui post interitum Neronis in urbem regressi sunt.* Cf. Momigliano (1981) 266: "The historian not only has to make sense of the event but also has to make sure that it was an event."

38. Cf. Corsi Zoli (1972).

39. On the significance of names, see above, n. 21.

40. Tac. *Ann.* 15.51.2: *erat navarchus in ea classe Volusius Proculus . . . is mulieri olim cognitus seu recens orta amicitia, dum merita erga Neronem sua et quam in irritum cecidissent aperit adicitque questus et destinationem vindictae, si facultas oreretur, spem dedit posse impelli et plures conciliare.*

41. Tac. *Ann.* 15.51.3: *ergo Epicharis plura; et omnia scelera principis orditur, neque senatui quidquam manere. sed provisum, quonam modo poenas eversae rei publicae daret: accingeretur modo navare operam et militum acerrimos ducere in partes, ac digna pretia exspectaret.*

42. Cf. Liv. 24.5; Curt. 6.8.15; V. Max. 3.3. ext. 1–5.

43. Cf. Dio 62.27.3: "The conduct of a woman named Epicharis also deserves mention. She had been included in the conspiracy and all its details had been entrusted to her without reserve; yet she revealed none of them, though often tortured in all the ways that the skill of Tigellinus could devise." tr. Loeb.

44. Sen. *Con.* 2.5.4: *explicatur crudelitatis adversus infelicem feminam adparatus et illa instrumenta virorum quoque animos ipso visu frangentia ad excutiendam muliebris pectoris*

*conscientiam proponuntur; instate ante denuntiationibus quam tormentis tyrannus et minando torquet: tacet. videt intentum tyranni vultum, videt oculos minaces: tacet. . . . flagellis caeduntur artus, verberibus corpus abrumpitur exprimiturque sanguis ipsis vitalibus: tacet.* tr. Loeb.

45. Sen. *Con.* 2.5.6: *describam nunc ego cruciatus et miram corporis patientiam inter tyrannica tormenta saevientia: extincti sanguine refovebantur ignes; in hoc desinebatur torqueri aliquando ut saepius posset. exquisita verbera, lamnae, eculeus, quidquid antiqua saevitia invenerat, quidquid et nova adiecerat . . . tacuit.* tr. Loeb, adapted.

46. On post-Vergilian obsessions with the melodramatic, the mysterious, and the horrifying, see Williams (1978) 254–261; note that alongside the poets Ovid, Lucan, Valerius, Seneca, and Statius, Williams includes Tacitus. In defense of Lucan's decadence, see Johnson (1987) 123–134, an application of his argument for the counter-classical sensibility (1970). On Statius, see Vessey (1973) 230; Henderson (1991) 47.

47. On the Elder Seneca's educational aims, see Bloomer (1997) 110–153.

48. Tac. *Ann.* 15.57.2: *clariore exemplo libertina mulier in tanta necessitate alienos ac prope ignotos protegendo, cum ingenui et viri et equites Romani senatoresque intacti tormentis carissima suorum quisque pignorum proderent.*

49. Examples of decent behavior were exceptional, *Hist.* 1.3.1; cf. Plin. *Ep.* 5.8.13, 7.33.9.

50. Syme (1958) 532–533; Kajanto (1970) 58; cf. Santoro-L'hoir (1992) 137. Like Griffin (1986) 199, van Hooff (1990) 18 notes that "the authors of antiquity who write for an élite readership raise from anonymity only those self-killers of low status who have some exemplary value."

51. Scafuro (1989) 137 suggests a similar exploitation of Hispala by Livy in his account of the Bacchanalia.

52. Tac. *Ann.* 15.53.2: *ut alii tradidere;* 15.53.3: *quod C. Plinius memorat.* Syme (1958) 534 believes Tacitus was able to interview the participants personally known to him.

53. Tac. *Ann.* 15.54.4: *nam cum secum servilis animus praemia perfidiae reputavit simulque immensa pecunia et potentia obversabantur, cessit fas et salus patroni et acceptae libertatis memoria.*

54. Cf. Tac. *Ag.* 2.4: *memoriam quoque ipsam cum voce perdidissemus, si tam in nostra potestate esset oblivisci quam tacere.* ("We should have lost memory as well as voice, if we had been as able to forget as to keep silent.")

55. Flavus' words were part of the tradition; see Dio 62.24.2. Laird (1999) 126–131 compares this passage to Seneca's dying words, reported in indirect discourse, and warns that the veracity of *ipsa verba* is not as straightforward as it seems.

56. See Pagán (2000), where I compare Tacitus' treatment of Arminius, Epicharis, Cremutius, and Caratacus. Similarly, in Statius' *Thebaid,* the most outspoken attacks on the tyrant come from those about to die; see Newlands (2002) 255.

57. Cf. the dying words of Drusus. At first pretending madness, he reviled Tiberius, but when it became clear that he was going to die, he delivered a studied and elaborate curse (*meditatas compositasque diras inprecabatur,* 6.24.2).

58. For MacMullen (1966) 46–94, the coincidence of Stoicism and opposition was due to the impulse of philosophers to say what they felt, regardless of the consequences. In discussing opposition to Nero, Warmington (1969) 142–154 argues that "the whole climate

of the intellectual and literary world of the Neronian age" was dominated by Stoicism (150). According to Griffin (1984) 171, however, only two of the victims of the aftermath of the Pisonian conspiracy mentioned by Tacitus adhered to Stoic principles. Griffin therefore denies the existence of a "Stoic" opposition. The persecuted did not share a common philosophy as much as they shared a common aristocratic legacy. See also Sullivan (1985) 115–152; Malitz (1985).

59. Waters (1970) 196.

60. Warrior (1998).

61. Cf. Suet. *Dom.* 21.1: *condicionem principum miserrimam aiebat, quibus de coniuratione comperta non crederetur nisi occisis.* ("He used to say that the lot of emperors was most wretched, because they were not believed about a proven conspiracy unless they were killed.") Cf. HA *V. Avid.* 2.5: *scis enim ipse quid avus tuus Hadrianus dixerit: misera condicio imperatorum, quibus de adfectata tyrannide nisi occisis non potest credi. eius autem exemplum ponere malui quam Domitiani, qui hoc primus dixisse fertur. tyrannorum enim etiam bona dicta non habent tantum auctoritatis quantum debent.* ("For you know yourself what your grandfather Hadrian said, 'Unhappy is the lot of emperors, who can never be trusted about claims to the throne, until after they are slain.' I have preferred, moreover, to quote this as his, rather than as Domitian's, who is reported to have said it first, for good sayings when uttered by tyrants have not so much weight as they deserve.")

62. Sal. *Cat.* 4.3: *igitur de Catilinae coniuratione* ("therefore about the conspiracy of Catiline"); Liv. 39.8.1: *cura ad intestinae coniurationis vindicatam avertit* ("attention turned to punishing a domestic conspiracy"); Tac. Ann. 15.48.1: *coepta simul et aucta coniuratione* ("when at the same time a conspiracy rose up and gained strength").

63. Sal. *Cat.* 17.3–4: *eo convenere senatorii ordinis P. Lentulus Sura* ("from the senatorial ranks joined . . ."); Liv. 39.17.6: *capita autem coniurationis constabat esse M. et C. Atinios de plebe Romana et Faliscum L. Opicernium et Minium Cerrinium Campanum* ("It is agreed, moreover, that the ringleaders of the conspiracy were the Roman plebeians Marcus and Gaius Atinius, Lucius Opicernius the Faliscian, and Minius Cerrinius from Campania"); Tac. *Ann.* 15.49.2–50.3: *promptissimos Subrium Flavum tribunum praetoriae cohortis . . . sed summum robur in Faenio Rufo praefecto videbatur* ("among the most eager was Subrius Flavus tribune of the praetorian cohort . . . but the greatest impetus seemed to stem from the praefect Faenius Rufus").

64. Sal. *Cat.* 53.1; Liv. 39.19.7; Tac. *Ann.* 15.73.1–74.1.

65. Sal. *Cat.* 24.3: *ea tempestate plurumos quoiusque generis homines adscivisse sibi dicitur, mulieres etiam aliquot* ("At that time it is said that he gathered for himself several of every sort of person, even some women"); Liv. 39.8.6: *mixti feminis mares, aetatis tenerae maioribus* ("males mixed with females, those of tender age with elders"); Tac. *Ann.* 15.48.1: *nomina dederant senatores eques miles, feminae etiam* ("there enlisted senators, equestrians, soldiers, even women") Cf. 15.54.1.

66. Sal. *Cat.* 48.1; Liv. 39.9.1, 39.11.3; Tac. *Ann.* 15.54.1.

67. Sal. *Cat.* 50.1; Liv. 39.19.3; Tac. *Ann.* 15.71.1.

68. Sal. *Cat.* 18.1: *sed antea item coniuravere pauci contra rem publicam, in quis Catilina fuit; de qua quam verissume potero dicam* ("But before this a few conspired against the re-

public among whom was Catiline; about which I shall speak as truthfully as I am able"); Liv. 39.9.1: *tandem indicium hoc maxime modo ad Postumium consulem pervenit* ("Finally information reached the consul Postumius in a way close to this"); Tac. *Ann.* 15.49.1: *nec tamen facile memoraverim* ("Still I could not easily recount").

69. See Barthes (1972) 150.

70. Sal. *Cat.* 22.1: *fuere ea tempestate qui dicerent;* Liv. 39.17.6: *dicebantur . . . constabat esse;* Tac. *Ann.* 15.53.2: *ut alii tradidere.*

71. Marincola (1997).

72. See the seminal study of "safe" speech by Ahl (1984).

73. Cf. Dio 53.19.6: ὅθενπερ καὶ ἐγὼ πάντα τὰ ἐξῆς, ὅσα γε καὶ ἀναγκαῖον ἔσται εἰπεῖν, ὡς που καὶ δεδήμωται φράσω, εἴτ᾽ ὄντως οὕτως εἴτε καὶ ἑτέρως πως ἔχει. προσέσται μέντοι τι αὐτοῖς καὶ τῆς ἐμῆς δοξασίας. ("Hence in my own narrative of later events, so far as they need to be mentioned, everything that I shall say will be in accordance with the reports that have been given out, whether it be really the truth or otherwise. In addition to these reports, however, my own opinion will be given." tr. Loeb.) Dio's honesty is misleading, for opinions are not just appended to the narrative, they are integral to it. See also Marincola (1997) 88–93.

## CHAPTER FOUR

1. For Josephus' study of Greek, see Hadas-Lebel (1993) 45–49.

2. Wiseman (1987) 167 and (1992) 1 notes that Josephus' narrative has attracted too little scholarly attention, given the importance of the event in Roman imperial history.

3. See Rutledge (2001) 162–164 for a brief summary of the conspiracies under Caligula.

4. Ferrill (1991) 121; Simpson (1980) 347; Barrett (1989) 155, cf. (1996) 62–70; see also Charlesworth (1933) 113–114; Faur (1973).

5. *CIL* 6.2029.d.

6. Dio 59.22.5–6: "In the first place, then, he put to death Lentulus Gaeticulus, who had an excellent reputation in every way and had been governor of Germany for ten years, for the reason that he was endeared to the soldiers. Another of his victims was Lepidus. . . ." tr. Loeb.

7. On the social and political connections of Gaeticulus in the circles of Sejanus, see Stewart (1953).

8. Barrett (1989) 82.

9. For the phrase *capax imperii,* see Tac. *Hist.* 1.49.4 and Damon (2003) *ad loc.*

10. Tac. *Ann.* 4.20.2: *hunc ego Lepidum temporibus illis gravem et sapientem virum fuisse comperior: nam pleraque ab saevis adulationibus aliorum in melius flexit.*

11. See Martin and Woodman (1989) 150: *sapiens* used only of Lepidus and ironically, of Seneca, in a speech of Nero (14.56.2).

12. Meise (1969) 108; Syme (1970) 48, (1986) 136.

13. Barrett (1989) 106–107.

14. Meise (1969) 108–122. Dio 59.22.7 specifies three daggers, presumably for Lepidus, Agrippina, and Julia; the connection to Gaeticulus remains tenuous.

15. Barrett (1989) 218.

16. Dio 54.15.2–3: οὐ γὰρ ἔστιν ἀκριβῶς τὰ τοιαῦτα τοῖς ἔξω αὐτῶν οὖσιν εἰδέναι· πολλὰ γὰρ ὧν ἂν ὁ κρατῶν πρὸς τιμωρίαν, ὡς καὶ ἐπιβεβουλευμένος, ἤτοι δι' ἑαυτοῦ ἢ καὶ διὰ τῆς γερουσίας πράξῃ, ὑποπτεύεται κατ' ἐπήρειαν, κἂν ὅτι μάλιστα δικαιότατα συμβῇ, γεγονέναι. tr. Loeb.

17. By pardoning Cinna, Augustus set a lasting example, followed by Marcus Aurelius: Dio 72.28; HA V. Marcus 25; see Bauman (2000) 84–85. See Charlesworth (1937) 112–113 on clementia (attributed to Tiberius, Caligula, Nero, and Vitellius) as a despotic mercy exercised by the conqueror or tyrant over powerless subjects to confirm inequality; Wirszubski (1950) 150–153; Bauman (2000) 77–78. See Bradley (1976) 249, (1991) 3715–3720 on clementia in Suetonius. Wallace-Hadrill (1981) argues against a canon of imperial virtues (as articulated on Augustus' golden shield, virtus, clementia, iustitia, pietas).

18. A.J. 18.181; see Levick (1976) 173–174 on the connection between Caligula's motives and Antonia's information.

19. A.J. 19.15–16: βούλομαι δι' ἀκριβείας τὸν πάντα περὶ αὐτοῦ λόγον διελθεῖν, ἄλλως τε ἐπειδὴ καὶ πολλὴν ἔχει πίστιν τοῦ θεοῦ τῆς δυνάμεως καὶ παραμυθίαν τοῖς ἐν τύχαις κειμένοις καὶ σωφρονισμὸν τοῖς οἰομένοις ἀίδιον τὴν εὐτυχίαν, ἀλλὰ μὴ ἐπιμεταφέρειν κακῶς ἀρετῆς αὐτῇ μὴ παραγενομένης.

20. Annius Vinicianus, son of Annius Pollio (Tac. Ann. 6.9.3), later conspired against Claudius (Dio 60.15.1). Josephus mistakenly calls him Minucianus twelve times. Furneaux (1896) ad 6.9 conjectures that Vinicianus was the nephew of M. Vinicius, husband of Caligula's sister Julia Livilla; see also Timpe (1962) 89 n. 2; Barrett (1989) 33, 108.

21. Levick (1990) 34 compares the assassination to the Catilinarian conspiracy, both confederations of members with divergent aims.

22. Cf. Sen. De Const. 18.2.

23. Cf. the speech of Postumius (Liv. 39.15–16) and the speeches of Cicero In Catil. The predominance of just one consul suggests a spirit of unity in the midst of the divisive act of conspiracy.

24. Plut. Caes. 69.3; Suet. Jul. 89; see Wiseman (1991) 102.

25. In Tacitus' imagination too, as he constructed the Pisonian conspiracy; see Woodman (1993) 107.

26. A.J. 19.54, 186; Weinstock (1971) 142. This detail shows that Josephus or his source (possibly Cluvius) was well versed in the accounts of the death of Julius Caesar, perhaps drawing upon Nicolas of Damascus, whom Josephus is seen to follow first-hand elsewhere, Schwartz (2002) 69–71.

27. A.J. 19.184: οὐδὲν παραπλησίως Κασσίῳ καὶ Βρούτῳ τοῖς Γάιον Ἰούλιον ἀνῃρηκόσιν.

28. Wiseman (1991) 78.

29. A.J. 19.187: ἔτει γὰρ ἑκατοστῷ, μεθ' ὃ τὴν δημοκρατίαν τὸ πρῶτον ἀφῃρέθησαν.

30. A.J. 19.15, 19.68, 19.107, 19.212. At 19.94, Wiseman (1991) reads Shilleto's suggestion

of μανθάνω ("I notice") but in the Loeb, Feldman retains the manuscript's συμβαίνει ("it happened that"). For the first person in Sallust, see above, pp. 32–33. Tacitus uses the first person five times in the Pisonian account (*Ann.* 15.49.1, 53.3, 54.1, 63.3, 67.3).

31. *A.J.* 19.212: ἀνώτερον ἔφην ("as I said above"), where Wiseman (1991) 86 assumes that Josephus has switched to a different source.

32. *A.J.* 19.68: δοκεῖν δὲ προσεποιεῖτο Κάλλιστος. The text is difficult; emendations yield δοκεῖ δὲ προσποιεῖσθαι. The Latin translation of Josephus made under the supervision of Cassiodorus at his estate Vivarium in Southern Italy in the sixth century makes the first person more explicit: *sed mihi videretur, quia fingebat haec Callistus.* On the principles governing translations in the period of late antiquity and the faithfulness of a translation to the original, see Blatt (1958) 18.

33. *A.J.* 19.107: οὐ μὴν ἐμοὶ πιθανὸς οὗτος ὁ λόγος . . . ἥγημαι ("This account, however, I cannot believe . . . I consider").

34. *B.J.* 1.9: ἀλλὰ τὰ μὲν ἔργα μετ᾽ ἀκριβείας ἀμφοτέρων διέξειμι.

35. Such is the thesis of Mader (2000): for *B.J.* 1.9, see p. 3. On Josephus' engagement with the generic convention, see Bilde (1988) 205; Marincola (1997) 168.

36. Seven times, including Wiseman's suggestion of a switch of sources at 19.212.

37. *A.J.* 19.61: καὶ τὸν Χαιρέαν τὸ μὲν πρῶτον ὑπιδέσθαι.

38. *A.J.* 19.88: Γάιον δ᾽ ἱστορεῖται παρὰ φύσιν τὴν ἑαυτοῦ εὐπροσηγορώτατον γενέσθαι κατ᾽ ἐκείνην τὴν ἡμέραν.

39. *A.J.* 19.196–197: οἱ μὲν γὰρ ἀποσημαίνειν ἔφασαν τὸν λόγον, ὡς συμβουλευομένης ἀποστάντα μανιῶν καὶ τοῦ εἰς τοὺς πολίτας ὠμοῦ μετρίως καὶ μετ᾽ ἀρετῆς ἐξηγεῖσθαι τῶν πραγμάτων, μὴ παρ᾽ αὐτὸν ἀπολέσθαι τρόπῳ τῷ αὐτοῦ χρώμενον. οἱ δέ, ὡς λόγου τοῦ περὶ τῶν συνωμοτῶν ἐπιφοιτήσαντος Γαΐῳ κελεύσειεν μηδὲν εἰς ἀναβολὰς ἀλλ᾽ ἐκ τοῦ ὀξέος πάντας μεταχειρισάμενον αὐτούς. . . . ("Some said that her words signified that she warned him to desist from his madness and barbarity to the citizens, to administer the government with moderation and virtue, and not to bring about his own destruction at their hands by following his own bent. Others said that a rumor had reached her concerning the conspirators and that she had bidden Gaius to do away with them all forthwith and without an instant's delay." tr. Loeb.)

40. *A.J.* 19.92: τοιγαροῦν, ὦ Κλούιε, τυραννοκτονίας ἀγὼν πρόκειται. καὶ ὁ Κλούιος, ὦ γενναῖε, φησίν, σίγα, μή τίς τ᾽ ἄλλος Ἀχαιῶν μῦθον ἀκούσῃ. Cf. *Iliad* 14.90–91: σίγα, μή τίς τ᾽ ἄλλος Ἀχαιῶν τοῦτον ἀκούσῃ / μῦθον. ("Silence, lest one of the Achaeans should hear this word.")

41. Mommsen (1870); Charlesworth (1933) 116–119; Townend (1964) 370–371; Ritter (1972); Momigliano (1975) esp. 809–810; Ferrill (1991) 161; Wiseman (1991) 111–118. Syme (1958) 179, 287, 293–294 is skeptical. *Contra* Timpe (1960) 500–501 and Feldman (1962). See also Hurley (2001) 14–15 on Cluvius as a source for Tacitus, Suetonius, Dio, Josephus, and Plutarch; Damon (2003) 22–23.

42. *A.J.* 19.44: Κλήμης δὲ τὴν μὲν διάνοιαν τὴν Χαιρέου φανερὸς ἦν ἐπαινῶν, σιγᾶν δ᾽ ἐκέλευε, μὴ καὶ φοιτῶντος εἰς πλείονας τοῦ λόγου καὶ διαχεομένων ὁπόσα κρύπτεσθαι καλῶς ἔχοι πρὶν τυχεῖν πράξαντας ἐκπύστου τοῦ ἐπιβουλεύματος γενομένου κολασθεῖεν.

43. The tale of Myrrha's incestuous love for her father Cinyras was the subject of the neoteric poem *Zmyrna* by Helvius Cinna (Cat. 95.1–2); for the fullest extant treatment, see Ovid *Met.* 10.298–502. The tale is so gruesome that Ovid's Orpheus issues a warning to his audience (300–303).

44. *A.J.* 19.94–95; however, Josephus is wrong. Caligula died in January, Philip in the autumn. See also Dio 59.29.3 and Suet. *Cal.* 57 for omens surrounding the death of Caligula.

45. *A.J.* 19.12, 14, 131. See Rutledge (2001) 33–34.

46. *A.J.* 19.86; on seating, see Rawson (1991).

47. For a survey of metaphorical uses of slavery in the works of Josephus, see Gibbs and Feldman (1986).

48. *A.J.* 19.42: ἐπὶ σωτηρίᾳ τοῦ δουλουμένου τά τε σώματα αὐτῶν καὶ τὰ φρονήματα.

49. *A.J.* 19.57: δουλώσει τε πατρίδος ἐλευθερωτάτης ἐπαλγοῦντι τῶν νόμων τῆς ἀρετῆς ἀφῃρημένης. ("I am tormented when I see my country reduced from unequalled freedom to slavery and robbed of its excellent laws." tr. Loeb.)

50. *A.J.* 19.261: καὶ Σαβῖνος εἷς τῶν Γαίου σφαγέων σφάζειν πρότερον αὐτὸν ἠπείλει παρελθὼν εἰς μέσους ἢ Κλαύδιον ἄρχοντα στήσεσθαι καὶ δουλοκρατίαν ἐπόψεσθαι καταλαβοῦσαν.

51. Wirszubski (1950) 163–167; Jens (1956); Syme (1958) 583; Roller (2001) 214–233.

52. Charlesworth (1933) 117–118.

53. *A.J.* 19.82: εἴ τις αὐτὸν Αἰγύπτιος κτείνειεν τὴν ὕβριν οὐχ ἡγησάμενος ἀνασχετὸν τοῖς ἐλευθέροις γεγονόσιν. This is precisely the humiliation that Epicharis brought upon the Pisonian conspirators.

54. On the emperor's German bodyguard, see Le Bohec (1994) 23; Noy (2000) 21; on the praetorian guard, see Campbell (1984) 109–120.

55. *A.J.* 19.33. On the identification of Pompedius, see Barrett (1989) 293 n. 24; on Timidius, see Rutledge (2001) 273.

56. Chilton (1955) 75; Bauman (1967) 55.

57. *A.J.* 19.35: Κυιντιλία δ' ἐπὶ τὴν βάσανον ἀγομένη τῶν συνιστόρων τινὸς ἐπιβαίνει τῷ ποδὶ ἀποσημαίνουσα θαρσεῖν καὶ μὴ τὰς βασάνους αὐτῆς δεδιέναι.

58. Gleason (2001) 51.

59. See Timpe (1962) 79; Barrett (1989) 158.

60. Wiseman (1991) 51.

61. Dio 59.26.4: Πομπώνιον γὰρ ἐπιβουλεῦσαι λεχθέντα οἱ ἀπέλυσεν, ἐπειδὴ ὑπὸ φίλου προεδόθη, καὶ τὴν ἑταίραν αὐτοῦ, ὅτι βασανισθεῖσα οὐδὲν ἐξεῖπεν, οὔτε τι κακὸν ἔδρασε καὶ προσέτι καὶ χρήμασιν ἐτίμησεν.

62. Suet. *Cal.* 16.4: *quoque magis nullius non boni exempli fautor videretur, mulieri libertinae octingenta donavit, quod excruciata gravissimis tormentis de scelere patroni reticuisset. quas ob res inter reliquos honores decretus est ei clipeus aureus.*

63. Thus the anecdote is generated and transmitted for the purpose of illustrating a moral lesson. See Saller (1980) 72 on the way such an anecdote contributes to the stereotype of Caligula as inhumanly cruel.

## CHAPTER FIVE

1. On Appian's bilingualism, see Famerie (1998) 27–32; Adams and Swain (2002) 18; Adams (2003) 472.

2. Barbu (1934).

3. Gabba (1956), qualified by Badian (1958); Rawson (1986) 112 is not willing to assign Pollio as the immediate source.

4. Swain (1996). For Plutarch, see Jones (1971); for Fronto, see Champlin (1980).

5. Bucher (2000).

6. Gowing (1992); Hose (1994).

7. Appian uses the first person sparingly, only eleven times each in Books 1 (1.3, 6, 16, 34, 55, 84, 86, 97, 100, 104, 115) and 2 (2.5, 18, 70, 86, 88, 92, 111, 113, 124, 149, 153).

8. Only Nic. Dam. 20 records that they were exiled. The entire episode is an instance of Caesar's obsession with his personal *dignitas* at the expense of the *res publica;* see Meier (1982) 4–5.

9. Cooper (1984) 11.

10. Tac. *Ann.* 1.8.6: *cum occisus dictator Caesar aliis pessimum, aliis pulcherrimum facinus videretur.*

11. Cic. *De Orat.* 2.311: *digredi tamen ab eo quod proposueris atque agas, permovendorum animorum causa saepe utile est.* ("To stir emotions, it is often useful to digress from what you have set out to do.") Cic. *Inv.* 1.27: *digressio aliquo extra causam aut criminationis aut similitudinis aut delectationis . . . causa interponitur.* ("Sometimes a digression beyond the topic is inserted for accusation, comparison, or sheer pleasure.")

12. Cic. *Fam.* 5.12.4: *nihil est enim aptius ad delectationem lectoris quam temporum varietates fortunaeque vicissitudines* ("For nothing is more suitable to the delight of the reader than variations of circumstances and the vicissitudes of fortune"); cf. Caes. *Gal.* 5.12–14, 6.11–28; Sal. *Jug.* 17–19; Tac. *Ann.* 5.2–10. According to Horsfall (1985) 199, "such geography appeals to a taste for the curious." See also Woodman (1988) 183.

13. Caesar's paternity of Brutus was merely rumor; Caesar's celebrated affair with Servilia (in the mid 60s B.C.E.) took place long after the birth of Brutus (in 85). On the year of Brutus' birth, see Woodman (1983) 173.

14. *B.C.* 2.112: ἀλλ' εἴτε ἀχάριστος ὢν ὁ Βροῦτος, εἴτε τὰ τῆς μητρὸς ἁμαρτήματα ἀγνοῶν ἢ ἀπιστῶν ἢ αἰδούμενος, εἴτε φιλελεύθερος ὢν ἄγαν καὶ τὴν πατρίδα προτιμῶν, εἴθ' ὅτι ἔκγονος ὢν Βροῦτον τοῦ πάλαι τοὺς βασιλέας ἐξελάσαντος ἐρεθιζόμενος καὶ ὀνειδιζόμενος μάλιστα ἐς τοῦτο ὑπὸ τοῦ δήμου (πολλὰ γὰρ τοῖς ἀνδριᾶσι τοῦ πάλαι Βροῦτου καὶ τῷ δικαστηρίῳ τοῦδε τοῦ Βροῦτου τοιάδε ἐπεγράφετο λάθρᾳ· Βροῦτε δωροδοκεῖς; Βροῦτε νεκρὸς εἶ; ἢ ὤφελές γε νῦν περιεῖναι ἢ ἀνάξιά σου τὰ ἔκγονα ἢ οὐδ' ἔκγονος εἶ σὺ τοῦδε, ταῦτα καί τοιουτότραπα ἄλλα πολλὰ τὸν νεανίαν ἐξέκαυσεν ἐπὶ τὸ ἔργον ὡς ἑαυτοῦ προγονικόν. tr. Loeb.

15. Gowing (1992) 180.

16. Suet. *Jul.* 80.3; Plut. *Brut.* 9.3; *Caes.* 62.7; cf. Dio 44.12.

17. Most likely Asinius Pollio, e.g., Tac. *Ann.* 4.34.4; see Gabba (1956); Syme (1958) 569; *contra* Rawson (1986) 112.

18. See Wiseman (1994), (1995), and (1998) for the hypothesis that the Roman historical tradition was created and perpetuated in dramatic performances.

19. *B.C.* 2.113: ἐμβαλὼν τὴν χεῖρα τῷ Βρούτῳ, τί ποιήσομεν, ἔφη, παρὰ τὸ βουλευτήριον, ἂν οἱ κόλακες τοῦ Καίσαρος γνώμην περὶ βασιλείας προθῶσι; καὶ ὁ Βροῦτος οὐκ ἔφη παρέσεσθαι τῷ βουλευτηρίῳ. ἐπανερομένου δὲ τοῦ Κασσίου· τί δ᾽ ἂν ἡμας καλῶσιν ὡς στρατηγούς, τί ποιήσομεν, ὦ ἀγαθὲ Βροῦτε; ἀμυνῶ τῇ πατρίδι, ἔφη, μέχρι θανάτου. καὶ ὁ Κάσσιος αὐτὸν ἀσπασάμενος, τίνα δ᾽, ἔφη, οὐ προσλήψῃ τῶν ἀρίστων οὕτω φρονῶν; tr. Loeb.

20. Nic. Dam. 19 says more than eighty men conspired against Caesar but names only Decimus, Cassius, and Brutus. Suet. *Jul.* 80.4 says more than sixty men participated but names only Decimus, Cassius, and Brutus. Livy *Per.* 116 names Brutus, Cassius, Decimus, and Trebonius as ringleaders. Vell. 2.56 calls Brutus and Cassius the leaders and mentions Decimus and Trebonius. Dio 44.14 declines to name them all for fear of boredom.

21. Appian deliberately avoids the calque συνωμοσία (*coniuratio*) and calls the assassination a plot ἐπιβουλή instead; according to Wheeler (1988) 42, the term often connotes treason. When Caesar's soldiers were defeated at Dyrrachium, they swore oaths to one another in Caesar's sight that they would not leave the battlefield unless victorious (κατὰ μέρη συνώμνυντο, *B.C.* 2.63, 73); such an oath resembles the original *coniuratio* of the early republic. Of the Catilinarian conspiracy, Appian says: "He formed a conspiracy with a number of senators and the so-called knights" (συνώμνυτό τισιν ἀπὸ τῆς βουλῆς καὶ τῶν καλουμένων ἱππέων, *B.C.* 2.2; see also 2.3: τοῖς συνωμόταις; 2.4: τὴν Λέντλου συνωμοσίαν). But Appian says that the assassins of Julius Caesar "pledged each other without oaths or sacrifices," ἄνευ τε ὅρκων καὶ ἄνευ σφαγίων (*B.C.* 2.114).

22. Bakhtin (1981) 84–258.

23. Morson (1994) 49, 118.

24. Bernstein (1994) 16, original emphasis. For a critique of Bakhtin, Morson, and Bernstein, see Pavel (1998).

25. *B.C.* 2.115: καί τις, αὐτῶν ὧδε ἐχόντων, τῆς Κάσκα χειρὸς λαβόμενος εἶπε· σὺ μὲν ὄντα με φίλον ἀπέκρυψας, Βροῦτος δ᾽ ἀνήνεγκέ μοι... ὁ δ᾽ ἐπιμειδιάσας ἔφη· πόθεν οὖν ἔσται σοι τὰ χρήματα τῆς ἀγορανομίας. tr. Loeb.

26. This is the one detail that is recorded in every source except the epitome of Livy: Nic. Dam. 19; Vell. 2.57; Suet. *Jul.* 81.4; Plut. *Caes.* 65; Florus 2.13.94; Dio 44.18.

27. Bettini (1991) 139.

28. *B.C.* 2.111: ταύτης δὲ σκοπῶν ἡγοῦμαι τῆς προσθήκης ἀφορμὴν λαβεῖν ἐγχειρήσεως.... The only other intrusion of the first person in chapters 111–117 gives direction to the reader ("about which I have spoken above," 2.113). On Appian's use of the first person to give opinion, see Gowing (1992) 166.

29. *B.C.* 4.136: "Porcia, the wife of Brutus and sister of the younger Cato, when she learned he had died in the manner described, although very strictly watched by domestics, seized some hot embers that they were carrying on a brazier, and swallowed them." tr. Loeb. Cf. *Cat. Min.* 73.4.

30. V. Max. 3.2.15: *quae, cum Bruti viri sui consilium quod de interficiendo ceperat Caesare ea nocte quam dies taeterrimi facti secutus est cognosset, egresso cubiculum Bruto cultellum*

*tonsorium quasi unguium resecandorum causa poposcit, eoque velut forte elapso se vulneravit. clamore deinde ancillarum in cubiculum revocatus, Brutus obiurgare eam coepit, quod tonsoris praeripuisset officium. cui secreto Porcia, "non est hoc" inquit "temerarium factum meum, sed in tali statu nostro amoris mei erga te certissimum indicium: experiri enim volui, si tibi propositum parum ex sententia cessisset, quam aequo animo me ferro essem interemptura."* tr. Loeb.

31. V. Max. 3.2.23a; Caes. *B.C.* 3.53.4; Luc. 6.230–262.

32. For Valerius' justification for her inclusion, see Bloomer (1992) 188.

33. Details perhaps provided by the memoirs of Porcia's son by Bibulus, Plu. *Brut.* 13.2. The only detail recounted by both Valerius and Plutarch is the type of instrument Porcia used (a manicure tool).

34. Plu. *Brut.* 13.4–5, tr. Loeb.

35. Parker (1998) 167.

36. Richlin (1999) 199.

37. Dio 44.13.2: μὴ καὶ ἄκουσά τι ἐκ βασάνων ἐξείπῃ.

38. Dio 44.13.3: σὺ μὲν, ὦ ἄνερ, καίτοι τῇ ψυχῇ μου πιστεύων ὅτι οὐδὲν ἐκλαλήσει, ὅμως ἠπίστεις τῷ σώματι, καὶ ἔπασχές γέ τι ἀνθρώπινον· ἐγὼ δὲ καὶ τοῦτο εὕρηκα σιωπᾶν δυνάμενον. tr. Loeb.

## CONCLUSION

1. Richard M. Nixon, quoted in Kutler (1997) xxiii.

2. Cf. the remarks of Ladouceur (1980) 253, 260, who doubts the credibility of Josephus' account of Masada; *contra* Cohen (1982). Broshi (1982) and Hadas-Lebel (1994) insist that Josephus be given credit for his accuracy, even if his accuracy was rare.

3. Catiline: Sal. *Cat.* 5.4, 14.7, 15.1; Caligula: Dio 59.3.3; Suet. *Cal.* 24.1, 36.1; Nero: Tac. *Ann.* 14.2, 15.37.

4. Barthes (1972) 153.

5. Plut. *Cat. Maior* 9.6, *Mor.* 507b–f; Gell. 1.23.

6. On the conspiracy, see Jones (1992) 193–196; Southern (1997) 117–118; Berriman and Todd (2001); Grainger (2003) 1–27.

7. Dio 67.15.3–4: ἤκουσα δὲ ἔγωγε καὶ ἐκεῖνο, ὅτι πάντας ἅμα αὐτοὺς ὁ Δομιτιανὸς ὑποπτεύσας ἀποκτεῖναι ἠθέλησε, καί σφων τὰ ὀνόματα ἐς σανίδιον φιλύρινον δίθυρον ἐσγράψας ὑπὸ τὸ προσκεφάλαιον ἐν τῇ κλίνῃ ἐν ᾗ ἀνεπαύετο ὑπέθηκε, καὶ αὐτὸ παιδίον τι τῶν γυμνῶν τῶν ψιθύρων καθεύδοντος αὐτοῦ μεθ' ἡμέραν ἀφελόμενον εἶχεν, οὐκ εἰδὸς ὅ τι φέροι, προστυχοῦσα δὲ αὐτῷ ἡ Δομιτία τά τε γεγραμμένα ἀνέγνω καὶ ἐμήνυσε καὶ ἐκείνοις, κἀκ τούτου καὶ ἄλλως διανοούμενοι συνετάχυναν τὴν ἐπιβουλήν.

8. Suet. *Aug.* 83: *pueris minutis, quos facie et garrulitate amabilis undique conquirebat* (". . . little boys whom he used to search everywhere for, such as were attractive for their pretty faces or their prattle"). Hadrian's whisperers were more pernicious, however; he was always ready to believe their rumors: HA *V. Had.* 15.2: *id tamen facile de amicis, quidquid insusurrabatur, audivit* ("Still he easily believed of his friends whatever was whispered to

him"). In Catullus 80.5–6, rumor whispers Gellius' sordid secret: *an vere fama susurrat / grandia te medii tenta vorare viri* (". . . whether rumor rightly whispers that you greedily eat the ample stiffness of a man's mid-section").

9. Dio 48.44.3: παιδίον τι τῶν ψιθύρων οἷα αἱ γυναῖκες γυμνὰ ὡς πλήθει ἀθύρουσαι τρέπουσιν, ἰδὸν χωρὶς μὲν τὴν Λιουίαν μετὰ τοῦ Καίσαρος χωρὶς δὲ τὸν Νέρωνα μεθ' ἑτέρου τινὸς κατακείμενον, προσῆλθέ τε αὐτῇ καὶ ἔφη, τί ποιεῖς ἐνταῦθα, κυρία; ὁ γὰρ ἀνήρ σου, δείξας αὐτὸν, ἐκεῖ κατάκειται.

10. *LSJ* s.v. ψιθυρίζω. The unnamed assassin in Plutarch's version of the Pisonian conspiracy whispered to the prisoner (προσψιθυρίσας, *Mor.* 505c).

11. App. *B.C.* 1.72 preserves an anecdote about a slave whose indiscreet whispers caused the death of M. Antonius the orator.

12. Suet. *Cal.* 49.3: *in secretis eius reperti sunt duo libelli diverso titulo, alteri gladius, alteri pugio index erat.*

13. HA *V. Comm.* 9.3: *quod per parvulum quendam proditum est, qui tabulam e cubiculo eiecit, in qua occidendorum erant nomina scripta.* Cf. the story told of Aurelian, HA *V. Aurelianus* 36.

14. Syme (1983) 137.

15. See Southern (1997) 119–125 on the psychology of suspicion of Domitian's character.

16. *ILS* 272, dated 140 C.E., does not mention the emperor Domitian at all but three times calls Domitia *Corbulonis filia*. On her survival, see Syme (1958) 300, 780, (1981) 50.

17. See Canning (2000) esp. 84–85; Porter (1999) 1–18.

18. Kutler (1997) xxiii.

# BIBLIOGRAPHY

Adams, J. N. 1982. *The Latin Sexual Vocabulary.* Baltimore, MD.

———. 1983. "Words for 'Prostitute' in Latin." *RhM* 126: 321–358.

———. 2003. *Bilingualism and the Latin Language.* Cambridge.

Adams, J. N., and Swain, S. 2002. "Introduction." In J. N. Adams, M. Janse, and S. Swain, eds. *Bilingualism in Ancient Society: Language Contact and the Written Text.* Oxford: 1–20.

Agamben, G. 1999. *Remnants of Auschwitz: The Witness and the Archive.* Trans. D. Heller-Roazen. New York.

Ahl, F. M. 1976. *Lucan: An Introduction.* Ithaca, NY.

———. 1984. "The Art of Safe Criticism in Greece and Rome." *AJP* 105: 174–208.

Arcellaschi, A. 1990. "Les *Bacchides* de Plaute et l'affaire des Bacchanales." In J. Blänsdorf, ed. *Theater und Gesellschaft im Imperium Romanum.* Tübingen: 35–44.

Archer, L. J., Fischler, S., and Wyke, M., eds. 1994. *Women in Ancient Societies: An Illusion of the Night.* New York.

Ash, R. 1999. *Ordering Anarchy: Armies and Leaders in Tacitus' Histories.* Ann Arbor.

———. 1999a. "An Exemplary Conflict: Tacitus' Parthian Battle Narrative (*Annals* 6.34–35)." *Phoenix* 53: 114–135.

———. 2002. "Epic Encounters? Ancient Historical Battle Narratives and the Epic Tradition." In D. Levene and D. Nelis, eds. *Clio and the Poets: Augustan Poetry and the Traditions of Ancient Historiography.* Leiden: 253–273.

Astin, A. E. 1978. *Cato the Censor.* Oxford.

Austin, R. G. 1988. *M. Tulli Ciceronis Pro M. Caelio Oratio.* Oxford.

Badian, E. 1958. "Appian and Asinius Pollio." *CR* 8: 159–162.

Bakhtin, M. M. 1981. *The Dialogic Imagination.* Trans. C. Emerson and M. Holquist. Austin, TX.

Bal, M. 1985. *Narratology: Introduction to the Theory of Narrative.* Trans. C. van Boheemen. Toronto.

———. 1991. *On Storytelling: Essays in Narratology.* Sonoma, CA.

Baldwin, B. 1967. "Executions, Trials, and Punishment in the Reign of Nero." *La Parola del passato* 22: 425–439.

Barbu, N. I. 1934. *Les Sourcès et l'Originalité d'Appien dans le deuxième livre des "Guerres civiles."* Paris.

Barrett, A. 1989. *Caligula: The Corruption of Power.* New York.

———. 1996. *Agrippina: Sex, Power, and Politics in the Early Empire.* New Haven.

Barthes, R. 1972. *Mythologies.* Trans. A. Lavers. New York.

———. 1974. *S / Z.* Trans. R. Miller. New York.

———. 1975. *The Pleasure of the Text.* Trans. R. Miller. New York.

———. 1982. "Tacitus and the Funerary Baroque." In S. Sontag, ed. *A Barthes Reader.* New York: 162–166.

———. 1986. *The Rustle of Language.* Trans. R. Howard. Berkeley.

Bartsch, S. 1994. *Actors in the Audience: Theatricality and Doublespeak from Nero to Hadrian.* Cambridge, MA.

Batstone, W. 1994. "Cicero's Construction of Consular *Ethos* in the *First Catilinarian.*" *TAPA* 124: 211–266.

Baty, S. P. 1995. *American Monroe: The Making of a Body Politic.* Berkeley.

Bauman, R. 1967. *The Crimen Maiestatis in the Roman Republic and Augustan Principate.* Johannesburg.

———. 1990. "The Suppression of the Bacchanals: Five Questions." *Historia* 39: 334–348.

———. 1992. *Women and Politics in Ancient Rome.* London.

———. 2000. *Human Rights in Ancient Rome.* London.

Beard, M., North, J., and Price, S. 1998. *Religions of Rome.* 2 vols. Cambridge.

Beesly, E. S. 1878. *Catiline, Clodius, and Tiberius.* London.

Belsey, C. 1980. *Critical Practice.* London.

Béquignon, Y. 1941. "Observations sur l'affaire des Bacchanales (Tite-Live, XXXIX, 8–19)." *RA* 17: 184–198.

Bernstein, M. A. 1994. *Foregone Conclusions: Against Apocalyptic History.* Berkeley.

Berriman, A. and Todd, M. 2001. "A Very Roman Coup: The Hidden War of Imperial Succession, AD 96–98." *Historia* 50: 312–331.

Berry, D. H. 1996. *Cicero "Pro P. Sulla Oratio."* Cambridge.

Bettini, M. 1991. *Anthropology and Roman Culture: Kinship, Time, Images of the Soul.* Trans. J. Van Sickle. Baltimore, MD.

Bilde, P. 1988. *Flavius Josephus between Jerusalem and Rome: His Life, His Works, and Their Importance.* Sheffield.

Blatt, F. 1958. *The Latin Josephus I: Introduction and Text. The Antiquities: Books I–V.* Vol. 30. Acta Jutlandica. Copenhagen.

Bleicken, J. 1959. "Urprung und Bedeutung der Provocation." *ZRG (RA)* 76: 325–377.

———. 1963. "Die Schwurszene auf den Münzen und Gemmen der römischen Republik." *Jahrbuch für Numismatik und Geldgeschichte* 13: 51–70.

Bloomer, W. M. 1992. *Valerius Maximus and the Rhetoric of the New Nobility.* Chapel Hill.

———. 1997. *Latinity and Literary Society at Rome.* Philadelphia.

Bömer, F. 1990. *Untersuchungen über die Religion der Sklaven in Griechenland und Rom. Dritter Teil: Die Wichtigsten Kulte der Griechischen Welt.* 2nd ed. Stuttgart.

Bonds, W. 1985. "Two Combats in the *Thebaid.*" *TAPA* 115: 225–235.

Bradley, K. R. 1976. "Imperial Virtues in Suetonius' *Caesares.*" *JIES* 4: 245–253.

———. 1984. *Slaves and Masters in the Roman Empire: A Study in Social Control.* Vol. 185. Collection Latomus. Brussels.

———. 1991. "The Imperial Ideal in Suetonius' *Caesares.*" *ANRW* 2.33.5: 3701–3732.

———. 1994. *Slavery and Society at Rome.* Cambridge.

Braund, S. M. 1996. *Juvenal "Satires" Book 1.* Cambridge.

———. 2002. *Latin Literature.* London.

Bringmann, K. 1972. "Sallusts Umgang mit der historischen Wahrheit in seiner Darstellung der catilinarischen Verschwörung." *Philologus* 116: 98–113.

Broshi, M. 1982. "The Credibility of Josephus." *JJS* 33: 379–384.

Bruhl, A. 1953. *"Liber Pater": Origine et expansion du culte Dionysiaque à Rome et dans le monde romaine.* Paris.

Brunt, P. A. 1957. "Three Passages from Asconius." *CR* 71: 193–195.

———. 1980. "Evidence Given under Torture in the Principate." *ZRG (RA)* 97: 256–265.

Bucher, G. S. 2000. "The Origins, Program, and Composition of Appian's *Roman History,*" *TAPA* 130: 411–458.

Buckland, W. W. 1969. *The Roman Law of Slavery: The Condition of the Slave in Private Law from Augustus to Justinian.* New York.

Burkert, W. 1998. "Le secret public et les mystères dits privés." *Ktema* 23: 375–381.

Caballos, A., Eck, W., and Fernández, F. 1996. *El Senadoconsulto de Gneo Pisón Padre.* Seville.

Campbell, J. B. 1984. *The Emperor and the Roman Army 31 BC–AD 235.* Oxford.

Canning, K. 2000. "The Body as Method? Reflections on the Place of the Body in Gender History." In L. Davidoff, K. McClelland, and E. Varikas, eds. *Gender and History: Retrospect and Prospect.* Oxford: 81–95.

Carroll, N. 2001. *Beyond Aesthetics: Philosophical Essays.* Cambridge.

Champlin, E. 1980. *Fronto and Antonine Rome.* Cambridge, MA.

———. 1989. "The Life and Times of Calpurnius Piso," *MH* 46: 101–124.

Charlesworth, M. P. 1933. "The Tradition about Caligula." *Cambridge Historical Journal* 4: 105–119.

———. 1937. "The Virtues of a Roman Emperor: Propaganda and the Creation of Belief." *Proceedings of the British Academy* 105–133.

Chilton, C. W. 1955. "The Roman Law of Treason under the Early Principate." *JRS* 45: 73–81.

Clarke, K. 2002. *"In arto et inglorius labor:* Tacitus's Anti-history." In A. Bowman, H. Cotton, M. Goodman, and S. Price, eds. *Representations of Empire: Rome and the Mediterranean World.* Oxford: 83–103. ·

Cobley, P. 2001. *Narrative.* Routledge.

Cohen, S. J. D. 1982. "Masada: Literary Tradition, Archaeological Remains, and the Credibility of Josephus." *JJS* 33: 385–405.

Coleman, K. M. 1993. Review of P. duBois 1991. *Torture and Truth.* London. *Gnomon* 65: 400–403.

Colledge, M. 1967. *The Parthians.* London.

Connors, C. 1994. "Famous Last Words: Authorship and Death in the *Satyricon* and Neronian Rome." In J. Elsner and J. Masters, eds. *Reflections of Nero: Culture, History, and Representation*. Chapel Hill: 225-235.

Cooper, H. H. A. 1984. *On Assassination*. Boulder, CO.

Corsi Zoli, D. 1972. "Aspetti inavvertiti della congiura pisoniana." *Studi Romani* 20: 329-339.

Cova, P. V. 1974. "Livio e la repressione dei Baccanali." *Atheneum* 52: 82-109.

Damon, C. 2003. *Tacitus "Histories" Book 1*. Cambridge.

Debevoise, N. 1938. *A Political History of Parthia*. Chicago.

Develin, R. 1983. "Tacitus and Techniques of Insidious Suggestion." *Antichthon* 17: 64-95.

Drexler, H. 1976. *Die catilinarische Verschwörung: Ein Quellenheft*. Darmstadt.

duBois, P. 1991. *Torture and Truth*. New York and London.

Dunn, F., and Cole, T., eds. 1992. *Beginnings in Classical Literature*. Vol. 29. Yale Classical Studies.

Earl, D. C. 1961. *The Political Thought of Sallust*. Cambridge.

————. 1963. "Two Passages of Sallust." *Hermes* 91: 125-127.

————. 1966. "The Early Career of Sallust." *Historia* 15: 302-311.

Eck, W. 1993. "Das s. c. de Cn. Pisone patre und seine Publikation in der Baetica." *Cahiers du Centre Gustave Glotz* 4: 189-208.

Edwards, C. 1993. *The Politics of Immorality in Ancient Rome*. Cambridge.

Famerie, E. 1998. *Le Latin et le Grec d'Appien*. Geneva.

Fantham, E. 1991. "*Stuprum:* Public Attitudes and Penalties for Sexual Offenses in Republican Rome." *EMC* 35: 267-291.

Faur, J. C. 1973. "La Première conspiration contra Caligula." *RBPh* 51: 13-50.

Feldman, L. 1962. "The Sources of Josephus' *Antiquities*, Book 19." *Latomus* 21: 320-333.

Ferrill, A. 1991. *Caligula Emperor of Rome*. New York.

Festugière, A. J. 1954. "Ce que Tite-Live nous apprend sur les mystères de Dionysos." *MEFRA* 66: 79-99.

Finley, M. I. 1980. *Ancient Slavery and Modern Ideology*. London.

Fitzgerald, W. 2000. *Slavery and the Roman Literary Imagination*. Cambridge.

Flower, H. forthcoming. "Rereading the Senatus Consultum de Bacchanalibus of 186 B.C."

Fowler, D. 1990. "Deviant Focalization in Virgil's *Aeneid*." *PCPhS* 216 (n.s. 36): 42-63.

Fraenkel, E. 1932. "Senatus Consultum de Bacchanalibus." *Hermes* 67: 369-396.

————. 1957. *Horace*. Oxford.

Frank, T. 1927. "The Bacchanalian Cult of 186 B.C." *CQ* 21: 128-132.

Frisch, H. 1947. "The First Catilinarian Conspiracy: A Study in Historical Conjecture." *C&M* 9: 10-36.

Furneaux, H. 1896. *The Annals of Tacitus*. Vol. 1, 2nd ed. Oxford.

————. 1907. *The Annals of Tacitus*. Vol. 2, revised by H. F. Pelham and C. D. Fisher. Oxford.

Gabba, E. 1956. *Appiano e la storia delle "Guerre civili."* Florence.

Gaida, E. 1934. *Die Schlactschilderungen in den "Antiquitates Romanae" des Dionys von Halikarnass*. Breslau.

Gallini, C. 1970. *Protesta e integrazione nella Roma antica.* Bari.

Gardner, J. 1991. *Women in Roman Law and Society.* Bloomington, IN.

Garnsey, P. 1970. *Social Status and Legal Privilege in the Roman Empire.* Oxford.

Gelzer, M. 1936. "Die Unterdrückung der Bacchanalien bei Livius." *Hermes* 71: 275–287.

Genette, G. 1980. *Narrative Discourse: An Essay in Method.* Trans. J. E. Lewin. Ithaca, NY.

Giancotti, F. 1971. *Strutture delle Monografie di Sallustio e di Tacito.* Florence.

Gibbs, J. G., and Feldman, L. H. 1986. "Josephus' Vocabulary for Slavery." *JQR* 76: 281–310.

Ginsburg, J. 1981. *Tradition and Theme in the "Annals" of Tacitus.* New York.

———. 1993. "*In maiores certamina:* Past and Present in the *Annals.*" In T. J. Luce and A. J. Woodman, eds. *Tacitus and the Tacitean Tradition.* Princeton, NJ: 86–103.

Gleason, M. 2001. "Mutilated Messengers: Body Language in Josephus." In S. Goldhill, ed. *Being Greek under Rome: Cultural Identity, the Second Sophistic, and the Development of Empire.* Cambridge: 50–85.

Goodyear, F. R. D. 1972. *The "Annals" of Tacitus Books 1–6, volume 2: "Annals" 1.1–54.* Cambridge.

Gowing, A. M. 1992. *The Triumviral Narratives of Appian and Cassius Dio.* Ann Arbor.

Grainger, J. D. 2003. *Nerva and the Roman Succession Crisis of AD 96–99.* London.

Griffin, M. 1984. *Nero: The End of a Dynasty.* London.

———. 1986. "Philosopy, Cato, and Roman Suicide." *G&R* 33: 64–77; 192–202.

———. 1995. "Tacitus, Tiberius, and the Principate." In I. Malkin and Z. W. Rubinsohn, eds. *Leaders and Masses in the Roman World: Studies in Honor of Zvi Yavetz.* Leiden: 33–57.

———. 1997. "The Senate's Story." *JRS* 87: 247–263.

Gruen, E. 1969. "Notes on the 'First Catilinarian Conspiracy'." *CP* 64: 20–24.

———. 1974. *The Last Generation of the Roman Republic.* Berkeley.

———. 1990. *Studies in Greek Culture and Roman Policy.* Berkeley.

Gunderson, E. 2003. *Declamation, Paternity, and Roman Identity: Authority and the Rhetorical Self.* Cambridge.

Habinek, T. 1998. *The Politics of Latin Literature: Writing, Identity, and Empire in Ancient Rome.* Princeton, NJ.

Hadas-Lebel, M. 1993. *Flavius Josephus: Eyewitness to Rome's First-Century Conquest of Judea.* Trans. R. Miller. New York.

———. 1994. "Flavius Josephus, Historian of Rome." In F. Parente and J. Sievers, eds. *Josephus and the History of the Greco-Roman Period: Essays in Memory of Morton Smith.* Leiden: 99–106.

Hardy, E. G. 1912. *Roman Laws and Charters.* Oxford.

———. 1917. "The Catilinarian Conspiracy in Its Context: A Re-study of the Evidence." *JRS* 7: 153–228.

Harrison, S. J. 1997. "The Survival and Supremacy of Rome: The Unity of the Shield of Aeneas," *JRS* 87: 70–76.

Hartog, F. 1988. *The Mirror of Herodotus: The Representation of the Other in the Writing of History.* Trans. J. Lloyd. Berkeley.

Haynes, H. 1996. "Narrative Anxiety in Tacitus' *Histories*." Ph.D. dissertation, University of Washington.

Henderson, J. 1991. "Statius' *Thebaid*/Form Premade," *PCPS* 37:30–80.

Henderson, M. I. 1950. "*De Commentariolo Petitionis*." *JRS* 40: 8–21.

Henrichs, A. 1978. "Greek Maenadism from Olympias to Messalina." *HSCP* 82: 121–160.

Herrmann, P. 1968. *Der römische Kaisereid*. Göttingen.

Hershkowitz, D. 1998. *The Madness of Epic: Reading Insanity from Homer to Statius*. Oxford.

Hinds, S. 1998. *Allusion and Intertext: Dynamics of Appropriation in Roman Poetry*. Cambridge.

Hock, R. P. 1988. "Servile Behavior in Sallust's *Bellum Catilinae*." *CW* 82: 13–24.

Hoff, J. 1994. *Nixon Reconsidered*. New York.

Holland, L. A. 1961. *Janus and the Bridge*. Rome.

Homeyer, H. 1961. "Klage um Cicero: Zu dem epischen Fragment des Cornelius Severus." *Annales Universitatis Saraviensis: Philosophie* 10: 327–334.

Horsfall, N. 1985. "Illusion and Reality in Latin Topographical Writing." *G&R* 32: 197–208.

———. 1987. "*Non viribus aequis:* Some Problems in Virgil's Battle Scenes." *G&R* 34: 48–55.

Hose, M. 1994. *Erneuerung der Vergangenheit: Die Historiker im Imperium Romanum von Florus bis Cassius Dio*. Stuttgart.

Hurley, D. W. 2001. *Suetonius Divus Claudius*. Cambridge.

Jed, S. 1989. *Chaste Thinking: The Rape of Lucretia and the Birth of Humanism*. Bloomington, IN.

Jens, W. 1956. "*Libertas* bei Tacitus." *Hermes* 84: 331–352.

Johnson, W. R. 1970. "The Problem of the Counter-classical Sensibility and Its Critics," *CSCA* 3: 123–151.

———. 1987. *Momentary Monsters: Lucan and His Heroes*. Ithaca, NY.

Jones, B. 1992. *The Emperor Domitian*. London.

Jones, C. P. 1971. *Plutarch and Rome*. Oxford.

de Jong, I. J. F. 1987. *Narrators and Focalizers: The Presentation of the Story in the "Iliad."* Amsterdam.

Joplin, P. 1990. "Ritual Work on Human Flesh: Livy's Lucretia and the Rape of the Body Politic." *Helios* 17: 51–70.

Joshel, S. 1992. "The Body Female and the Body Politic: Livy's Lucretia and Verginia." In A. Richlin, ed. *Pornography and Representation in Greece and Rome*. Oxford: 112–130.

———. 1997. "Female Desire and the Discourse of Empire: Tacitus's Messalina." In J. Hallett and M. Skinner, eds. *Roman Sexualities*. Princeton, NJ: 221–254.

Kajanto, I. 1970. "Tacitus on the Slaves: An Interpretation of the *Annales* XIV.42–45." *Arctos* n.s. 6: 43–60.

Kaplan, A. 1968. *Catiline: The Man and His Role in the Roman Revolution*. New York.

Kaplan, M. 1979. "*Agrippina semper atrox:* A Study in Tacitus' Characterization of Women." *Studies in Latin Literature and Roman History* 1: 410–417.

Kellner, H. 1989. *Language and Historical Representation: Getting the Story Crooked.* Madison, WI.

Kent, J. P. C. 1978. *Roman Coins.* London.

Kermode, F. 1967. *The Sense of an Ending.* Oxford.

Koestermann, E. 1968. *Cornelius Tacitus: "Annalen."* Vol. IV: Books 14–16. Heidelberg.

Kraus, C. and A. J. Woodman. 1997. *Latin Historians.* Oxford.

Kutler, S. 1990. *The Wars of Watergate: The Last Crisis of Richard Nixon.* New York.

———. 1997. *Abuse of Power: The New Nixon Tapes.* New York.

La Penna, A. 1959. "Il Significato dei proemi Sallustiani." *Maia* 11: 23–43.

Ladouceur, D. 1980. "Masada: A Consideration of the Literary Evidence." *GRBS* 21: 245–260.

Laird, A. 1999. *Powers of Expression, Expressions of Power: Speech Presentation in Latin Literature.* Oxford.

———. 2000. "Design and Designation in Virgil's *Aeneid*, Tacitus' *Annals*, and Michelangelo's *Conversion of Saint Paul*." In A. Sharrock and H. Morales, eds. *Intratextuality: Greek and Roman Textual Relations.* Oxford: 143–170.

Last, H. 1948. "Sallust and Caesar in the *Bellum Catilinae*." In *Mélanges de philologie, de littérature et d'histoire anciennes offerts à J. Marouzeau.* Paris: 355–369.

Le Bohec, Y. 1994. *The Imperial Roman Army.* London.

Leeman, A. D. 1954. "Sallusts Prologe und seine Auffassung von der Historiographie." *Mnemosyne* 7: 323–339.

Levene, D. S. 2000. "Sallust's *Catiline* and Cato the Censor," *CQ* 50: 170–191.

Levi, M. A. 1969. "Bacchanalia, foedus e foederati." *Klearchos* 11: 15–23.

Levick, B. 1976. *Tiberius the Politician.* London.

———. 1990. *Claudius.* New Haven.

Linderski, J. 1984. "Rome, Aphrodisias and the *Res Gestae*: The *Genera Militiae* and the Status of Octavian." *JRS* 74: 74–80.

Lintott, A. 1968. *Violence in Republican Rome.* Oxford.

———. 1999. *The Constitution of the Roman Republic.* Oxford.

Lucas, J. 1974. *Les Obsessions de Tacite.* Leiden.

Luce, T. J. 1989. "Ancient Views on the Causes of Bias in Historical Writing." *CP* 84: 16–31.

Macherey, P. 1978. *A Theory of Literary Production.* Trans. G. Wall. London.

MacMullen, R. 1966. *Enemies of the Roman Order.* London.

Mader, G. 2000. *Josephus and the Politics of Historiography: Apologetic and Impression Management in the "Bellum Judaicum."* Leiden.

Magie, D. 1950. *Roman Rule in Asia Minor to the End of the Third Century after Christ,* 2 vols. Princeton, NJ.

Malitz, J. 1985. "Helvidius Priscus und Vespasian: Zur Geschichte der stoischen Senatsopposition." *Hermes* 113: 231–246.

Mankin, D. 1995. *Horace "Epodes."* Cambridge.

Marincola, J. 1997. *Authority and Tradition in Ancient Historiography.* Cambridge.

Marrs, J. 1989. *Crossfire: The Plot That Killed Kennedy.* New York.

Martin, R. H. 1955. "Tacitus and the Death of Augustus." *CQ* 5: 123–128.

————. 1981. *Tacitus*. Bristol.

Martin, R. H., and Woodman, A. J. 1989. *Tacitus "Annals" Book 4*. Cambridge.

McCarthy, K. 2000. *Slaves, Masters, and the Art of Authority in Plautine Comedy*. Princeton, NJ.

McDonald, A. H. 1944. "Rome and the Italian Confederation (200–186 B.C.)." *JRS* 34: 11–33.

McGinn, T. 1998. *Prostitution, Sexuality, and the Law in Ancient Rome*. Oxford.

McHale, B. 1978. "Free Indirect Discourse: A Survey of Recent Accounts." *PTL: A Journal for Descriptive Poetics and Theory of Literature* 3: 249–287.

McKeown, J. 1987–1998. *Ovid. "Amores." Text, Prolegomena, and Commentary in Four Volumes*. Leeds.

Méautis, G. 1940. "Aspects religieux de l'affaire des Bacchanales." *REA* 42: 476–485.

Meier, C. 1982. *Caesar*. Trans. D. McLintock. New York.

Meise, E. 1969. *Untersuchungen zur Geschichte der Julisch-Claudischen Dynastie*. Munich.

Mensching, E. 1967. "Zu den namentlichen Zitaten in Tacitus' *Historien* und *Annalen*." *Hermes* 95: 457–469.

Mitford, T. B. 1960. "A Cypriot Oath of Allegiance to Tiberius." *JRS* 50: 75–79.

Momigliano, A. 1975. "Osservazioni sulle fonti per la storia di Caligola, Claudio, Nerone." In *Quinto contributo alla storia degli studi classici e del mondo antico*. Rome: 799–836.

————. 1981. "The Rhetoric of History and the History of Rhetoric: On Hayden White's Tropes." *Comparative Criticism* 3: 259–268.

Mommsen, T. 1870. "Cornelius Tacitus und Cluvius Rufus." *Hermes* 4: 395–425.

Morson, G. S. 1994. *Narrative and Freedom: The Shadows of Time*. New Haven.

Murray, J. A. H., ed. 1872. *The Complaynt of Scotlande*. London.

Newlands, C. E. 2002. *Statius' "Silvae" and the Poetics of Empire*. Cambridge.

Nicolet, C. 1980. *The World of the Citizen in Republican Rome*. Trans. P. S. Falla. Berkeley.

Nilsson, M. 1957. *The Dionysiac Mysteries of the Hellenistic and Roman Age*. Lund.

Nippel, W. 1995. *Public Order in Ancient Rome*. Cambridge.

————. 1997. "Orgien, Ritualmorde und Verschwörung? Die Bacchanalian-Prozesse des Jahres 186 v. Chr." In U. Manthe and J. von Ungern-Sterberg, eds. *Grosse Prozesse der römischen Antike*. Munich: 65–73.

Nixon, R. M. 1978. *The Memoirs of Richard Nixon*. New York.

Nörr, D. 1983. "C. Cassius Longinus: Der Jurist als Rhetor (Bemerkungen zu Tacitus, *Ann*. 14.42–45)." In H. Heinen, K. Stroheker, and G. Walser, eds. *Althistorische Studien: Festschrift H. Bengtson*. Weisbaden: 187–222.

North, J. 1979. "Religious Toleration in Republican Rome." *PCPS* 205 (n.s. 25): 85–103.

————. 1992. "The Development of Religious Pluralism." In J. Lieu, J. North, and T. Rajak, eds. *The Jews among Pagans and Christians in the Roman Empire*. London: 174–193.

Noy, D. 2000. *Foreigners at Rome: Citizens and Strangers*. London.

O'Gorman, E. 2000. *Irony and Misreading in the "Annals" of Tacitus*. Cambridge.

Oakley, S. P. 1998. *A Commentary on Livy Books VI–X*. Vol. 2, Books VII–VIII. Oxford.

————. 2000. Review of A. J. Woodman and R. H. Martin 1996. *The "Annals" of Tacitus Book 3*. Cambridge. *BMCR* 2000.01.28.

Ogilvie, R. M. 1965. *A Commentary on Livy Books 1–5*. Oxford.

Pagán, V. E. 1999. "Beyond Teutoburg: Transgression and Transformation in Tacitus *Annales* 1.61–62." *CP* 94: 302–320.

————. 2000. "Distant Voices of Freedom in the *Annales* of Tacitus." *Studies in Latin Literature and Roman History* 10: 358–369.

————. 2000a. "The Mourning after: Statius *Thebaid* 12." *AJP* 121: 423–452.

Pailler, J.-M. 1988. *Bacchanalia: La répression de 186 a.v. J.-C. à Rome et en Italie: Vestiges, images, tradition*. Rome.

Palmer, R. E. A. 1989 [1998]. *"Bullae Insignia Ingenuitatis."* American Journal of Ancient History 14: 1–69.

Parker, H. 1998. "Loyal Slaves and Loyal Wives: The Crisis of the Outsider-within and Roman *exemplum* Literature." In S. Joshel and S. Murnaghan, eds. *Women and Slaves in Greco-Roman Culture: Differential Equations*. New York: 152–173.

Patzer, H. 1970. "Sallust und Thukydides." In V. Pöschl, ed. *Sallust*. Darmstadt: 102–120.

Paul, G. M. 1966. "Sallust." In T. A. Dorey, ed. *Latin Historians*. London: 85–113.

————. 1982. *"Urbs Capta*: Sketch of an Ancient Literary Motif." *Phoenix* 36: 144–155.

————. 1985. "Sallust's Sempronia: The Portrait of a Lady." *Papers of the Liverpool Latin Seminar* 5: 9–22.

Pauw, D. A. 1980. "Impersonal Expressions and Unidentified Spokesmen in Greek and Roman Historiography and Biography." *Acta Classica* 23: 83–95.

Pavel, T. 1998. "Freedom, from Romance to the Novel: Three Anti-Utopian American Critics." *New Literary History* 29: 579–598.

Plass, P. 1995. *The Game of Death in Ancient Rome: Arena Sport and Political Suicide*. Madison, WI.

Plathner, H.-G. 1934. *Die Schlachtschilderungen bei Livius*. Breslau.

Porter, J. I., ed. 1999. *Constructions of the Classical Body*. Ann Arbor, MI.

Potter, D. 1998. "*Senatus consultum de Cn. Pisone*." *JRA* 11:437–457.

Premerstein, A. v. 1937. *Vom Werden und Wesen des Prinzipats*. Abhandlungen der Bayerischen Akademie der Wissenschaften, Philosophisch-historische Abteilung. Munich.

Prince, G. 1982. *Narratology: The Form and Functioning of Narrative*. Berlin.

Rabinowitz, P. 1987. *Before Reading: Narrative Conventions and the Politics of Interpretation*. Ithaca, NY.

Rambaud, M. 1946. "Les Prologues de Salluste et la démonstration morale dans son oevre." *REL* 24: 115–130.

Ramsey, J. T. 1984. *Sallust's "Bellum Catilinae."* Chico, CA.

Rawson, E. 1986. "Cassius and Brutus: The Memory of the Liberators." In I. Moxon, J. Smart, and A. J. Woodman, eds. *Past Perspectives: Studies in Greek and Roman Historical Writing*. Cambridge: 101–119.

————. 1991. *"Discrimina Ordinum*: The *Lex Julia Theatralis."* In *Roman Culture and Society: Collected Papers*. Oxford: 508–545.

Redfield, J. 1990. "From Sex to Politics: The Rites of Artemis Triklaria and Dionysos Aisymnetes at Patras." In D. Halperin, J. Winkler, and F. Zeitlin, eds. *Before Sexuality: The Construction of Erotic Experience in the Ancient Greek World*. Princeton, NJ: 115–134.

Reynolds, L. D., ed. 1991. *C. Sallusti Crispi: Catilina, Iugurtha, Historiarum Fragmenta Selecta, Appendix Sallustiana*. Oxford Classical Texts. Oxford.

Richlin, A. 1992. *The Garden of Priapus: Sexuality and Aggression in Roman Humor*, Revised Edition. Oxford.

———. 1999. "Cicero's Head." In J. I. Porter, ed. *Constructions of the Classical Body*. Ann Arbor: 190–211.

Ritter, H. W. 1972. "Cluvius Rufus bei Josephus?" *RhM* 115: 85–91.

Roberts, D., Dunn, F., and Fowler, D., eds. 1997. *Classical Closure: Reading the End in Greek and Latin Literature*. Princeton, NJ.

Robin, P. 1979. "*Bacchanal, Bacchanalia, Bacchanalis*." *Pallas* 26: 63–75.

Roller, M. B. 2001. *Constructing Autocracy: Aristocrats and Emperors in Julio-Claudian Rome*. Princeton, NJ.

Rood, T. 1998. *Thucydides: Narrative and Explanation*. Oxford.

Rossi, A. 1997. "Battle Scenes in Virgil: Analysis of Narrative Techniques." Ph.D. dissertation, Harvard University.

———. 2002. "The Fall of Troy: Between Tradition and Genre." In D. Levene and D. Nelis, eds. *Clio and the Poets: Augustan Poetry and the Traditions of Ancient Historiography*. Leiden: 231–251.

Rousselle, R. 1989. "Persons in Livy's Account of the Bacchic Persecution." *Studies in Latin Literature and Roman History* 5: 55–65.

Rudich, V. 1993. *Political Dissidents under Nero: The Price of Dissimulation*. London.

Rutland, L. 1978. "Women as Makers of Kings in Tacitus' *Annals*." *CW* 72: 15–29.

Rutledge, S. 2001. *Imperial Inquisitions: Prosecutors and Informants from Tiberius to Domitian*. London.

Ryberg, I. S. 1942. "Tacitus' Art of Innuendo." *TAPA* 73: 383–404.

Saller, R. 1980. "Anecdotes as Historical Evidence for the Principate." *G&R* 27: 69–83.

Santoro-L'hoir, F. 1992. *The Rhetoric of Gender Terms: "Man," "Woman," and the Portrayal of Character in Latin Prose*. Leiden.

———. 1994. "Tacitus and Women's Usurpation of Power." *CW* 88: 5–25.

Scafuro, A. 1989. "Livy's Comic Narrative of the Bacchanalia." *Helios* 16: 119–142.

Scanlon, T. 1980. *The Influence of Thucydides on Sallust*. Heidelberg.

Schmal, S. 2001. *Sallust*. Hildesheim.

Schwartz, D. R. 2002. "Rome and the Jews: Josephus on 'Freedom' and 'Autonomy'." In A. Bowman, H. Cotton, M. Goodman, and S. Price, eds. *Representations of Empire: Rome and the Mediterranean World*. Oxford: 65–81.

Seager, R. 1964. "The First Catilinarian Conspiracy." *Historia* 13: 338–347.

Shackleton Bailey, D. R., ed. 1977. *Cicero: "Epistulae Ad Familiares."* Vol. I, 62–47 B.C. Cambridge.

Sherwin-White, A. N. 1966. *The Letters of Pliny: A Historical and Social Commentary*. Oxford.

————. 1984. *Roman Foreign Policy in the East 168 B.C. to A.D. 1.* London.

Shumate, N. 1997. "Compulsory Pretense and the 'Theatricalization of Experience' in Tacitus." *Studies in Latin Literature and Roman History* 8: 364–403.

Simpson, C. J. 1980. "The 'Conspiracy' of A.D. 39." *Latomus* 168: 347–366.

Sinclair, P. 1991. "Rhetorical Generalizations in *Annales* 1–6: A Review of the Problem of Innuendo and Tacitus' Integrity." *ANRW* 2.33.4: 2795–2831.

————. 1995. *Tacitus the Sententious Historian: A Sociology of Rhetoric in "Annales" 1–6.* University Park, PA.

Skard, E. 1932. "Studien zur Sprache der 'Epistulae ad Caesarem'." *SO* 10: 61–98.

Skinner, M. B. 1997. "*Quod multo fit aliter in Graecia.*" In J. Hallett and M. Skinner, eds. *Roman Sexualities.* Princeton, NJ: 3–25.

Sloan, B., and Hill, J. 1992. *JFK: The Last Dissenting Witness.* Gretna, LA.

Southern, P. 1997. *Domitian: Tragic Tyrant.* Bloomington, IN.

Stevens, C. E. 1963. "The Plotting of B.C. 66/65." *Latomus* 22: 397–435.

Stewart, Z. 1953. "Sejanus, Gaeticulus, and Seneca," *AJP* 74: 70–85.

Stockert, W. 1972. "Die Anspielungen auf die Bacchanalien in der *Aulularia* (406–414) und anderen Plautuskomödien." In R. Hanslik, A. Lesky, and H. Schwabl, eds. *Antidosis: Festschrift für Walter Kraus zum 70 Geburtstag.* Vienna: 398–407.

Stockton, D. 1971. *Cicero: A Political Biography.* Oxford.

Sturken, M. 1997. *Tangled Memories: The Vietnam War, the AIDS Epidemic, and the Politics of Remembering.* Berkeley.

Sullivan, J. 1985. *Literature and Politics in the Age of Nero.* Ithaca, NY.

Swain, S. 1996. *Hellenism and Empire: Language, Classicism, and Power in the Greek World AD 50–250.* Oxford.

Syme, R. 1939. *The Roman Revolution.* Oxford.

————. 1958. *Tacitus.* 2 vols. Oxford.

————. 1964. *Sallust.* Berkeley.

————. 1970. *Ten Studies in Tacitus.* Oxford.

————. 1974. "History or Biography: The Case of Tiberius Caesar." *Historia* 23: 481–496.

————. 1978. *History in Ovid.* Oxford.

————. 1981. "Princesses and Others in Tacitus." *G&R* 28: 40–52.

————. 1983. "Domitian: The Last Years." *Chiron* 13: 121–146.

————. 1984. "How Tacitus Wrote *"Annals"* 1–3." In A. Birley, ed. *Roman Papers III.* Oxford: 1014–1042.

————. 1986. *The Augustan Aristocracy.* Oxford.

Talbert, R. 1999. "Tacitus and the Senatus Consultum de Cn. Pisone Patre." *AJP* 120: 89–97.

Tarditi, G. 1954. "La Questione dei Baccanali à Roma nel 186 a.c." *La Parola del passato* 9: 265–287.

Taylor, L. R. 1966. *Party Politics in the Age of Caesar.* Berkeley.

Thomas, R. F. 1988. *Virgil "Georgics."* 2 vols. Cambridge.

Thompson, J. 1967. *Six Seconds in Dallas: A Micro-Study of the Kennedy Assassination.* New York.

Tiffou, E. 1973. *Essai sur la pensée morale de Salluste à la lumière de ses prologues*. Paris.

Timpe, D. 1960. "Römische Geschichte bei Flavius Josephus." *Historia* 9: 474–502.

———. 1962. *Untersuchungen zur Kontinuität des Frühen Prinzipats*. Wiesbaden.

Townend, G. B. 1964. "Cluvius Rufus in the *Histories* of Tacitus." *AJP* 85: 337–377.

Toynbee, A. 1965. *Hannibal's Legacy: The Hannibalic War's Effects on Roman Life*. Vol. 2. Oxford.

Trask, R. B. 1994. *Pictures of the Pain: Photography and the Assassination of President Kennedy*. Danvers, MA.

Treggiari, S. 1991. *Roman Marriage: "Iusti Coniuges" from the Time of Cicero to the Time of Ulpian*. Oxford.

van Hooff, A. 1990. *From Autothanasia to Suicide: Self-Killing in Classical Antiquity*. London.

van Neste, R. 2002. "Structure and Cohesion in Titus: Problems and Method." *Bible Translator* 53: 118–133.

Vandiver, E. 1999. "The Founding Mothers of Livy's Rome: The Sabine Women and Lucretia." In F. B. Titchener and R. F. Moorton, eds. *The Eye Expanded: Life and the Arts in Greco-Roman Antiquity*. Berkeley: 206–232.

Varner, E. R., ed. 2000. *From Caligula to Constantine: Tyranny and Transformation in Roman Portraiture*. Atlanta, GA.

Vasaly, A. 1993. *Representations: Images of the World in Ciceronian Oratory*. Berkeley.

Verstraete, B. C. 1980. "Slavery and the Social Dynamics of Male Homosexual Relations in Ancient Rome." *Journal of Homosexuality* 5: 227–236.

Vessey, D. 1973. *Statius and the "Thebaid."* Cambridge.

Vretska, K. 1970. "Der Aufbau des *Bellum Catilinae*." In V. Pöschl, ed. *Sallust*. Darmstadt: 74–101.

———. 1976. *C. Sallustius Crispus: De Catilinae Coniuratione*. 2 vols. Heidelberg.

Wacholder, B. 1962. *Nicolaus of Damascus*. Berkeley.

Walker, B. 1952. *The "Annals" of Tacitus: A Study in the Writing of History*. Manchester.

Wallace-Hadrill, A. 1981. "The Emperor and His Virtues." *Historia* 30: 298–323.

Walsh, P. G. 1994. *Livy Book XXXIX (187–183 B.C.)*. Warminster.

———. 1996. "Making a Drama out of a Crisis: Livy on the Bacchanalia." *G&R* 43: 188–203.

Walters, J. 1997. "Invading the Roman Body: Manliness and Impenetrability in Roman Thought." In J. Hallett and M. Skinner, eds. *Roman Sexualities*. Princeton, NJ: 29–43.

Warmington, B. H. 1969. *Nero: Reality and Legend*. New York.

Warrior, V. 1998. "The Roman Bid to Control Bacchic Worship." In S. Esposito, ed. *The "Bacchae" of Euripides*. Newburyport, MA: 100–105.

Waters, K. H. 1970. "Cicero, Sallust, and Catiline." *Historia* 19: 195–215.

Watson, A. 1974. "*Enuptio Gentis*." In A. Watson, ed. *Daube Noster: Essays in Legal History for David Daube*. Edinburgh: 331–341.

———. 1987. *Roman Slave Law*. Baltimore, MD.

Weinstock, S. 1971. *Divus Julius*. Oxford.

Wellesley, K. 1969. "Tacitus as a Military Historian." In T. A. Dorey, ed. *Tacitus*. London: 63–97.

Wells, S. 1985. *The Dialectics of Representation*. Baltimore, MD.

Wheeler, E. L. 1988. *Stratagem and the Vocabulary of Military Trickery*. Leiden.

White, H. 1973. *Metahistory: The Historical Imagination in Nineteenth-Century Europe*. Baltimore, MD.

———. 1978. *Tropics of Discourse: Essays in Cultural Criticism*. Baltimore, MD.

Whitehead, D. 1979. "Tacitus and the Loaded Alternative." *Latomus* 38: 474–495.

Wilkins, A. T. 1994. *Villain or Hero: Sallust's Portrayal of Catiline*. New York.

Willcock, M. M. 1983. "Battle Scenes in the *Aeneid*." *PCPS* n.s. 29: 87–99.

Wille, G. 1983. *Der Aufbau der Werke des Tacitus*. Amsterdam.

Williams, C. A. 1999. *Roman Homosexuality: Ideologies of Masculinity in Classical Antiquity*. Oxford.

Williams, G. 1968. *Tradition and Originality in Roman Poetry*. Oxford.

———. 1978. *Change and Decline: Roman Literature in the Early Empire*. Berkeley.

Williams, J. H. C. 2001. *Beyond the Rubicon: Romans and Gauls in Republican Italy*. Oxford.

Wirszubski, C. 1950. *Libertas as a Political Idea at Rome during the Late Republic and Early Principate*. Cambridge.

Wiseman, T. P. 1985. *Catullus and His World: A Reappraisal*. Cambridge.

———. 1987. "Josephus on the Palatine." In *Roman Studies Literary and Historical*. Liverpool: 167–175.

———. 1991. *Flavius Josephus: Death of an Emperor*. Exeter.

———. 1992. *Talking to Virgil: A Miscellany*. Exeter.

———. 1993. "Lying Historians: Seven Types of Mendacity." In C. Gill and T. P. Wiseman, eds. *Lies and Fiction in the Ancient World*. Austin, TX: 122–146.

———. 1994. *Historiography and Imagination*. Exeter.

———. 1995. *Remus: A Roman Myth*. Cambridge.

———. 1998. *Roman Drama and Roman History*. Exeter.

Wolf, J. G. 1988. *Das Senatusconsultum Silanianum und die Senatsrede des C. Cassius Longinus aus dem Jahre 61 n. Chr*. Heidelberg.

Woodman, A. J. 1983. *Velleius Paterculus: The Caesarian and Augustan Narratives (2.41–93)*. Cambridge.

———. 1988. *Rhetoric in Classical Historiography: Four Studies*. Portland, OR.

———. 1989. "Virgil the Historian: *Aeneid* 8.626–62 and Livy." In J. Diggle, J. B. Hall, and H. D. Jocelyn, eds. *Studies in Latin Literature and its Tradition in Honour of C. O. Brink*. Cambridge: 132–145.

———. 1993. "Amateur Dramatics at the Court of Nero: *Annals* 15.48–74." In T. J. Luce and A. J. Woodman, eds. *Tacitus and the Tacitean Tradition*. Princeton, NJ: 104–128.

———. 1995. "A Death in the First Act: Tacitus, *Annals* 1.6." *Papers of the Leeds International Latin Seminar* 8: 257–273.

———. 1998. *Tacitus Reviewed*. Oxford.

Woodman, A. J., and Martin, R. H. 1996. *The "Annals" of Tacitus Book 3.* Cambridge.

Yavetz, Z. 1963. "The Failure of Catiline's Conspiracy." *Historia* 12: 485–499.

Zetzel, J. E. G. 1995. *Cicero "De Re Publica" Selections.* Cambridge.

Ziolkowski, A. 1993. "*Urbs Direpta,* or How the Romans Sacked Cities." In J. Rich and G. Shipley, eds. *War and Society in the Roman World.* London: 69–91.

# GENERAL INDEX

Adams, J. N., 58, 148n.63, 159n.1

Adultery, 15, 41–42, 49, 58, 79. *See also* Sexuality

Adverbs, 88–89

Aebutia, 52–53, 62

Aebutius, 52–53, 61, 62, 64, 83, 87, 128, 148n.61

Aemelius Lepidus, Marcus, 95, 96, 97, 99, 111, 155n.6, 156n.14

Aemelius Regulus, 99–103

Aeneas, 6, 8, 10, 39, 142n.9

Agrippina the Elder, 69

Agrippina the Younger, 5, 72, 73, 96–97, 156n.14

Allobroges, 31, 46–49, 123

Alternative explanations, 77, 113–114

Annalistic history, 89, 109–110, 130

Annius Vinicianus, 99–104, 156n.20

Antonia, 69, 98

Antony, 14, 44, 100, 105, 111, 116, 118

*Aporia* (difficulty), 89, 150n.14

Appian: alternative explanations given by, 113–114; on Caesar's assassination, 6, 8, 10, 110–119, 124, 130, 160n.21; career and writings of, 109–110; on Catilinarian conspiracy, 7, 41, 45, 47, 160n.21; on Cato's suicide attempt, 150n.8; compared with other writers of conspiracy narratives, 7, 22, 110, 123–124; conversation between Brutus and Cassius in, 114–115; on Crassus and Pompey, 29; Greek language used by, 15; and hermeneutics of assassination, 111–119; importance of, 15; naming of conspirators by, 115, 119; narrative strategies and rhetorical devices of, 22, 110–119, 159n.7, 160n.28; on Porcia, 120; scholarship on, 110; sources of, 110

Asinius Pollio, 59–60, 110, 159n.17

Assassination: aborted attempts against Caligula, 94–98; of Caesar, 6, 8, 10, 87, 100–101, 108–119, 124, 125, 130, 156n.26, 160nn.20–21; of Caligula, 5, 6, 8, 10, 87, 94, 98–108, 111, 119–120, 124, 129, 130; Cooper on, 112; of Domitian, 5; of J. F. Kennedy, 2–3, 65–68, 149n.77; omens and portents concerning, 10, 103, 116, 118, 158n.44; Porcia's involvement in Caesar's assassination, 120–122, 128; Quintilia's involvement in Caligula's assassination, 105–107, 119, 122, 124, 128, 129; rewards for assassins, 100. *See also* Conspiracy

Augustus: biography of, 8; birthday of, 9, 136n.24; and Caesar's assassination, 10; Caligula's descent from, 97; conspiracies against, 97–98; death of, 5; golden shield of, 156n.17; marriage of, 127; moral reforms of, 148n.47; oath of allegiance to, 14; pardons of conspirators by, 97–98, 156n.17; successor for, 96; Tacitus on, 68, 77

Author component of narratology, 19–20, 23

Authority in ancient historiography, 32, 37, 45, 89

Bacchanalia and Bacchantes: initiation and practices of, 52, 53, 56–59, 61, 62, 64, 65; oath taken by members, 54; and physical and sexual abuse, 57–61, 64, 124–125; in Plautus and other Latin authors, 9, 57, 61; and senatorial decree banning cult of Bacchus, 4, 7, 51–57, 60–61, 89, 123

Bacchanalian affair: betrayal of, 52–53, 64–65, 83, 90, 93, 119, 122; and Cato the Elder, 51–52; charges against conspirators, 55; chronology of, 89; compared with other conspiracy narratives, 87–90, 123–124; debate on existence of, 86; and Hispala, 52, 53, 56, 58, 61–67, 83, 87, 107, 115, 119, 121, 122, 124, 128, 153n.51; impact of, 90; Livy on, 4–5, 7, 50–67, 74, 87–90, 93, 123, 124–125, 129, 130, 136n.25, 137nn.28,37; punishment of conspirators, 53, 80, 87; and senatorial decree banning cult of Bacchus, 4, 7, 51–57, 60–61, 89, 123; and slaves, 50, 56–61, 80; sources on, 51–53; and women, 50, 52–53, 56, 61–67; and xenophobia, 54–56

Backshadowing, 117–118

Bakhtin, M., 116–117

Bal, M., 36

Balbus, 59–60

Barbu, N. I., 110

Barrett, A., 95

Barthes, R., 22, 39, 125, 151n.17

Bauman, R., 55

Bernstein, M., 117

Betrayal: of aborted assassination attempt against Caligula, 97; of Bacchanalian affair, 52–53, 64–65, 83, 87, 90, 93, 119, 122; of Catilinarian conspiracy, 30, 39, 41, 42–47, 49, 83, 87, 93, 119, 122; of conspiracy generally, 5, 6; of Pisonian conspiracy, 74, 80, 83–87, 93, 119; rewards for informants, 47, 48, 53, 64, 65, 84–85, 87, 90; by slaves, 82, 103–104; by women, 42–46, 64–65, 68–69, 83, 93, 119, 126

Body: inviolability of male citizen body, 59–61, 80, 124–125; knowledge held in female body, 42–48, 52, 61, 62, 64, 73–74, 79–80, 105, 106, 107, 126, 128; mutilated body of Quintilia, 106, 129; self-mutilation of, 120–122, 128; silence of, 122; of slaves, 18, 59, 80; slave's access to master's body, 17. *See also* Rape; Sexuality; Torture

Body language, 105–106

Body politic metaphor, 38

Boundary violation, 80, 87, 107, 124–125, 129. *See also* Public/private spaces

Bradley, K. R., 18, 139n.68

Bruhl, A., 56

Bucolianus, 115, 119

Burrus, 73, 77

Caesar: and affair with Servilia, 42, 159n.13; assassination of, 6, 8, 10, 87, 100–101, 108–119, 124, 125, 130, 156n.26, 160nn.20–21; and attempted warnings about assassination plot, 118; Brutus' relationship with, 113–114, 159n.13; and Catilinarian conspiracy, 33, 35, 40, 59, 80, 87; and Cato, 40, 120, 148n.52; and Cleopatra, 105; and colony of Urso, 12; *coniuratio* used by, 12; as consul, 30; crossing of Rubicon by, 90; eponymous wife and mistress of, 79; and first Catilinarian conspiracy, 142n.10; first consulship of, 100–101; honors for, 111–112; oaths of soldiers of, 160n.21; omens before assassination of, 10, 116, 118; and personal *dignitas*, 111, 159n.8; Pompey's campaign against, 113; Porcia's knowledge of assassination plot against, 120–122, 128; sources on assassination of, 109, 112; speech against capital punishment by, 31, 40, 59, 80, 87; uprisings of Gauls against, 12; worship of Bacchus during rule of, 55

Caesonia, 97, 102, 157n.39

Caligula: aborted assassination attempts against, 94–98, 111, 155n.6; assassination of, 5, 6, 8, 10, 87, 94, 98–108, 111, 119–120, 124, 129, 130, 158n.44; and *clementia*, 97, 156n.17; omens and portents on assassination of, 103, 158n.44; Quintilia's involvement in assassination of, 105–107, 119, 124, 128, 129; sexuality of, 94, 96, 125; slaves as informants for, 104; sources on, 94–95, 101–102; successor for, 96; torture ordered by, 18, 105–107, 121, 128, 140n.77; tyrannical behavior and reign of, 93, 94–96, 98, 101–103, 111, 127, 158n.63; youth of, 98

Callistus, 97, 99, 101

Calpurnia, 5, 79, 116, 118

Calpurnius Piso, Gaius, 77, 84, 85, 93, 150n.9

Calpurnius Piso, Gnaeus, 44, 68, 69–72

Capital punishment. *See* Punishment

Casca, 118–119

Cassius, 10, 100, 105, 108, 109, 113–115, 119, 125, 128, 160n.20

Cassius Chaerea, 99–108

Catilinarian conspiracy: and Allobroges at Mulvian Bridge, 31, 46–49, 123; Appian on, 160n.21; betrayal of, 30, 39, 41, 42–47, 49, 83, 87, 93, 119, 122; and Cataline's last battle, 31, 37, 40–41; and Catiline's sexuality, 34; catalogue of conspirators in, 34–35; chronology and date of, 9, 27, 89; and Cicero, 7, 8, 9, 27, 31, 36, 39–48, 50, 83, 129, 136n.22, 137n.37, 145n.51; compared with other

conspiracy narratives, 87–90, 123–124, 156n.21; and conspirators' drinking of human blood, 33; debate on existence of, 86; first Catilinarian conspiracy, 30, 32, 34, 39–40; Fulvia's betrayal of, 31, 42–46, 47, 48, 49, 83, 87, 90, 107, 115, 119, 121, 122, 123, 124, 128; impact of, 90; and oaths, 33, 47, 48, 116; overview of, 5–6; punishment of conspirators, 31, 40, 47, 59, 80, 145n.1; rhetorical devices on, 32–37, 49, 101; Sallust on, 5, 7, 8, 9, 27, 32–50, 75, 87–90, 93, 110, 115, 123, 124, 125, 130, 136n.22, 154n.68; sources on, 7, 8–9, 51; suspense in *Bellum Catilinae* on, 37–41, 49; unnamed sources on, 34–35, 88; women's involvement in, 41–46, 87

Catiline: character of, 8, 34–37, 41, 75, 129, 135n.11, 155n.68; as conspirator, 5, 28–31, 35, 36, 38–41, 43, 45–48, 124, 136n.22, 143n.26; and consulship elections, 30–31; impact of, 90; last battle of, 40; rivalry between Cicero and, 13, 29, 31, 86, 129; sexuality of, 34, 35, 36–37, 41–42, 125; Vergil on, 8. *See also* Catilinarian conspiracy

Cato the Elder: and Bacchanalian affair, 51, 53, 145n.1; echoed in Sallust, 49; on *lex Oppia*, 11, 49; negative attitude toward women, 49

Cato the Younger: and Caesar, 40, 120, 148n.52; and Catilinarian conspiracy, 31, 33, 39, 47, 87, 145n.1; daughter of, 120–122; suicide of, 120, 150n.8

Causality, 23, 36, 44, 45, 48, 72, 111, 114, 117, 119, 126–127, 130

Celebratory history, 6, 9–10

Characterization, 36–37, 40, 41, 49

Cicero: and Catilinarian conspiracy, 7, 8, 9, 27, 31, 36, 39–48, 50, 83, 86, 90, 122, 129, 130, 136n.22, 137n.37, 145n.51; *De Lege Manilia* by, 29; on digressions, 113; exile of, 90; on extortion charge against Fonteius, 13; government offices for, 29, 30, 46; on history, 152n.36; as orator, 29; on political background of Catilinarian conspiracy, 28; rivalry between Catiline and, 13, 29, 31, 86, 129; on Verres, 12, 60, 145n.47; wife of, 44; on women's involvement in Catilinarian conspiracy, 41

Cinna, 97–98, 156n.17

Civil war, 6, 8, 112–113

Claudius: accession of, 94, 100, 104; Antonia as daughter of, 77; and Caligula's assassination, 10, 100, 104, 108; conspiracies against, 5, 79, 156n.20; death of, 68; Messalina as wife of, 9; suicide of freedman of, 72; Tacitus on, 70; torture ordered by, 18; and trial of Piso, 70

Clemens, 99, 103, 104

*Clementia* (despotic mercy), 97–98, 156n.17

Cleopatra, 79, 105

Cluvius Rufus, 102, 156n.26, 157n.41

Commodus, 5, 127

Common sense, 78, 152n.36

Confessions, 85–86

*Coniuratio*, 11–14, 54–56, 87, 123, 160n.21

Conspiracy: and containment strategy, 6, 16, 22–23, 56, 61, 88, 90, 98–99; and counterconspiracy, 48, 67, 86–87, 108, 128, 129–131; debates on existence of, 86–87, 95; early examples of, in Roman history, 4–6; etymology of, 11; exceptionality of, 126; foreigners' involvement in, 5, 54–56, 105; historical study of, 14–15; initiation compared with, 59; literary study of, 15–24; meaning of, 90; pardons of conspirators, 97–98, 156n.17; rhetoric of, 19–24, 32–37, 49, 88–89, 101, 124; in Roman literary imagination, 7–10, 123; slaves' involvement in, 5, 17–18, 19; typology of conspiracy narratives, 19–24,

87–90; vocabulary of, 10–14. *See also* Assassination; Betrayal; Women; and specific conspiracies and conspirators

Containment strategy, 6, 16, 22–23, 56, 61, 88, 90, 98–99

Continuity. *See* Narrative continuity

Cornelius Cethegus, Publius, 8, 30

Cornelius Lentulus Gaeticulus, Gnaeus, 95–98, 111, 155n.6, 156n.14

Cornelius Lentulus Sura, Publius, 8, 9, 30, 31, 36, 46, 47

Cornelius Sulla, Publius, 8, 30

Cornelius Sulla, Servius, 8

Counterconspiracy, 48, 67, 86–87, 108, 128, 129–131

Crassus, 28–31, 34, 35, 111, 141n.5, 142n.10

Cremutius Cordus, 10, 86, 153n.56

Curius, 42–46, 47, 48, 83, 87, 115, 128, 144n.45

Dean, John, 2, 130, 135n.4

Deictic markers of space or time, 19–20

Delay, 22, 23–24, 37–41, 49, 113–114, 115, 119

Description, 21–22, 23

Deterrence, 6, 22, 40, 98–99, 124, 129. *See also* Containment strategy

Digresssion, 22, 32, 37–41, 49, 113

Dio: on assassination attempt against Nero, 8; on Caesar's assassination, 7, 109; on Caligula, 94–98; Cluvius as source for, 157n.41; on Commodus, 5; on conspiracy against Domitian, 126–128; opinions of, in historical narratives by, 155n.73; on Porcia, 120, 121–122; on Quintilia, 106–107; on republican versus imperial historiography, 75; scholarship on, 110

Diodorus Siculus, 7, 43–44, 45

Direct discourse (*oratio recta*), 20, 40, 47, 86, 114

Discourse, 20–21, 22, 40, 47, 141n.83

Distant voice of freedom, 86

Diversion, 22, 37–41, 115
Domitia, 126–128, 162n.16
Domitian, 5, 93, 126–129, 154n.61, 162n.16
Dyrrhachium, battle of, 113, 120

Eighteen-and-a-half-minute gap, 1, 2, 76, 130
Epicharis, 68–69, 73–74, 76–83, 84, 87, 106, 107, 115, 122, 124, 128–129, 140n.77, 152n.43, 153n.56
Epistemological gap, 39–40, 46, 88, 89, 109, 110, 131
Ethnicity. See Foreigners
Evidence: etymology of, 3; gaps in, 1–4, 76, 88, 130; problems of different types of, 139n.61. See also Sources
Exceptionality, 49, 81–82, 107, 119–122, 126
Execution. See Punishment
Eyewitness, 58, 61–62, 64–65

Fabius Sanga, Quintus, 47, 48, 145n.51
Faenius Rufus, 73, 77, 85
Fantham, E., 58
Faur, J. C., 95
Fear, 6, 17, 19, 22, 24, 65, 89, 90, 99, 103, 123, 124
Ferrill, A., 95
First Catilinarian conspiracy, 30, 32, 34, 39–40, 142n.10. See also Catilinarian conspiracy
First person, 19–20, 21, 32–33, 34, 37, 49, 70, 71, 88, 101, 119, 124, 126, 157n.30, 159n.7, 160n.28
Flower, H., 60
Focalization, 21, 22, 49, 115–116, 119, 124, 141n.83. See also Point of view
Foreigners: and Bacchanalian affair, 54–56; and Caligula's assassination, 99–100, 105; expulsion of, from Rome, 28; involvement of, in conspiracies, 5, 105; negative attitudes against, 13, 105; and xenophobia, 54–56, 124
Foreshadowing, 116–118

Frank, T., 56
Freedom: from constraints of time, 116–117; contrasted with slavery, 38–39, 104–105, 125, 158n.49; distant voice of freedom, 86; as negative condition, 143n.25
Free indirect discourse, 21
Fulvia, 31, 42–46, 47, 48, 49, 83, 87, 90, 107, 115, 119, 121, 122, 123, 124, 128, 144n.45

Gabba, E., 110
Gabinius, 30, 46, 47, 48–49
Gardner, J., 58
Garnsey, P., 18, 140n.77
Gelzer, M., 53
Gender. See Women
Germanicus, 44, 69–70, 72, 77, 143n.31
Gleason, M., 105
Gruen, E., 56, 60, 64, 141n.5, 142n.10

Habinek, T., 13
Haldeman, H. R., 1–2
Hannibalic war (218/217 B.C.E.), 13, 54
Hermeneutics, 22, 23, 24, 111–119, 123. See also Suspense
Hill, J., 65–67
Hispala, 52, 53, 56, 58, 61–67, 83, 87, 107, 115, 119, 121, 122, 124, 128, 148nn.60–61, 149n.69, 153n.51
Historiography. See specific historians
Homosexuality, 58–59, 96, 148nn.46–47
Horace, 8, 22
Human sacrifice, 34, 37

Ignorance, 71–72, 74–78, 88–90. See also Limits of knowledge
Imperial versus republican historiography, 75–76, 151n.28
Impersonal statements, 35, 37
Improbability, 34, 37, 77–78
Indefinite pronouns and adverbs, 35–36, 37, 45, 49, 77, 90, 124

Indeterminacy, 71–72, 74–78, 88–90, 97, 124

Indirect discourse (*oratio obliqua*), 21, 22, 40, 153n.55

Informants. *See* Betrayal

Initiation, 52, 53, 56–59, 61, 62, 64, 65

Janus, 13, 19, 41, 130

Jews, 93–94, 98–99, 130

Josephus: on body language, 105–106; on Caesar's assassination, 10, 100–101, 156n.26; on Caligula's assassination, 5, 6, 8, 93, 94, 99–108, 111, 119, 124, 125, 129, 130, 156n.20; compared with other writers of conspiracy narratives, 7, 22, 104, 110, 111, 123–124; on foreigners, 105; Greek language used by, 15; importance of, 15, 97; on Masada, 161n.2; narrative strategies and rhetorical devices of, 22, 101, 119; pro-republican underpinnings of narrative of, 104; on Quintilia, 105–107, 122, 124; reliability of, 102, 161n.2; on Sejanus, 98; on slavery, 103–105; sources of, 101–102, 157nn.31,41; unnamed sources of, 101–102; and Vespasian, 93; writings by, 93–94

Joshel, S., 45

Julius Caesar. *See* Caesar

Junius Brutus, Decimus, 42, 46, 109, 115, 116, 160n.20

Junius Brutus, Lucius, 6, 63

Junius Brutus, Marcus, 10, 42, 100, 105, 108, 109, 113–116, 118–122, 125, 128, 159n.13, 160nn.20,29

Junius Silanus, 31, 72

Kennedy, J. F., 2–3, 65–67, 130, 139n.64, 149n.77

Kutler, S., 2, 76, 130

Levene, D. S., 49

*Lex Oppia*, 11, 44, 49

*Lex Plautia de vi*, 54

Licinius Murena, Lucius, 28, 31

Limits of knowledge, 1–4, 7, 32, 33, 36, 39–40, 71–72, 74–78, 88, 130. *See also* Epistemological gap; Ignorance

Lintott, A., 55

Livia, 5, 44, 68, 69, 97–98, 127

Livilla, 96–97

Livy: on Bacchanalian affair, 4–5, 7, 50–67, 87–90, 93, 123, 124–125, 129, 130, 136n.25, 137nn.28,37; on Caesar's assassination, 10, 109; compared with other writers of conspiracy narratives, 7, 22, 87–90, 123–124; on foundation myths and legends, 9, 45, 62–64; on Hispala, 52, 53, 56, 58, 61–67, 83, 87, 107, 122, 124, 153n.51; on military oaths before battle of Cannae (216 B.C.E.), 11; narrative strategies of, 22, 124; reliability of, 53, 61, 62, 65; on Romulus' death, 4; on women wanting repeal of *lex Oppia*, 44; and xenophobia, 54–56

Loyalty tale, 121

Lucan, 8, 9, 73, 81, 150n.8, 153n.46

Lucceius, 27, 130

Lucretia, 45, 62, 63–64

*Maiestas* (slander against *princeps* or his family), 105

Mamertine Prison, 29–30

Manlius, Gaius, 31, 36, 90

Manumission of slaves, 17, 52, 61–62, 84

Marincola, J., 89

Martin, R. H., 72, 144n.40

McCarthy, K., 17

McDonald, A. H., 53, 56

McHale, B., 21

Méautis, G., 53

Messalina, 9, 79

Milichus, 68–69, 74, 83–87, 128, 151n.21; wife of, 68–69, 85, 107, 119, 122, 128

Mimesis, 20, 111, 115, 119

Mode of presentation, 20–21, 23, 123

Morality and moralizing statements, 9, 38, 39, 55–56, 81–82, 90, 107–108, 125
Morson, G., 117
*Mos maiorum* (ancestral custom), 14
Mulvian Bridge skirmish, 31, 46–49
Mystery. *See* Suspense
Mystery cults, 54–56, 148n.49. *See also* Bacchanalian affair

Narcissus, 72, 79
Narrative, definition of, 20
Narrative continuity: in Appian's narrative of Caesar's assassination, 119; in conspiracy narratives generally, 23, 24, 87–88, 123, 130; in Livy's narrative on Bacchanalian affair, 53, 64, 87–88; in Sallust's narrative on Catilinarian conspiracy, 32–37, 43, 87–88; in Tacitus, 71–72, 87–88
Narratology: author component of, 19–20, 23; critique of, 123–131; purpose of, 19; reader component of, 22–24; of successful versus betrayed conspiracies, 5–6, 123–124; text component of, 20–24. *See also* specific narrative strategies
Natalis, Antonius, 73, 80, 84, 85
Nero: assassination plots against, 7–8, 68, 73–80, 84–85, 123–124; betrayal of Pisonian conspiracy to, 74, 80, 83–86; and *clementia*, 156n.17; counter-conspiracy by, 86, 129; Proculus' hostility toward, 73–74, 79–80; punishment of Pisonian conspirators by, 9, 73, 74, 79, 80–81, 86, 87; sexuality of, 125; Stoicism and opposition to, 153n.58; Subrius Flavus' hatred of, 85–86; terror under, 5, 72–73, 76, 151n.17; torture ordered by, 18, 80–83, 121, 128, 140n.77. *See also* Pisonian conspiracy
Nicolaus of Damascus, 8, 109, 110, 156n.26
Nilsson, M., 56

Nixon, R. M., 1–2, 3, 76, 123, 130
Nonius Asprenas, 70, 99, 103
North, J., 55

Oaths, 11–14, 33, 47, 48, 54, 115–116, 160n.21
Octavia, 18, 72–73
Omens, 10, 36, 102, 103, 116, 118, 158n.44
*Oratio obliqua* (indirect discourse), 21, 22, 40, 153n.55
*Oratio recta* (direct discourse), 20, 40, 47, 86, 114
Oswald, L. H., 66

Pardons of conspirators, 97–98, 156n.17
Parker, H., 121
Paul, G. M., 16–17
Petronius, 9, 73, 150n.8
Physical abuse by Bacchantes, 57–61, 64, 124–125
Pillow talk, 44–45, 63, 82–83, 88, 106
Pisonian conspiracy: betrayal of, 80, 83–87, 93, 119; chronology and date of, 74, 75, 89; compared with other conspiracy narratives, 87–90, 123–124; debate on existence of, 86; description of, 5–6, 73–78; dual beginnings of narrative on, 74–76; and Epicharis, 68–69, 73–74, 76–83, 84, 87, 106, 107, 115, 122, 124, 128–129; impact of, 90; and Milichus, 68–69, 74, 83–87, 128; Plutarch on, 83–84, 162n.10; punishment of conspirators, 9, 73, 74, 79, 80–81, 86, 87; and relationship between Proculus and Epicharius, 73–74, 79–80, 87, 115, 128; sources on, 9–10, 77–78, 84, 137n.37; and Stoicism, 153n.58; Tacitus on, 5, 68, 72–90, 87–90, 93, 123–124, 125, 129, 130, 137n.37; and torture of Epicharis, 80, 87, 106, 107, 122, 124, 128–129
Plancina, 44, 69
Plautius Lateranus, 73, 77, 84

Pliny, 9, 17, 77–78

Plot, 20, 36

Plutarch: on assassination attempt against
Nero, 8; on Caesar's assassination, 10,
109, 114; on Catilinarian conspiracy,
7, 31, 45, 47, 48; Cluvius as source
for, 157n.41; on Pisonian conspiracy,
83–84, 162n.10; on Porcia, 120, 121,
161n.33; scholarship on, 110

Point of view, 21, 23, 36–37, 115–116, 119.
See also Focalization

Poison, 49, 68, 72

Pompedius, 105, 106, 107

Pompey, 28–29, 30, 90, 113

Pomponius, 107

Porcia, 111, 120–122, 128, 160n.29, 161n.33

Postumius, 52–53, 58–59, 61, 64–65, 74,
87, 129

Preface, 37–39, 49

Presuppositions, 20, 22, 23, 39

Private spaces. See Public/private spaces

Proculus, Volusius, 73–74, 79–80, 83, 87,
115, 128

Promiscuity. See Adultery; Sexuality

Pronouns: distributive pronouns, 36; first
person, 19–20, 21, 32–33, 34, 37, 49,
70, 71, 88, 101, 119, 124, 126, 157n.30,
159n.7, 160n.28; indefinite pronouns,
35–36, 37, 45, 49, 124; third person, 21,
33, 37, 49, 101–102, 110, 114

Prostitution, 41, 61–62, 79, 122, 148nn.60,
63

Provocatio (appeal), 60

Public/private spaces, 5, 17–19, 24, 44–46,
48–49, 53, 62, 80, 82–84, 87–88, 107,
125. See also Secrecy

Punishment: of assassins of Caligula, 99,
100, 108; of Bacchantes, 53, 87, 89, 90;
Caesar's speech against capital punishment, 31, 40, 59, 80, 87; of Catilinarian
conspirators, 31, 40, 47, 59, 80, 87,
145n.1; of children, 8, 99; of conspirators in aborted assassination attempts

against Caligula, 97, 98, 99, 111, 155n.6;
of Pisonian conspirators, 9, 73, 74, 79,
80–81, 86, 87; of Sejanus and fellow-
conspirators, 98; of slaves, 17–18. See
also Torture

Quintilia, 105–107, 119, 122, 124, 128, 129,
140n.77

Quirito and quiritatio, 59–60

Quoquo modo, 45, 77, 90

Rape, 45, 58–59, 63, 98, 148n.46

Readership, 22–24

Repetition, 23, 64, 74–76, 119

Republican versus imperial historiography, 75–76, 151n.28

Res publica, 5, 49, 123, 159n.8

Res repetundae (extortion), 12–13

Retrogression, 39

Revelation, 11, 20, 42–46, 49, 83, 87,
110–119. See also Betrayal

Rewards: for assassins, 100; following torture, 106, 107; for informants, 47, 48,
53, 64, 65, 84–85, 87, 90

Rhetoric of conspiracy: of Appian, 159n.7,
160n.28; of Josephus, 101; overview
of, 19–24, 88–89, 124; of Sallust, 32–
37, 49, 101. See also specific rhetorical
strategies and specific authors

Romulus, 4, 6, 10, 116, 120

Sabinus, 99, 100, 103, 104

Sallust: on Allobroges at Mulvian Bridge,
46–49, 123; on Catilinarian conspiracy,
5, 7, 8, 9, 27, 32–50, 75, 87–90, 93,
110, 115, 123, 124, 125, 130, 136n.22,
154n.68; compared with other writers
of conspiracy narratives, 7, 22, 50, 87–
90, 104, 123–124; on first Catilinarian
conspiracy, 39–40; on Fulvia, 42–46,
47, 48, 49, 87, 90, 122, 123, 124; on
moral crisis at Rome, 55, 56; narrative
strategies and rhetorical devices of,

22, 32–37, 49, 101, 119, 124; reliability of, 33, 35, 76; on rumors of human sacrifice, 34, 37; on Sempronia, 16–17, 40, 42, 49; success of *Bellum Catilinae* by, 136n.19; suspense used by, in *Bellum Catilinae*, 37–41, 49; and title of *Bellum Catilinae*, 137n.37; unnamed sources of, 34–35, 88, 124

Scaevinus, Flavius, 73, 74, 80, 84–85

Scafuro, A., 61–62, 64, 153n.51

*Scortum nobile* (noble prostitute), 61–62, 148n.60

Secrecy: and assassination, 109, 115, 118, 120–122; and conspiracy, 5, 30, 32, 44, 48, 49, 50, 59, 64–65, 83, 86–90, 93, 95, 102–108, 124, 126, 131; and epistemological gap, 39–40, 46, 88, 89, 109, 110, 131; and initiation, 59, 62, 83. *See also* Public/private spaces; Silence

Sejanus, 68, 95, 98

Self-mutilation, 120–122, 128

Sempronia, 16–17, 35–36, 40, 42, 49

*Senatus consultum*, 31, 55

*Senatus consultum de Bacchanalibus*, 4, 7, 51–57, 60–61, 89, 123, 147n.18

*Senatus consultum Pisone patre* (SCPP), 69–70

Seneca the Elder, 81

Seneca the Younger, 8, 9, 73, 75, 81, 94, 97–98, 150n.8, 153nn.46,55

Separate subjectivity, 17, 18

Servilia, 42, 159n.13

Servius, 11, 13

Servius Tullius, 4, 62

Sexual abuse by Bacchantes, 57–59, 61, 64, 124–125

Sexual assualt. *See* Rape

Sexuality: and adultery, 15, 41–42, 49, 58, 79; affair of Fulvia and Curius, 42–46, 47, 48, 87, 107, 128; affair of Hispala and Aebutius, 52, 61, 62, 64, 83, 87, 128; affair of Pompedius and Quintilia, 105, 106, 107, 128; affair of Proculus

and Epicharius, 73–74, 79–80, 87, 115, 128; of Caligula, 94, 96, 125; of Catiline, 34, 35, 36–37, 41–42, 125; of Domitian, 126–127, 161n.8; homosexuality, 58–59, 96, 148nn.46–47; of Nero, 125; and pillow talk, 44–45, 63, 82–83, 88, 106; and prostitution, 41, 61–62, 79, 122, 148nn.60,63; of women, 15, 16, 17, 41–42, 49, 78–79, 105, 106, 126

Sideshadowing, 117

Silence, 11, 17–18, 23, 30, 50, 64–66, 80–85, 89–90, 94, 102–103, 109, 122, 125, 131, 140n.70, 153n.54. *See also* Secrecy

Simpson, C. J., 95

Singularity. *See* Exceptionality

Skard, E., 32

Slaves: and Bacchanalian affair, 50, 56–61, 80; betrayal of conspiracies by, 82, 103–104; bodies of, 18, 59, 80; as Caligula's informants, 104; distinction between freedom and slavery, 38–39, 80, 104–105, 125, 158n.49; involvement of, in conspiracies, 5, 17–18, 79; manumission of, 17, 52, 61–62, 84; negative attitudes toward, 13; revolts and resistance of, 12, 13, 17, 29, 139n.68; and senate, 104; separate subjectivity of, 17, 18; silence of, 17–18, 140n.70; torture of, 17–18, 136n.28, 140n.73

Sources: of Appian, 110; on Bacchanalian affair, 51–53; on Caesar's assassination, 109, 112; on Caligula's reign and assassination, 94–95, 101–102; on Catilinarian conspiracy, 7, 8–9, 51; of Josephus, 101–102, 157n.31; on Pisonian conspiracy, 9–10, 77–78, 84, 137n.37; unnamed sources, 34–35, 70, 88–89, 101–102, 124, 142n.18; women's treatment in, 15–17, 49

Specter, A., 66

Stoicism, 82, 96, 153n.58

Story, definition of, 20

*Stuprum,* 58–59, 61, 64, 87
Subrius Flavus, 73, 75, 85–86, 153n.55
Suetonius: on assassination attempt against
  Nero, 7–8; on Augustus, 9, 14, 136n.24;
  on Caesar's assassination, 10, 109,
  114; on Caligula, 94–96, 103–104; on
  Catilinarian conspiracy, 7; Cluvius as
  source for, 157n.41; on Quintilia, 107
Suicide, 9, 63, 69–71, 72, 74, 79, 80, 82,
  100, 120, 128, 150nn.8,10, 153n.50,
  160n.29
Sulla, dictator, 28, 54, 56
Suspense: in Appian's narrative of Caesar's
  assassination, 111–119, 124; and assassination, 112; in conspiracy narratives
  generally, 22, 23, 24, 124; in Sallust's
  *Bellum Catilinae,* 37–41, 49, 123. *See
  also* Hermeneutics
Syme, R., 96, 127, 142n.10, 151n.31,
  152n.35, 153n.52

Tacitus: alternative explanations given by,
  77; on battle of Idistaviso, 150n.15;
  on Caesar's assassination, 112, 125; on
  Cicero, 8; compared with other writers
  of conspiracy narratives, 7, 22, 87–90,
  104, 123–124; conspiracy as focus of
  generally, 68; and dating of beginning
  of *Annales,* 151n.31; on Epicharis, 68–
  69, 73–74, 76–83, 84, 87, 106, 107,
  122, 124; on Gaeticulus, 95; and indeterminacy, 71–72, 74–78; interviews
  of conspirators by, 153n.52; on Lepidus, 96; on Messalina, 9, 79; names
  as meaningful in, 151n.21; narrative
  strategies of, 22, 71–72, 87–88, 124; on
  Pisonian conspiracy, 5, 68, 72–80, 87–
  90, 93, 123–124, 125, 129, 130, 137n.37;
  on Piso's writing, 150n.9; reliability of,
  77–78; and republican versus imperial
  historiography, 75–76, 151n.28; and
  sequence of campaigns in the East,
  150n.5; sources of, 9–10, 77–78, 84,

137n.37, 157n.41; on suicides, 69–71,
  150n.8; temporal ordering of events by,
  21; on Tiberius, 98, 152nn.33–34; on
  topics of history, 6; on trial and death
  of Piso, 69–72, 77; unnamed sources
  of, 70, 88, 124, 142n.18
Tanaquil, 4, 5
Tarditi, G., 53, 56
Tarquinius Priscus, Lucius, 4, 5, 62
Tarquinius Superbus, Lucius, 4, 62–63
Telltale tablet, 118, 126–128
Text: as component of narratology, 20–
  24; definition of, 20
Theatricality, 114–115, 119, 151n.23, 160n.18
Third person, 21, 33, 37, 49, 101–102, 110,
  114
Tiberius: and *clementia,* 156n.17; con-
  spiracy of Sejanus against, 95, 98;
  death of, 68, 93; Drusus' hatred of,
  153n.57; and Germanicus, 143n.31;
  Livia and rise to power of, 5, 68; Livia's
  intercession with, for Plancina, 44, 69;
  reign of, 76, 94, 95, 96; Tacitus on, 98,
  152nn.33–34; torture ordered by, 18;
  and trial of Piso, 69–70
Torture, 17–19, 80–85, 87, 105–107,
  119, 121–122, 124, 128–129, 136n.28,
  140n.73, 152n.43
Toynbee, A., 54
Trebonius, Gaius, 109, 118, 160n.20
Treggiari, S., 58
Trojan War, 11, 137n.38
Truth, 33, 98, 101. *See also* Verisimilitude
Tullia, 62–63
Typology, 19–24, 87–90

Umbrenus, Publius, 46, 47, 48–49
Uncertainty. *See* Indeterminacy
Unnamed sources on, 34–35, 70, 88–89,
  101–102, 124, 142n.18

Valerius Maximus, 8, 10, 44, 109, 120, 121,
  153n.46, 161n.33

Velleius Paterculus, 7, 8, 109

Vergil, 8, 9, 10, 65, 136n.19

Verisimilitude, 37, 71, 86

Verres, 12, 29, 60, 145n.47

Vespasian, 93, 95

Violence, 5, 6, 16, 22, 38, 45, 68, 72–73, 80–81, 87, 94, 112–113. *See also* Assassination; Civil war; Torture

Vitellius, 69, 156n.17

Vocabulary of conspiracy, 10–14

Volturcius, 47–49

Warren Commission, 3, 66, 67, 130

Watergate, 1–2, 76, 130

Waters, K. H., 86

Whispering, 83–84, 126–127, 161n.8, 162nn.10–11

Williams, C. A., 58

Williams, G., 42, 153n.46

Women: in Bacchanalian affair, 50, 52–53, 56, 61–67, 87; barrenness of, 81; betrayal of conspiracies by, 42–46, 64–65, 68–69, 83, 93, 119, 126; and Caesar's assassination, 120–122; and Caligula's assassination, 105–107; in Catilinarian conspiracy, 41–46, 87; as *clarius exemplum*, 81–82, 107, 119–122; high-born, noble women of Roman republic, 45, 62, 63–64, 119–122; immorality of noble women, 35–36, 42, 62–63, 64; and inability to keep secrets, 49, 126; involvement of, in conspiracies generally, 4, 5–6, 8, 15–17, 19, 87, 126–127, 126–129, 128–129, 139n.64, 140n.77, 152n.43; litigiousness of, 44; Livy on founding of Roman republic and, 45; and oaths, 11; and pillow talk, 44–45, 63, 82–83, 88, 106; in Pisonian conspiracy, 68–69, 73–74, 76–83, 87; and prostitution, 41, 61–62, 79, 122, 148nn.60,63; sexuality of, 15, 16, 17, 41–42, 49, 78–79, 105, 106, 126; torture of, 80–82, 83, 87, 105–107, 119, 121–122, 124, 128–129, 136n.28, 140n.77; treatment of, in ancient sources, 15–17, 49. *See also* specific women

Woodman, A. J., 72, 144n.40, 151n.23

Woods, Rose Mary, 1

Xenophobia, 54–56, 124

Yavetz, Z., 28

Zapruder film, 2–3, 4

"Zigzag history," 39

# INDEX LOCORUM

Ampelius
  19.5: 137n.36
  27.5: 136n.21

Appian
  *Civil Wars:* 109, 110
  1–2: 110, 113
  1.3: 159n.7
  1.6: 112, 159n.7
  1.16: 159n.7
  1.34: 159n.7
  1.55: 159n.7
  1.72: 162n.11
  1.84: 159n.7
  1.86: 159n.7
  1.97: 159n.7
  1.100: 159n.7
  1.104: 159n.7
  1.115: 159n.7
  2.1: 7
  2.1.2: 143n.37
  2.1.3: 45
  2.1.4: 145n.51
  2.2: 160n.21
  2.3: 144n.45, 160n.21
  2.4: 160n.21
  2.5: 159n.7
  2.18: 159n.7
  2.39: 113
  2.63: 160n.21
  2.70: 159n.7

  2.73: 160n.21
  2.86: 159n.7
  2.88: 159n.7
  2.92: 159n.7
  2.106: 111
  2.108: 111
  2.109: 111
  2.110: 112
  2.111: 115, 119, 159n.7, 160n.28
  2.111–117: 6, 8, 119
  2.112: 113, 159n.14
  2.113: 114, 115, 159n.7, 160nn.19,28
  2.114: 115, 116, 160n.21
  2.115: 116, 160n.25
  2.116: 118, 137n.34
  2.117: 137n.35
  2.124: 159n.7
  2.149: 159n.7
  2.153: 159n.7
  3.46: 139n.54
  3.58: 139n.54
  4.32–34: 44
  4.136: 160n.29
  *Roman History:* 109

Aristotle, *Poetica* 1451a36–38: 135n.7

Asconius, *In Toga Candida*
  92: 30
  93.10: 30

Augustine
  Confessiones, 2.5.11: 135n.12
  De civitate Dei
    6.9: 137n.29, 148n.58
    18.13: 148n.58

Augustus
  Res Gestae, 25.2: 13–14, 139n.53

Caesar
  Bellum Civile, 3.53.4: 161n.31
  Bellum Gallicum
    2.1.1: 12
    3.3: 12
    3.8.3: 12
    3.10.2: 12
    4.30.3: 12
    5.12–14: 159n.12
    5.27.4: 12
    6.11–28: 159n.12
    6.44.1: 12
    8.1: 12
    8.2.2: 12
    23.3: 12

Cato
  frag. 68 Malcovati: 145n.1
  frag. 240 Malcovati: 49

Catullus
  80.5–6: 162n.8
  95.1–2: 158n.43

Cicero
  Brutus, 62: 151n.28
  De Inventione, 1.27: 159n.11
  De Legibus, 2.15: 148n.58
  De Lege Manilia: 29
  De Oratore
    2.15.62: 152n.36
    2.311: 159n.11
  De Republica, 2.54: 148n.52
  Epistulae ad Atticum, 2.1.3: 141n.3

Epistulae ad Familiares
  5.12.2: 141n.1
  5.12.4: 159n.12
  10.32.3: 148n.53
  In Catilinam: 7, 27, 28, 156n.23
    1.24: 144n.44
    2.7: 143n.34
    2.8–10: 40
    2.11: 138–139n.48
    3: 48–49
    3.1.1: 144n.44
    3.9: 136n.21, 145n.54
    4.5: 48
  In Pisonem: 7
  In Toga Candida: 7
  In Verrem
    2.1.136–137: 145n.47
    2.3.68: 138n.45
    2.5.10–14: 138n.45
    2.5.17: 138n.45
    2.5.162: 148n.54
  Pro Caelio, 70: 146n.12
  Pro Cluentio, 177: 140n.75
  Pro Cornelio: 7
  Pro Fonteio, 21.3: 138n.46
  Pro Milone, 9: 148n.46
  Pro Murena: 7
  Pro Sestio, 101: 143n.35
  Pro Sulla: 7

Corpus Inscriptionum Latinarum
  6.2029.d: 155n.5
  I² 581: 7

Curtius Rufus 6.11.21: 140n.75

Dio (Cassius Dio)
  37.29–42: 7
  37.33.1: 145n.51
  37.34.1: 145n.51
  44.12: 159n.16
  44.12–22: 8
  44.13.2: 161n.37

44.13.3: 161n.38
44.14: 160n.20
44.14.3: 142n.17
44.17.1: 137n.34
44.18: 160n.26
44.18.4: 137n.34
44.19.5: 137n.35
45.13.5: 139n.54
48.44.3: 162n.9
50.6.6: 14
53.19.2: 151n.28
53.19.3: 151n.28
53.19.6: 155n.73
54.15.2–3: 156n.16
55.14–22: 98
57.3.2: 139n.55
59.3.3: 161n.3
59.22.5–6: 155n.6
59.22.5–8: 97
59.22.7: 156n.14
59.25.3: 96
59.25.7: 97
59.26.4: 107, 158n.61
59.29: 8
59.29.3: 158n.44
60.4.5–6: 137n.32
60.15.1: 156n.20
62.24–28: 8
62.24.2: 153n.55
62.27.3: 152n.43
67.15.3–4: 161n.7
72.28: 156n.17

Diodorus Siculus
37.11: 139n.54
40.5: 7, 144nn.45,46

Eutropius
6.15: 136n.23
6.25: 137n.35

Florus
2.12: 7, 136n.19

2.13.94: 160n.26
2.13.95: 137n.35

Frontinus *Strategemata* 4.1.4: 138n.40

Fronto
*Ad Antoninum Pium*, 3.1.2: 136n.19
*Ad Caesarem*, 3.12.2: 136n.19

Gellius
1.23: 161n.5
3.1.1: 136n.19
4.15.1: 136n.19
6.17.7: 136n.19
12.9.2: 136n.19
20.6.14: 136n.19

Historia Augusta
*Aurelianus* 36: 162n.13
*Avidius Cassius* 2.5: 154n.61
*Clodius Albinus* 12.10: 137n.31
*Commodus* 9.3: 162n.13
*Hadrian* 15.2: 161n.8
*Marcus Aurelius* 25: 156n.17
*Pescennius Niger* 9.1–2: 137n.31

Horace
*Ars Poetica*, 343–344: 141n.85
*Carmina*
1.2.1–2: 137n.34
1.15.7: 137n.38
*Epodes*, 16.6: 136n.13

Hyginus, *Fabulae*
15: 138n.38
95: 138n.38

*Inscriptiones Latinae Selectae*
18: 7, 145n.2
18.13: 137n.37
190: 139n.55
272: 162n.16
6087.106: 138n.43

Josephus
  *Jewish Antiquities:* 93–94
  18.181: 156n.18
  19: 94
  19.1–273: 6
  19.9: 102
  19.12: 158n.45
  19.14: 158n.45
  19.15: 156n.30
  19.15–16: 156n.19
  19.19: 102
  19.33: 158n.55
  19.35: 158n.57
  19.42: 158n.48
  19.44: 157n.42
  19.48: 103
  19.51: 103
  19.54: 156n.26
  19.57: 158n.49
  19.61: 157n.37
  19.62: 103
  19.68: 156n.30, 157n.32
  19.82: 158n.53
  19.86: 158n.46
  19.87: 103
  19.88: 157n.38
  19.91: 103
  19.92: 157n.40
  19.94–95: 158n.44
  19.94: 156n.30
  19.95: 102
  19.103: 104
  19.107: 156n.30, 157n.33
  19.110: 102
  19.112: 102
  19.116: 104
  19.131: 158n.45
  19.132–133: 103
  19.181: 104
  19.184: 156n.27
  19.186: 156n.26
  19.187: 156n.29

  19.196–197: 157n.39
  19.212: 156n.30, 157n.36
  19.227: 104
  19.232: 104
  19.242: 104
  19.248: 104
  19.261: 158n.50
  20.267: 93
  *Jewish War:* 101, 105–106
  1.3: 93
  1.9: 157n.34

Juvenal
  2.27: 136n.15
  8.231–244: 136n.15
  10.286–288: 136n.15
  14.41: 136n.15

Livy
  1: 9–10, 62
  1.16.4: 4
  1.40: 4
  1.41: 4
  1.46.7: 62
  1.57.10: 63
  1.59.1: 63
  2.3–5: 4
  8.18: 136n.14
  8.40: 151n.28
  22.38.2–4: 138n.40
  24.5: 152n.42
  34.1.7: 44
  34.2–4: 49
  34.2.3: 138n.38
  39.6.7: 56
  39.8–9.1: 52
  39.8–19: 5
  39.8.1: 137n.37, 154n.62
  39.8.3: 146n.3
  39.8.5: 124
  39.8.6: 154n.65
  39.8.7–8: 55

39.8.7: 147n.39
39.8.8: 59, 64, 147n.39
39.9.1: 90, 154n.66, 155n.68
39.9.5: 148n.60
39.9.6: 87
39.10.1: 62
39.10.5: 52, 62
39.10.7: 59, 64, 147n.40
39.11: 52
39.11.3: 148n.64
39.12.1: 61
39.12.2: 149n.71
39.12.5: 149n.72
39.12.6: 149n.68
39.13: 53
39.13.1–2: 149n.69
39.13.2: 64, 87
39.13.3: 65
39.13.5: 65, 87
39.13.63: 87
39.14: 53
39.14.1: 149n.73
39.14.3: 144n.40
39.15–16: 53, 156n.23
39.15.5: 74
39.15.13: 58
39.15.14: 59
39.17.6: 5, 154n.63, 155n.70
39.18: 53
39.18.4: 87
39.19: 53
39.19.3: 154n.67
39.19.4–7: 149n.74
39.19.7: 154n.64
*Per.*, 116: 137n.35, 160n.20

Lucan
1.674–675: 136n.26
2.541: 8
6.230–262: 161n.31
6.793: 136n.13
7.64: 136n.13

Manilius *Astronomica*, 3.7: 137n.38

Martial
5.69: 136n.18
9.70: 136nn.13,18

Mela 2.45.5: 138n.38

Nicolaus of Damascus *Augustus:* 8
19: 160nn.20,26
20: 159n.8
24: 137n.35

Obsequens 67: 137n.34

Orosius 6.6.5: 136n.22

Ovid
*Amores,* 2.8.27–28: 144n.40
*Fasti,* 5.518: 10
*Metamorphoses*
10.298–502: 158n.43
10.300–303: 158n.43
12.6: 137n.38
15.763: 10

Plautus
*Amphitruo*
702–704: 57, 147n.34
703–704: 136n.25
*Aulularia*
408: 136n.25
408–410: 57, 147n.35
*Bacchides,* 371–372: 136n.25
*Casina,* 978–982: 136n.25
*Menaechmi,* 835: 136n.25
*Miles Gloriosus*
857–858: 136n.25
1016: 136n.25

Pliny, *Epistulae*
3.14.5: 140n.69
5.8.13: 153n.49

7.33.9: 153n.49
10.96.8: 136n.28

Plutarch
  Brutus, 120
  9.3: 159n.16
  13.2: 161n.33
  13.4–5: 161n.34
  53.4: 128
  Caesar
  62.7: 159n.16
  63.1–6: 137n.34
  65: 160n.26
  66: 137n.35
  69.3: 156n.24
  Cato Maior, 9.6: 49, 161n.5
  Cato Minor, 73.4: 160n.29
  Cicero
  10.5: 28
  14–22: 7
  15: 31
  16.2: 45, 144n.45
  18.7: 145n.53
  Crassus, 13: 29
  Marius, 14.3: 148n.46
  Moralia (De Garrulitate)
  505c: 162n.10
  505c–d: 8, 83
  507b–f: 161n.5
  Pompey, 33–24: 142n.8
  Sulla, 10.6: 139n.54

Propertius 1.3.5–6: 136n.26

Quintilian
  Instituto oratoria, 5.10.3: 136n.21
[Quintilian]
  Declamationes Maiores
  3: 148n.46
  306.13.1: 138n.38

Sallust
  Bellum Catilinae: 28, 55

1.1: 32
1.1–2: 143n.24
4.3: 33, 38, 137n.37, 154n.62
5: 40, 75
5.4: 161n.3
5.5: 36
5.7: 32
5.9: 39
6.1: 38, 39, 142n.15
7–10: 56
7.7: 33
8: 39
9.1: 39
9.4: 33
11.4: 56
11.6–13: 42
12.2: 147n.22
13.1: 33
14.7: 34, 142n.13, 161n.3
15.1: 35, 161n.3
15.2: 142nn.13,15
15.4: 36
16.1: 32
17.3–4: 154n.63
17.3–7: 142n.16
17.4: 35
17.5: 35
17.6: 35
17.7: 35, 142nn.13–14
18.1: 154n.68
18.2: 30, 33, 39
18.3: 30
19.1: 30
19.5: 32, 34
19.6: 39
20.1: 32, 36
20.6: 143n.26
22.1: 33, 139n.54, 142nn.13–14, 155n.70
22.3: 33, 142n.13
23.3: 87
23.3–5: 144n.41
23.4: 90
24.3: 124, 142nn.13–14, 154n.65

24.3–4: 143n.36
24.4: 36
25: 40
25.1: 42
25.2: 36
26.4: 32
27.1: 36
28.2: 144n.45
30.2: 36
31: 146n.12
31.4: 36
31.6: 141n.3
32.1: 36
32.2: 35
36.4–39.5: 40
39.5: 136n.20
40.1: 36
40.3: 46, 47
40.5: 42
40.6: 46
41.3: 46
43.2: 142n.13
44.1: 47, 48
44.2: 47
44.3: 48
44.4: 47
44.5: 47
45: 48
46.2: 36
47.2: 136n.21
48.1: 143n.28, 154n.66
48.3: 35, 142n.13
48.7: 35, 142nn.13–14
48.9: 33
50: 48
50.1: 47, 154n.67
51–53.1: 87
51.22: 148n.52
51.40: 35
52.1: 40
52.36: 47
52.4: 145n.1
52.6: 143n.27

52.7: 145n.1
53–54: 40
53.1: 40, 154n.64
53.2–4: 33
53.6: 33
54: 33
55.1: 32, 36
57.1: 32
57.2: 32, 36
57.5: 36
58: 40
59.3: 142nn.13,15
59.5: 40
61.9: 32, 41
*Bellum Iugurthinum:* 32
17–19: 159n.12
[Sallust]
*In Ciceronem,* 2.3: 146n.12


*Senatus Consultum de Pisone Patre*
109–120: 145n.48


Seneca
*Controversiae*
2.5: 81
2.5.4: 152n.44
2.5.6: 153n.45
*Suasoriae*
6.26.5–7: 136n.17
7.14: 136n.18


Seneca
*De Clementia:* 97–98
9: 98
*De Constantia,* 18.2: 156n.22
*Dialogi*
5.18.2: 135n.12
6.20.5: 135n.12
*Troades,* 672–677: 136n.26


Servius
*Aeneid*
1.6: 136n.19

1.195: 136n.19
1.298: 136n.19
1.378: 136n.19
1.488: 136n.19
7.614: 138n.41
8.1: 138n.41
8.5: 139n.49
*Georgics,* 2.499: 136n.19

Silius Italicus 4.774–777: 136n.26

Statius
 *Achilleid,* 1.36: 137n.38
 *Thebaid:* 153n.56
 5.92–94: 136n.26
 5.162–163: 138n.38

Suetonius
 *Augustus*
 5.1: 136n.24
 17.2: 14
 83: 161n.8
 94.5: 136n.24
 *Caligula:* 8
 8.2: 95
 15.4: 104
 16.4: 158n.62
 24.1: 161n.3
 24.3: 96
 25.1: 94
 26.3: 94
 26.5: 94
 27.4: 94
 28: 94
 30.1: 94
 36.1: 94, 161n.3
 37–40: 95
 46.1: 96
 49.3: 162n.12
 51: 95
 55: 95
 55.3: 95
 57: 158n.44

*Claudius*
 1.1: 144n.41
 9.1: 95
 *Domitian,* 21.1: 154n.61
 *Julius*
 11: 29
 14: 7
 17: 7, 144n.45
 80.3: 159n.16
 80.4: 160n.20
 81.1–2: 137n.34
 81.4: 160n.26
 82: 137n.35
 89: 156n.24
 *Nero:* 7–8
 *Vespasian,* 2.4: 95

Tacitus
 *Agricola,* 2.4: 153n.54
 *Annales:* 104, 106
 1: 21
 1.1–10: 68
 1.1.3: 141n.88
 1.4.1: 76
 1.6: 151n.29
 1.6.1: 76
 1.7: 139n.55
 1.8.6: 159n.10
 1.11.4: 77
 1.13.2: 96
 2–3: 68
 2.18.1: 150n.15
 2.26.2: 143n.31
 3.10–19: 69
 3.13.1–2: 69
 3.13.2: 69
 3.14.2: 69
 3.14.3–4: 69
 3.15: 71, 145n.48
 3.15.1: 69
 3.15.3: 150n.7
 3.16: 69, 71
 3.16.1: 70, 72, 150n.6

3.17: 69, 145n.48
3.18.3: 70
3.18.3–4: 70
3.18.4: 149n.4
3.19.2: 144n.40, 150nn.13,15, 152n.34
3.24.3: 151n.31
4.1: 151n.25
4.20: 96
4.20.2: 155n.10
4.32.1: 6
4.34.2: 86
4.34.4: 159n.17
4.35.3: 137n.36
4.60.2: 85
5.2–10: 159n.12
5.9: 98
6.9.3: 156n.20
6.24.2: 153n.57
6.30.3: 95
6.30.4: 95
6.38: 152n.34
11.31: 9
11.37.4: 79
13.1: 76
13.8–15.31: 150n.5
14.2: 161n.3
14.43–44: 140n.69
14.51.1: 77
14.56.2: 155n.11
14.60.3: 140n.76
14.65.2: 73
15–16: 74
15.37: 161n.3
15.48: 75
15.48–74: 5
15.48.1: 76, 137n.37, 151n.24, 154nn.62,65
15.49: 75
15.49.1: 76, 151n.26, 155n.68, 157n.30
15.49.2–50.3: 154n.63
15.49.2: 73
15.50.4: 75
15.51: 73
15.51.1: 78, 151n.32

15.51.2: 87, 152n.40
15.51.3: 152n.41
15.52: 74
15.53: 74, 84
15.53.2: 153n.52, 155n.70
15.53.3: 90, 153n.52
15.53.3–4: 152n.34
15.53.4: 144n.40
15.54.1: 84, 124, 154n.66
15.54.3: 84
15.54.4: 153n.53
15.55.1: 85
15.55.4: 85
15.57: 80, 87
15.57.2: 153n.48
15.64: 150n.8
15.66.2: 85
15.67.1: 85–86
15.67.2: 86
15.70: 150n.8
15.71.1: 87, 154n.67
15.73.1: 78
15.73.1–74.1: 154n.64
15.73.2.: 152n.37
16.19: 150n.8
16.34: 150n.8
53.3.: 157n.30
54.1: 157n.30
63.3: 157n.30
67.3: 157n.30
*Dialogus,* 37.6: 136n.18
*Historiae*
1.3.1: 153n.49
1.49.4: 155n.9
2.13: 82
2.49: 150n.8
16.18: 82
16.19: 82
16.20: 83

Tertullian *Apologeticum,* 6.7: 137n.29

Thucydides 1.1.2: 141n.88

Valerius Maximus
  *Facta et Dicta Memorabilia:* 109
  1.6.13: 137n.34
  3.2.15: 160n.30
  3.2.23a: 161n.31
  4.5.6: 137n.35
  5.8.5: 136n.20
  6.1.12: 148n.46
  6.3.7: 148n.58
  8.3: 44
  8.11.2: 137n.34
  9.1.9: 136n.20

Varro, *De Lingua Latina* 6.68: 59

Velleius Paterculus
  2.34–35: 7
  2.56: 160n.20

2.56.3–59.1: 8
2.57: 160n.26
2.57.2: 137n.34

Vergil
  *Aeneid:* 9–10
  4.301–303: 136n.26
  4.426: 137n.38
  4.469–470: 136n.26
  5.121: 135n.12, 142n.9
  6.46–51: 149n.70
  6.77–80: 149n.70
  8.668–670: 135n.12
  *Georgics:* 10
  1.463–497: 137n.34

Zonaras 10.11.D: 137n.35